STAGE CRAFTS

CHRIS HOGGETT **Stage Crafts**

St. Martin's Press   New York

St. Martin's Press, Inc., 175 Fifth Ave.,
New York, N.Y. 10010.
Manufactured in the United States of America
Library of Congress Catalog Card Number: 76–10554
ISBN: 312-75495-7
Library of Congress Cataloging in Publication Data

Hoggett, Chris.
   Stage crafts.

   Bibliography: p.
   Includes index.
   1. Stage management.   I. Title.
PN2085.H6   1976   792'.025   76–10554

Contents

	Introduction	1
1	ACTING AREA	3
2	ROSTRA	27
3	FLATS	47
4	DESIGN	71
5	PAINTING & PRINTING	107
6	PROPERTIES	133
7	LIGHTING	173
8	ARMS & ARMOUR	193
9	COSTUME ACCESSORIES	225
10	MAKE-UP & MASKS	243
11	Glossary . List of materials . List of suppliers . Book list . Index	269

Each section has a detailed list of contents on the first page.

Acknowledgements

My grateful thanks are due to all those who have assisted me in the preparation of this book:

Photographs—Norman D. Sutherland, Cheltenham Camera Club, for giving many hours to photographing the various settings shown in the design section (pages 82 to 106) and on pages 116–120, 125–129, 136, 140, 143, 146, 153, 166, 188, 189, 191, 236, 254, 256, 268 (top) and 282; John Pilston for the make-up section and pages 105 and 188; Rev. J. B. Abrami for pages 117, 121–123, 127, 144, 267 and 268 (right); Matthew Ruane for pages 84 (foot), 130 and 131; Patrick Gibson for page 104.

Permission to reproduce photographs—Professor John Holgate, Guildhall School of Music and Drama, for page 268 (foot); Cheltenham Newspaper Co. Ltd. for page 240; Rank Strand Electric Ltd. and W. J. Furse & Co. Ltd. for photographs of their lamps and equipment in the lighting section.

David Hall of St. Mary's College, Cheltenham, for permission to reproduce on page 179 details of simple lighting control equipment of his own design and manufacture.

The Rev. J. E. Maguire, O. Carm., headmaster of Whitefriars School, Cheltenham for his support and interest over many years of school productions; the Rev. B. Cunliffe, O. Carm., for lighting most of the productions shown in this book; the boys of the school for their assistance in making properties and scenery.

Peter and Sheila Mander for their helpful suggestions and criticism for the section on make-up; Peter Etheredge for his advice on painting and stage-lighting.

My wife for her constant help and support throughout the preparation of the book.

C.H., Cheltenham, 1975

Introduction

This book is intended for all those who seek information on methods of design, construction and decoration for the stage. It is also intended as a source book in the various techniques of painting, printing and modelling suitable for the theatre.

The purpose throughout is to provide a practical visual approach – all constructional methods clearly seen with a minimum of text. Many techniques can be only lightly sketched in and it is hoped that those seeking further information will follow up the books listed in the reference section at the back of this book.

The layout of the book is straightforward: divided into eleven sections, it starts literally from ground level and develops gradually towards the final visual appearance of a production.

The sections

1 using an empty space, the construction of stage and superstructures, masking off the front, sides and back of the stage with curtains;

2 basic building units for independent stages, making rostra, steps, staircases and mobile units:

3 building the 'walls' of the stage: flats, their types and construction;

4 planning and design: the use of all the materials shown in sections 1–3, methods of planning, drawings, models and types of setting – ten examples:

5 decorating the set: painting of flats and cloths; printing and painting techniques;

6 furnishing the set: the design and manufacture of all 'properties' other than furniture;

7 lighting the set: types of lamp, equipment, arrangement of lights, lighting rehearsals;

8 arms and armour, dressing the characters;

9 costume accessories;

10 the final touches: make-up of characters;

11 glossary, index, list of suppliers, tools, materials, books, etc.

The acting area 1

STAGE BUILDING · CURTAINS · CLOTHS

The acting area 4
The empty space 6
Seating arrangements using rostra 7
Flexible wooden rostra 8
Metal frame and boards 10
Superstructures 12
Proscenium stage 14
Positioning of cloths, borders and wings . . . 16
Curtains and cloths 18
Proscenium curtains 20
Curtains and backcloths 22
Gauzes and cut-cloths 24
Fixing a temporary cyclorama 26

THE ACTING AREA

The acting area may be an empty hall, a proscenium stage, a set of rostra or a set of curtains or screens – with or without staging. Sometimes a garden may be used for an outdoor production.

Whatever the area or space, check all dimensions carefully and all the facilities available round the space. Give thought to the possibility of experimenting with the area, keeping in mind the demands of the text and the director's concept of the play.

Certain essential questions should be answered before planning a production: will more than one level be needed for the movement of the play? Is the width of the hall or stage sufficient for storage of scenery and properties? Is there enough depth for a gangway behind the backcloth? Are the exits suitably placed?

Queries of this kind must be dealt with before the making of any preliminary sketches and plans.

These two pages show some of the solutions to filling and changing an acting area. The pages following deal with the various examples in more detail.

The empty space
(see page 6)

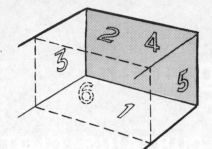

The empty space: consider it as an empty box enclosed by six sides – five planes consisting of floor, ceiling, three walls and an imaginary open side towards the audience.

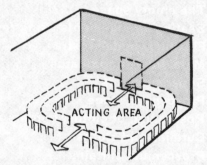

Theatre-in-the-round: the empty space used as an acting area with seats encircling the space.

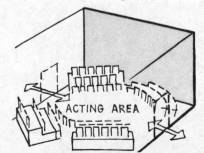

Arena space: seats raised on temporary rostra or platforms. (Arena seating is rarely permanent except in the Greek and Roman amphi-theatres.)

Flexible wooden rostra, or metal frame and boards
(see pages 8–9)

The play may be staged on any level above the audience or be arranged on many levels. A stage that allows a wide variety of level and shape is that shown in **a** and **b**. (See pages 40–41 for the rostra staging units.)

If rostra or normal staging are not available, tubular steel or slotted angle framing can be used as a structure with duck-boarding to make the level.

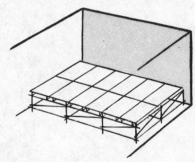

Metal frame and boards

Superstructures
(see pages 12–13)

If the ceiling of a hall is unsuitable for fixing or hanging equipment and drapes, one can consider the possibility of a superstructure. Provided that there is sufficient height, a metal structure of angle or tubular steel can be built on or off the sides of the stage as a freestanding unit.

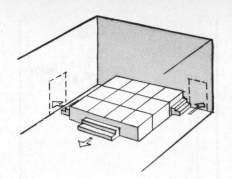

a *Twelve rostra units with three sets of steps.*

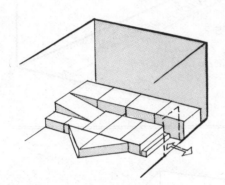

b *Rostra units arranged on two levels and with triangular apron and a ramp.*

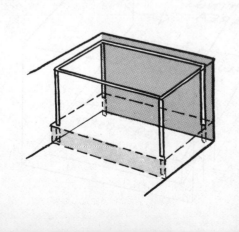

Proscenium stage and aprons

(see pages 14–15)

Many halls already have a stage, often with a substantial proscenium opening and a complete set of drapes. Do not feel confined and unable to adapt this arrangement – rather consider the possibilities inherent in the apron front, a ramp down to the auditorium, steps and exits to the sides of the proscenium. Even the introduction of a new entrance/exit area may be considered if it helps the movement of players. Any idea should be considered if economically possible.

It may seem obvious to stage a play on an existing stage, but if the auditorium is large certain productions may be better suited to a central arena type of setting. Possibly a long gangway could be projected out from the stage with the audience arranged round it – rather like a fashion show! Always be prepared to experiment with the facilities at hand.

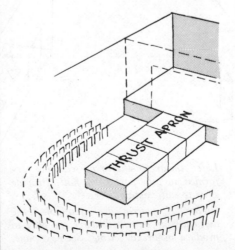

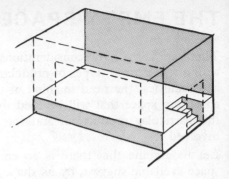

A permanent stage or a rostra stage built out to the full width of the hall (dotted lines indicate proscenium opening above).

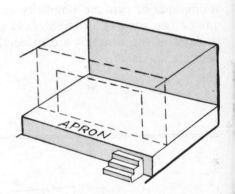

As above, but with an apron fitted in front. The apron could be on a lower level.

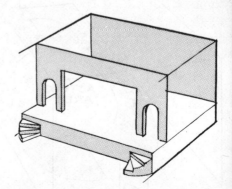

As above, but with proscenium altered to accommodate side entrances and steps.

THE EMPTY SPACE

There are some basic considerations when planning an acting space for all types of production: the dimensions and facilities, the need to think of the hall or room as an empty space that will be used to full advantage for the particular production, and the practical problems involved.

Let us assume that there is an empty hall. Does the space available suggest, by its shape, size and, possibly, colour, a suitable acting area without making any fundamental alterations?

Two rows of benches arranged on three sides of the hall and a curtain against the fourth side would offer an acting area of extreme simplicity and economy. Where one or two rows of children could sit on the floor just in front of the benches, a considerable audience would be accommodated.

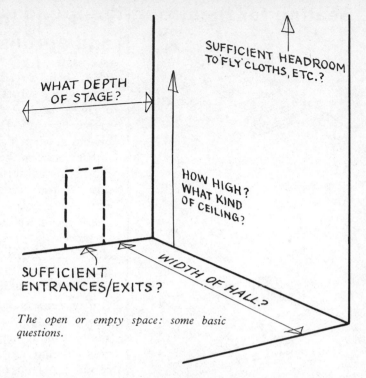

The open or empty space: some basic questions.

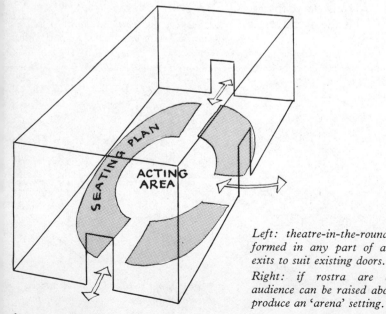

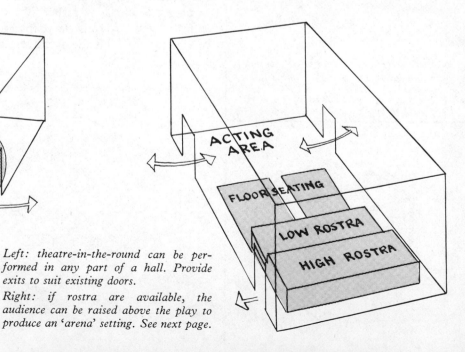

Left: theatre-in-the-round can be performed in any part of a hall. Provide exits to suit existing doors.

Right: if rostra are available, the audience can be raised above the play to produce an 'arena' setting. See next page.

Seating for theatre-in-the-round or 'arena' productions

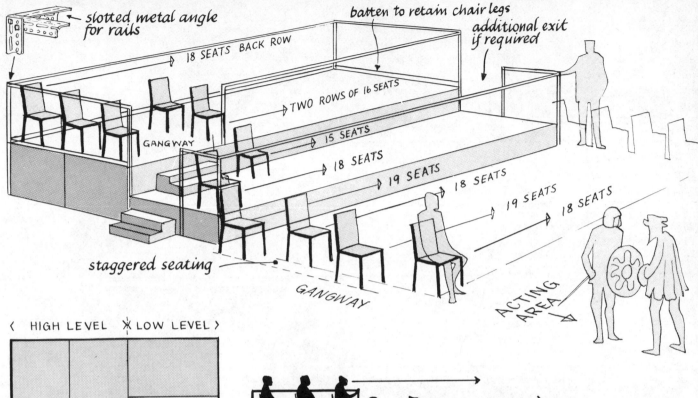

slotted metal angle for rails

batten to retain chair legs

additional exit if required

18 SEATS BACK ROW

TWO ROWS OF 16 SEATS

15 SEATS

18 SEATS

19 SEATS

18 SEATS

19 SEATS

18 SEATS

GANGWAY

staggered seating

GANGWAY

ACTING AREA

< HIGH LEVEL ✳ LOW LEVEL >

ACTING AREA

Above: side elevation shows eye levels. If the ground-level seating is staggered, there will be better visibility.

Left: plan view of rostra layout. Two lines of higher rostra at the back, one line of lower rostra at the front.

With flexible rostra staging it is easy to adapt to all types of production. Here the usual role of the rostrum has been reversed – the audience replacing the actors.

The rails round the raised seating are essential for safety and to meet existing fire regulations – see note on page 281.

With sufficient rostra two sides can be built up to make a semi-arena setting.

7

FLEXIBLE WOODEN ROSTRA

With approximately 12 rostra (in proportions 6 × 4 × 3) and 4 rostra (6 × 4 × 1½) a great variety of shapes can be erected – note the three variations on the next page. If the building has an existing narrow stage, a large apron may be built with the rostra if the heights relate (small adjustments can be made by placing blocks beneath the rostra to increase the height).

'Horseshoe' layout – entrance through side door and centre gangway.

Using a corner of the hall.

Theatre-in-the-round.

Fascia boards

Rostra staging can be covered in front by fascia boards. Make them from 9 mm plywood cut to fit two, three or more rostra. Alternatives to plywood are hardboard or pinboard.

a 12 × 3 plywood fascia to cover three rostra

glued and screwed

turn. keys

9mm. plywood

REAR SIDE

equals thickness of rostra leg

9

METAL FRAME AND BOARDS

If a permanent stage or rostra unit system is not available, a quick and practical stage can be assembled from a metal frame structure with duck-boards to cover the top. Tubular scaffolding and duck-boards can be hired from most large building contractors or suppliers. If scaffolding is not available, slotted metal angle (such as Dexion in U.K.) is an excellent alternative. Again, if duck-boards are difficult to obtain large sheets of composition chip-board (such as Weyroc in U.K.) or block-board are good substitutes provided that they are secured and strengthened on the underside with wood or metal strips – see the inset illustration.

The noise problem of actors' movements on boards that rest on a metal frame can be alleviated by covering with tarpaulin (also obtainable on hire or loan from some builders). Old canvas and underfelt are another useful sound-proofing. The footwear of the actors can also decrease the noise.

The amount of framing and boarding needed will depend on the space available and on the needs of the production.

duckboard

scaffolding

Above: elevation showing duck-boards resting on metal frame. Allow clearance between the top of frame uprights and the underside of the boards.

joint pin used for connecting tubes end to end

TARPAULIN (Stage cloth)

DUCKBOARD

coupler for connecting tubing... ...at right-angles

base plate or rubber feet to protect the floor

swivel coupler connects tubes at any angle

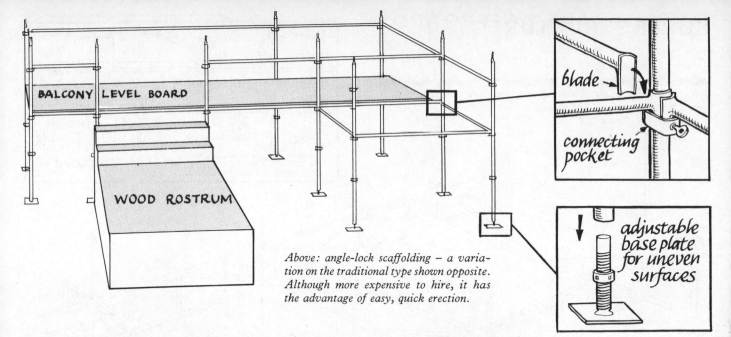

BALCONY LEVEL BOARD

WOOD ROSTRUM

blade →

connecting pocket

Above: angle-lock scaffolding – a variation on the traditional type shown opposite. Although more expensive to hire, it has the advantage of easy, quick erection.

adjustable base plate for uneven surfaces

Below: slotted angle frame with boards. Heavy-duty or medium frame are both suitable for staging.

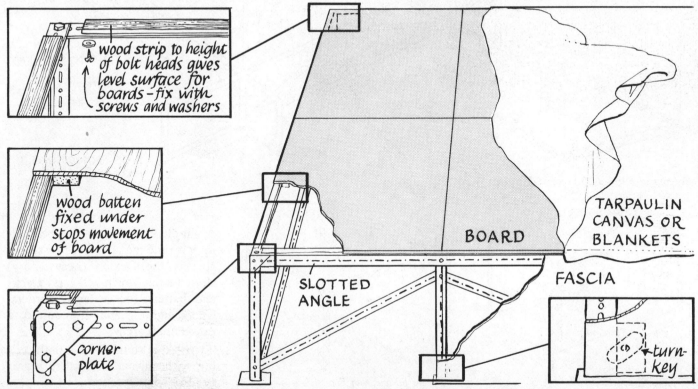

wood strip to height of bolt heads gives level surface for boards – fix with screws and washers

wood batten fixed under stops movement of board

corner plate

SLOTTED ANGLE

BOARD

TARPAULIN CANVAS OR BLANKETS

FASCIA

turn-key

II

SUPERSTRUCTURES

Right: a cross-section through ceiling showing the lifting mechanism for a suspended superstructure. By lowering the structure to floor level, borders, wings, lighting and the structure itself are easily assembled and dismantled.

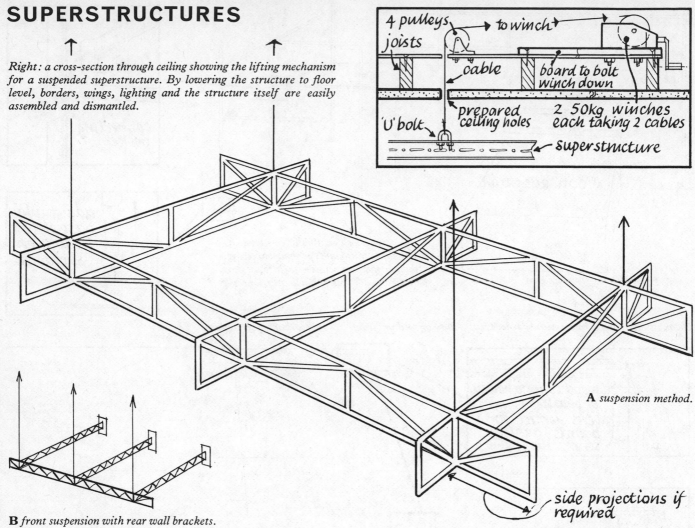

4 pulleys
joists
to winch
cable
board to bolt
winch down
'U' bolt
prepared
ceiling holes
2 50kg winches
each taking 2 cables
superstructure

A *suspension method.*

side projections if required

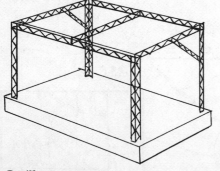

B *front suspension with rear wall brackets.*

C *pillar supports.*

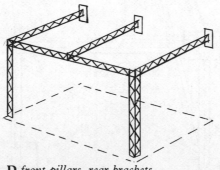

D *front pillars, rear brackets.*

A simple grid system can be built up with the metal angle. Most suitable is the Dexion (heavy duty) slotted angle which will carry tracks and battens for curtains, borders, wings, lighting and, if required, a proscenium arch.

Type '**A**' is suitable for a high ceiling with substantial timber beams or girder construction.

Frame construction

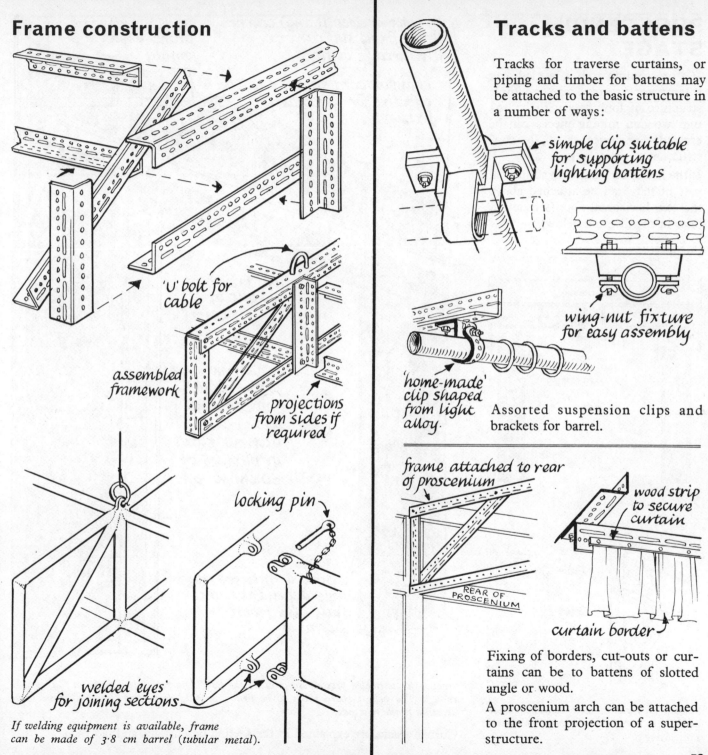

'U' bolt for cable

assembled framework

projections from sides if required

welded 'eyes' for joining sections

locking pin

If welding equipment is available, frame can be made of 3·8 cm barrel (tubular metal).

Tracks and battens

Tracks for traverse curtains, or piping and timber for battens may be attached to the basic structure in a number of ways:

simple clip suitable for supporting lighting battens

wing-nut fixture for easy assembly

'home-made' clip shaped from light alloy.

Assorted suspension clips and brackets for barrel.

frame attached to rear of proscenium

REAR OF PROSCENIUM

wood strip to secure curtain

curtain border

Fixing of borders, cut-outs or curtains can be to battens of slotted angle or wood.

A proscenium arch can be attached to the front projection of a super-structure.

PROSCENIUM STAGE

If a proscenium arch is needed over a temporary rostra stage, a simple structure of four flats with 50×25 mm wooden joining pieces can be erected. See pages 48–49 for construction of plain flats.

If the hall is very high, an additional pair of flats can be attached above the two horizontal flats (see dotted lines in the diagram below).

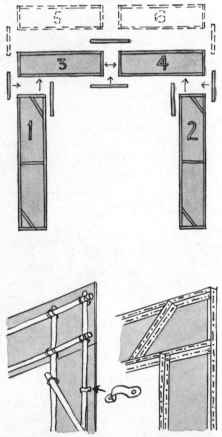

Above: an alternative to wooden framework is the barrel (tubular metal) or metal slotted angle.

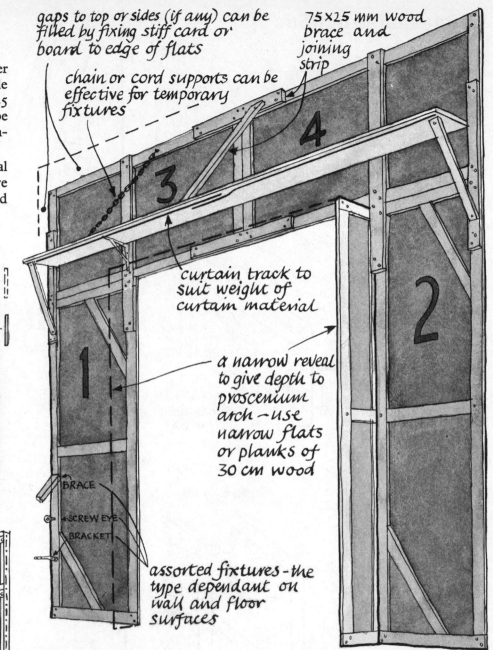

gaps to top or sides (if any) can be filled by fixing stiff card or board to edge of flats

chain or cord supports can be effective for temporary fixtures

75×25 mm wood brace and joining strip

curtain track to suit weight of curtain material

a narrow reveal to give depth to proscenium arch – use narrow flats or planks of 30 cm wood

BRACE

SCREW EYE

BRACKET

assorted fixtures – the type dependant on wall and floor surfaces

Above: the assembled proscenium arch. If the hall is narrow, one horizontal flat may be enough. The pelmet board needs to be firmly braced; supporting flats will have to be attached to the rear side.

Curtain tracks are explained in the section on curtains and cloths.

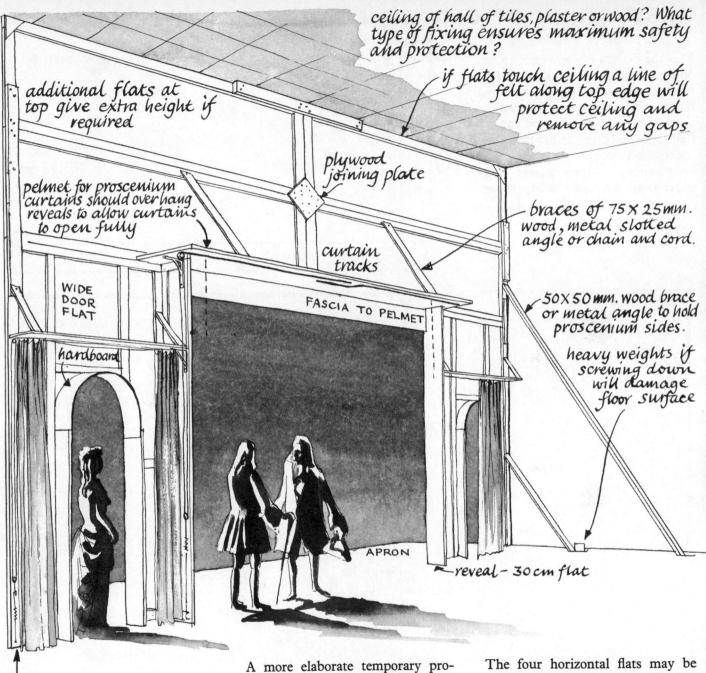

ceiling of hall of tiles, plaster or wood? What type of fixing ensures maximum safety and protection?

if flats touch ceiling a line of felt along top edge will protect ceiling and remove any gaps

additional flats at top give extra height if required

plywood joining plate

pelmet for proscenium curtains should over hang reveals to allow curtains to open fully

braces of 75 x 25 mm. wood, metal slotted angle or chain and cord.

curtain tracks

WIDE DOOR FLAT

FASCIA TO PELMET

50 x 50 mm. wood brace or metal angle to hold proscenium sides.

hardboard

heavy weights if screwing down will damage floor surface

APRON

reveal – 30 cm flat

continuous cord for sets of curtains (see page 20)

A more elaborate temporary proscenium consisting of two wide-door flats with rounded arches. Each arch has an independent curtain track system.

The four horizontal flats may be reduced to two if larger flats are available, or a special flat can be constructed – see the section on flats.

15

POSITIONING OF CLOTHS, BORDERS & WINGS

Masking a stage, whether permanent or erected for the occasion, requires careful planning. The backcloth, borders and wings must be placed in relation to the proscenium edges. Before considering the borders, the background cloth or curtain should be positioned approximately one metre from the back wall to allow a free passageway behind.

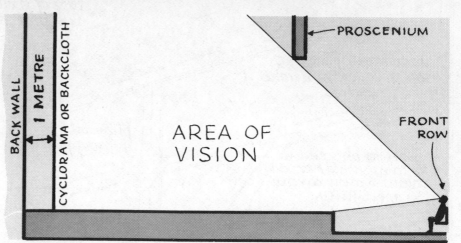

BACK WALL

1 METRE

CYCLORAMA OR BACKCLOTH

AREA OF VISION

PROSCENIUM

FRONT ROW

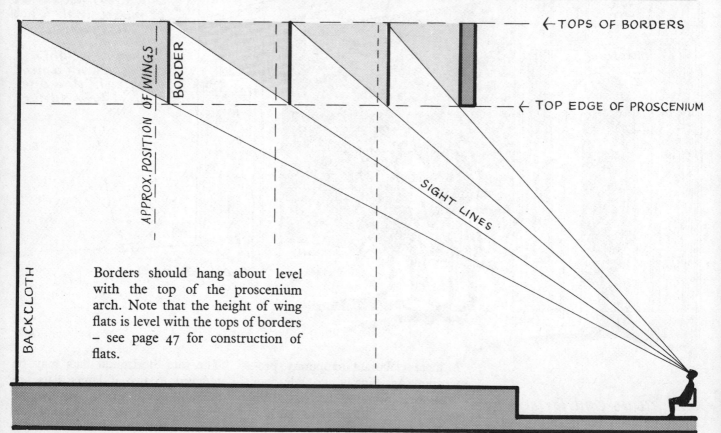

TOPS OF BORDERS

TOP EDGE OF PROSCENIUM

APPROX. POSITION OF WINGS

BORDER

SIGHT LINES

BACKCLOTH

Borders should hang about level with the top of the proscenium arch. Note that the height of wing flats is level with the tops of borders – see page 47 for construction of flats.

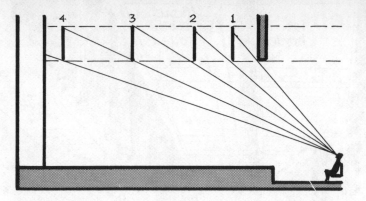

The deeper the stage the more borders will be needed. (Note how the spacing widens towards the backcloth.)

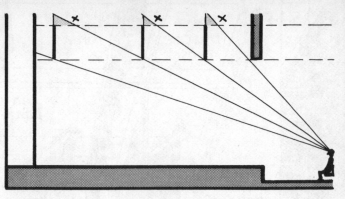

Incorrect positioning: the shaded area, called the 'non-masking triangle', is wasteful of material and may not mask the lighting battens.

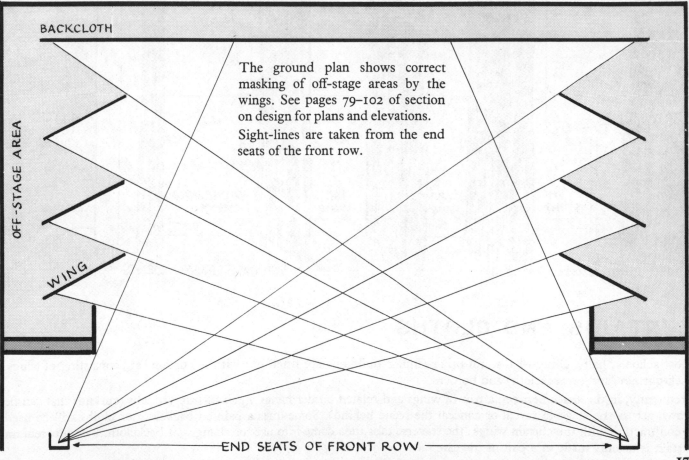

BACKCLOTH

OFF-STAGE AREA

WING

The ground plan shows correct masking of off-stage areas by the wings. See pages 79–102 of section on design for plans and elevations.

Sight-lines are taken from the end seats of the front row.

←——————— END SEATS OF FRONT ROW ———————→

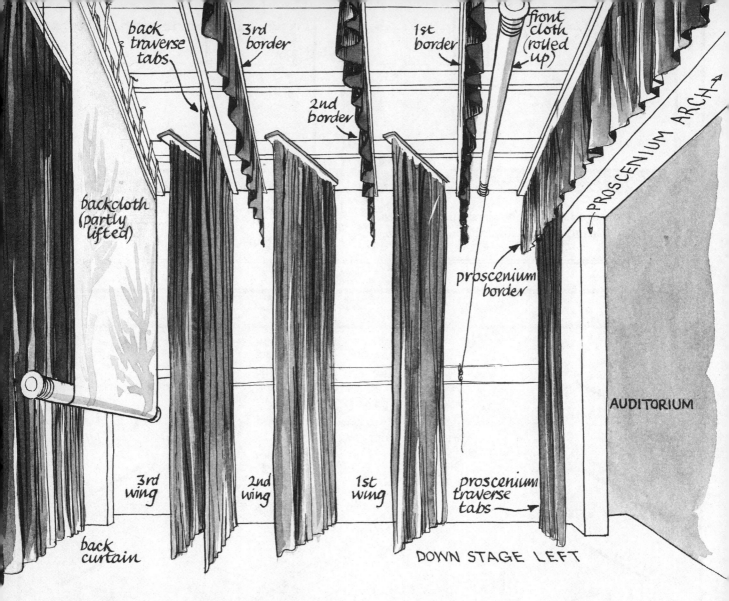

back traverse tabs

3rd border

1st border

front cloth (rolled up)

2nd border

backcloth (partly lifted)

PROSCENIUM ARCH →

proscenium border

AUDITORIUM

3rd wing

2nd wing

1st wing

proscenium traverse tabs →

back curtain

DOWN STAGE LEFT

CURTAINS AND CLOTHS

Most schools, halls, church-halls and other similar buildings are fitted out with a 'curtain set', consisting of wings, back-curtain (and/or backcloth) and borders.

Frequently, in the space between a pair of wings and related border hangs a pair of traverse tabs (curtains that can be drawn across the stage to reveal or conceal the scene behind). Sometimes a painted backcloth or cloths will be used in conjunction with the curtain wings: the traverse tabs then come into use for changes of backcloth. The proscenium curtain is usually made of a pair of traverse tabs.

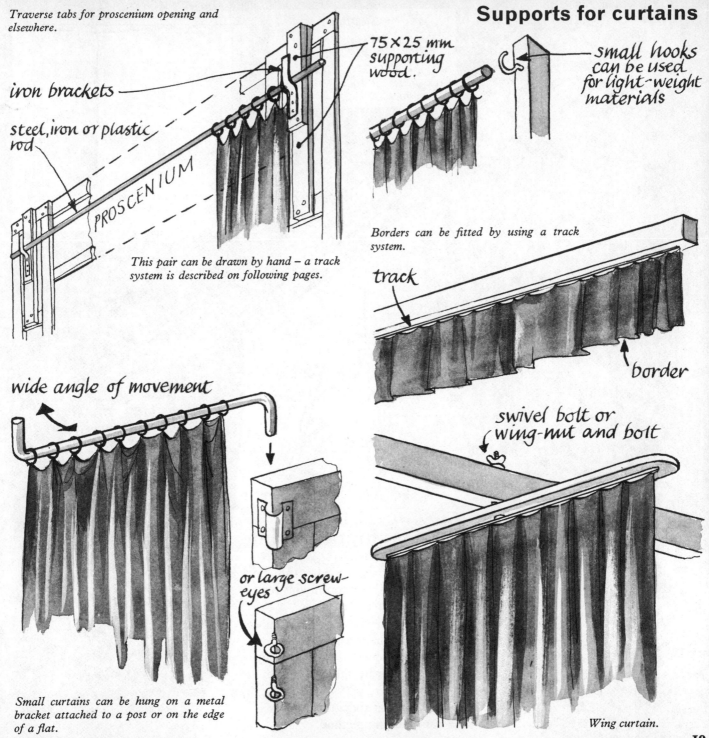

Traverse tabs for proscenium opening and elsewhere.

Supports for curtains

iron brackets

steel, iron or plastic rod

PROSCENIUM

75 × 25 mm supporting wood.

small hooks can be used for light-weight materials

This pair can be drawn by hand – a track system is described on following pages.

Borders can be fitted by using a track system.

track

border

wide angle of movement

or large screw-eyes

swivel bolt or wing-nut and bolt

Small curtains can be hung on a metal bracket attached to a post or on the edge of a flat.

Wing curtain.

300 mm × 25 mm PELMET BOARD

A diagrammatic view of pulley system and fixing of tabs 'x' to the continuous cord.

Proscenium curtains

A pair of traverse tabs can be operated by using a continuous cord fixed over four pulleys.

The low pulley should be firmly attached to the floor – a tension spring fitted between the low pulley and the floor will help to keep the cord taut.

A windlass (see above) may replace the hand-pulling method.

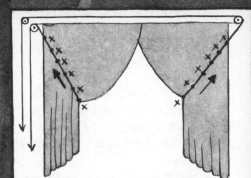

Diagrammatic view of pulleys and fixing sets of ties 'x' to the cords.

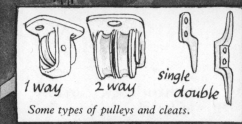

1 way   2 way   single double

Some types of pulleys and cleats.

The winch. Useful for raising and lowering heavy curtains, cloths and superstructures (see page 12).

Alternative curtains

With this type of curtains, the two cords are pulled simultaneously and tied over cleats. Some theatres use small hand windlasses for the same operation.

The traverse style is often preferred.

21

lightly tack curtain to lintel

approx 1 metre from curtain to back wall

LINTEL

wood block to protect floor

A quick assembly of backcloth or curtain

If a performance is to take place in unfamiliar surroundings, a useful method of hanging back-curtains is to wedge them against the ceiling, as shown.

A preliminary survey and note of dimensions is needed and then the lengths of timber cut as shown.

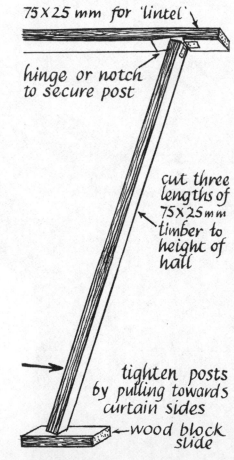

75 × 25 mm for 'lintel'

hinge or notch to secure post

cut three lengths of 75 × 25 mm timber to height of hall

tighten posts by pulling towards curtain sides

wood block slide

Arrangement of supports.

Rolling up a backcloth

A backcloth may be hired or purchased from the appropriate supplier – see page 276. If it is desired to 'fly' the cloth, assemble as shown. Use two pieces of 50 × 25 mm timber to 'sandwich' the cloth and tapes at the top edge, securing with screws. A cylinder attached to the cloth may be hired or made from a long wooden pole or metal tube. Metal will be suitable only if of a light alloy such as aluminium that can be drilled and attached to the lower edge of the cloth.

Pulleys should be arranged as shown, spaced out to fit the width of the cloth. See previous page but one for types of pulley.

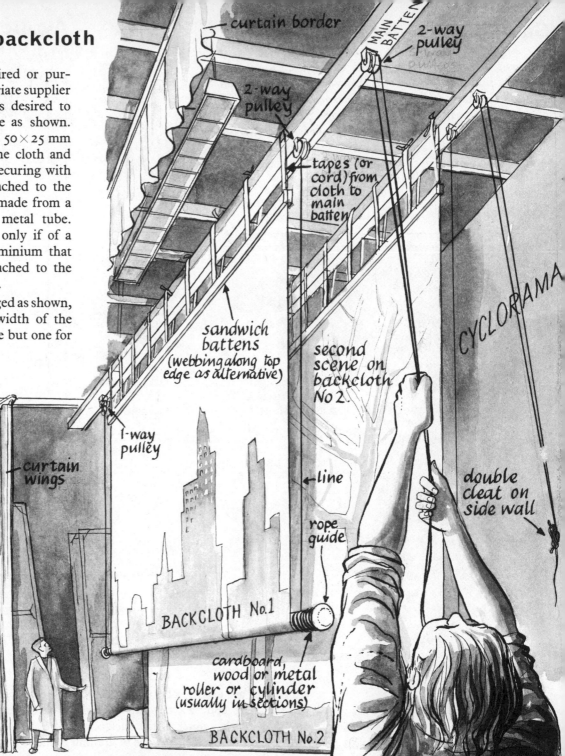

curtain border

MAIN BATTEN

2-way pulley

2-way pulley

tapes (or cord) from cloth to main batten

2-way pulley

CYCLORAMA

sandwich battens (webbing along top edge as alternative)

second scene on backcloth No 2

line

rope guide

double cleat on side wall

1-way pulley

curtain wings

BACKCLOTH No.1

cardboard, wood or metal roller or cylinder (usually in sections)

BACKCLOTH No.2

Gauzes and cut-cloths

Gauzes are thin, semi-transparent cloths used to achieve effects of illusion and surprise. They are frequently used in transformation scenes and where atmospheric effects of mist or fog are required. The more gauzes used, the more realism is achieved in the mist scenes. The whole quality of surprise and illusion is dependent on the correct placing of lights – which will be fully discussed in the section on lighting.

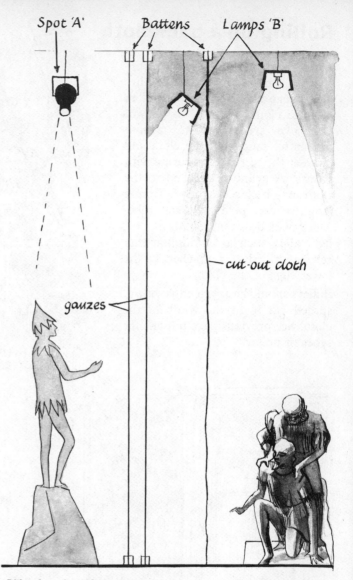

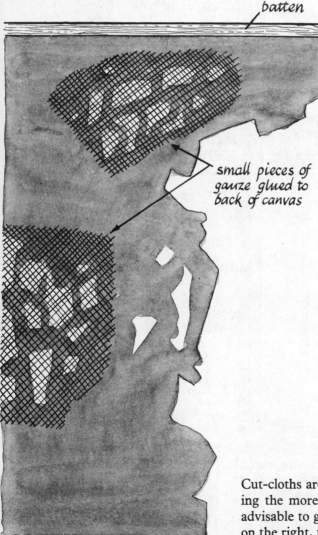

*Side elevation of the scene on the right: the standing figure is soon to appear before the figures crouching. This will occur the moment that spot **A** is lit – if the **B** lights are dimmed or cut off, the intensity of the effect will be increased.*

Cut-cloths are used for decorative effects. Pieces of gauze are for strengthening the more complex cut-out shapes. If the cut-out is very intricate, it is advisable to glue gauze to the back of the complete surface area. In the scene on the right, the cut-out shape of arching branches is achieved by this means.

cut-out cloth

bottom of
gauze

ground row
with ramp

ground row

rock 'props'

rock 'props'

*The dotted figure will appear only when spot **A** is on. The silhouette is achieved by lighting the gauze curtains immediately in the front. All other lamps are off. The effect of this kind of lighting technique on a painted gauze is illustrated on page 127.*

25

Fixing a temporary cyclorama

The skycloth or cyclorama should fill the back wall of the hall and can be easily assembled as shown. Build the framework of metal slotted angle to the height of the hall, allowing approximately 30 mm for inserting wedges. Further bracing can be added where appropriate. Ensure that the cloth is taped at top and sides and attached to the frame as shown. A barrel (tubular metal) is inserted in the pocket to pull the cloth taut.

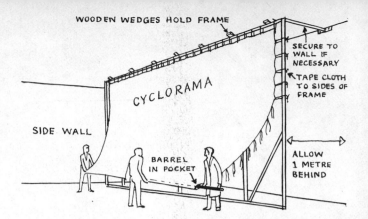

A street scene from 'Fiddler on the Roof'. The silhouette effect is achieved by batten lighting on a temporary cyclorama as illustrated at the top of the page. The house construction is shown on page 46. The setting was built in a school hall by 15 and 16 year old boys as part of a craft course. Other scenes from the production are shown on pages 70 and 282.

Rostra

2

CONSTRUCTION · RAMPS · STEPS · TRUCKS

Rostra construction 28
Ramps 32
Triangles and curves 32
Steps 34
A basic 4-level rostra system 40
Trucks and revolving settings 42

ROSTRA

Rostra, considered as building units for all kinds of stage-building, are most versatile pieces of equipment.

As rectangular boxes they can be built into stages or can make new levels on an existing stage. In the form of ramps or steps they allow movement from one level to another and, with wheels or castor runners, they are the basis of mobile set pieces – useful for quick scene changes.

Rigid, non-collapsible rostra are also suitable for staging but are difficult to store away unless a large amount of storage space is available. One useful purpose for a rigid rostrum could be that of a wardrobe – ideal where space for clothing is inadequate – see drawing.

The construction of the basic unit shown here is of a collapsible type for convenience of storage. Variations of shape and size are shown in this section. They include the ramp, triangular and semi-circular rostra, steps and staircases, and spiral and curving assemblies.

An example of a basic rostra stage with a ramp and five individual step units making a four-level set is shown on pages 40–41. It is also featured in the section on design as the arrangement used for a production of 'The Merchant of Venice' (see pages 92–93).

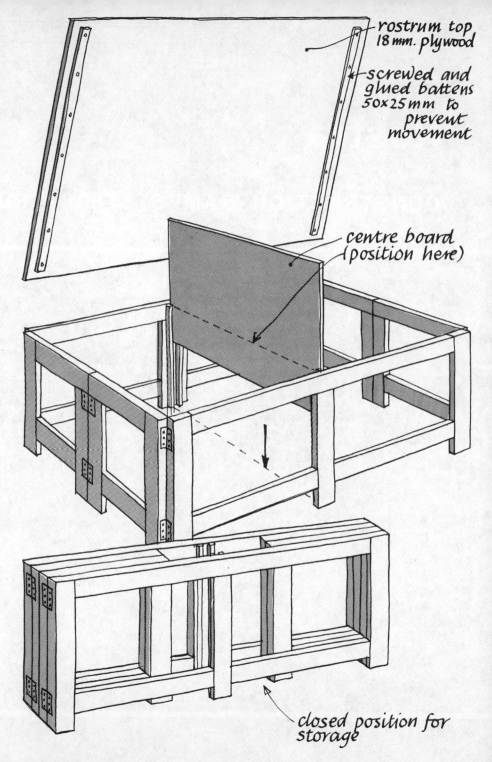

rostrum top
18 mm. plywood

screwed and glued battens
50 × 25 mm to prevent movement

centre board (position here)

closed position for storage

28

Collapsible rostra–1

Drawings and plans on these pages show the construction of a large rostrum measuring $6 \times 4 \times 3$. Whatever the size, a top board of 18 mm plywood and a 12 mm centre-board will be necessary. Chip- or blockboard may be substituted for the centre-board if more convenient.

A number of such rostra will be suitable for building an independent stage. (The height of 3 units is always optional – some people may prefer a lower level.)

This type of rostra is seen in the stage assembly on page 99.

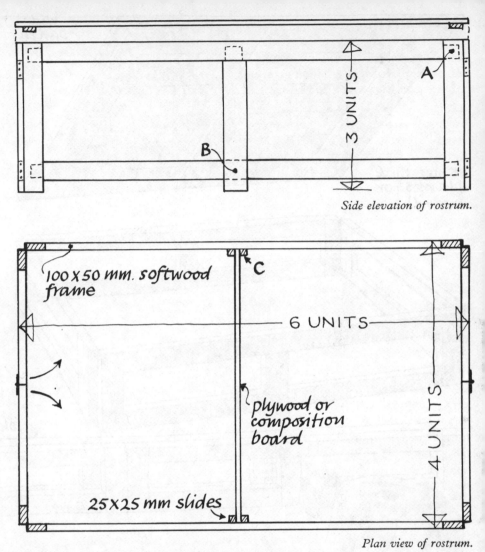

Side elevation of rostrum.

Plan view of rostrum.

rostrum for stage and/or wardrobe

plywood top and sides

rostrum top and back of wardrobe

rail

flush fitting lock

bolts

rigid framework

Wardrobe: the frame must be of a fixed type or be braced at the back to keep it rigid. Sides and top can, as required, be covered with thin plywood or hardboard. Doors are added at the front.

100 × 50 mm. softwood frame

C

6 UNITS

4 UNITS

3 UNITS

A

B

plywood or composition board

25 × 25 mm slides

*Mortice and tenon joint as at **A**.*

*Halving joint as at **B**.*

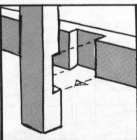

*Slides for centre-board as at **C**.*

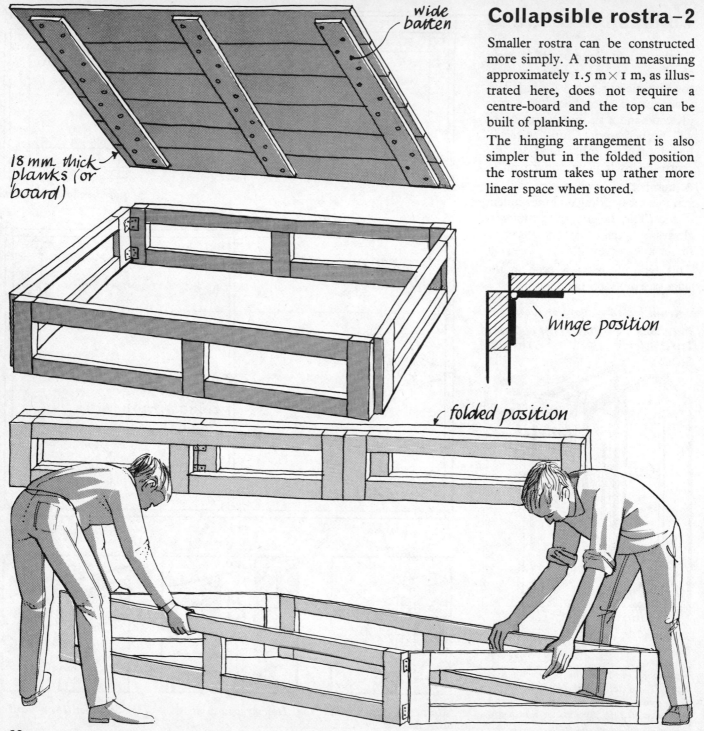

wide batten

18 mm thick planks (or board)

Collapsible rostra-2

Smaller rostra can be constructed more simply. A rostrum measuring approximately 1.5 m × 1 m, as illustrated here, does not require a centre-board and the top can be built of planking.

The hinging arrangement is also simpler but in the folded position the rostrum takes up rather more linear space when stored.

hinge position

folded position

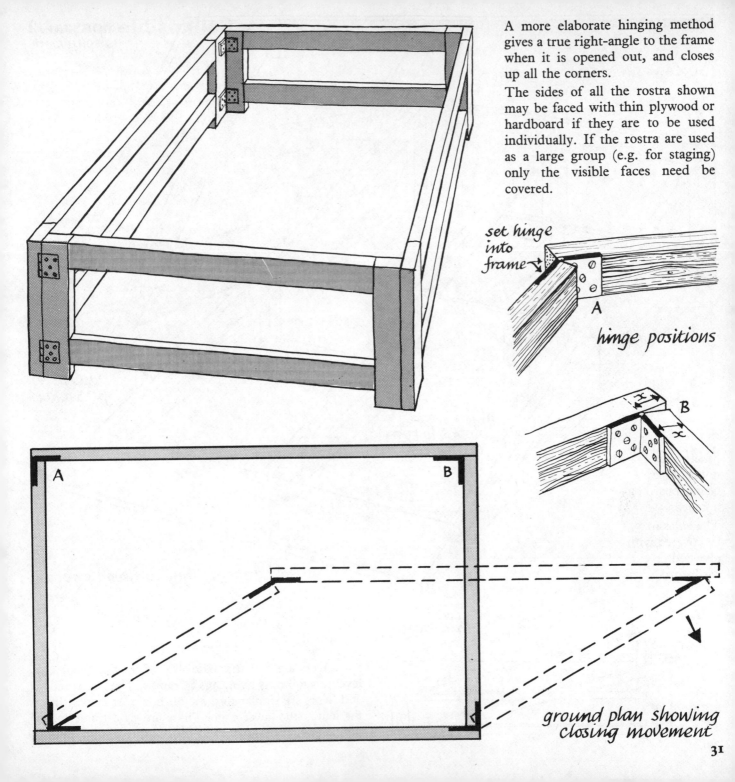

A more elaborate hinging method gives a true right-angle to the frame when it is opened out, and closes up all the corners.

The sides of all the rostra shown may be faced with thin plywood or hardboard if they are to be used individually. If the rostra are used as a large group (e.g. for staging) only the visible faces need be covered.

set hinge into frame

A

hinge positions

B

ground plan showing closing movement

Ramps

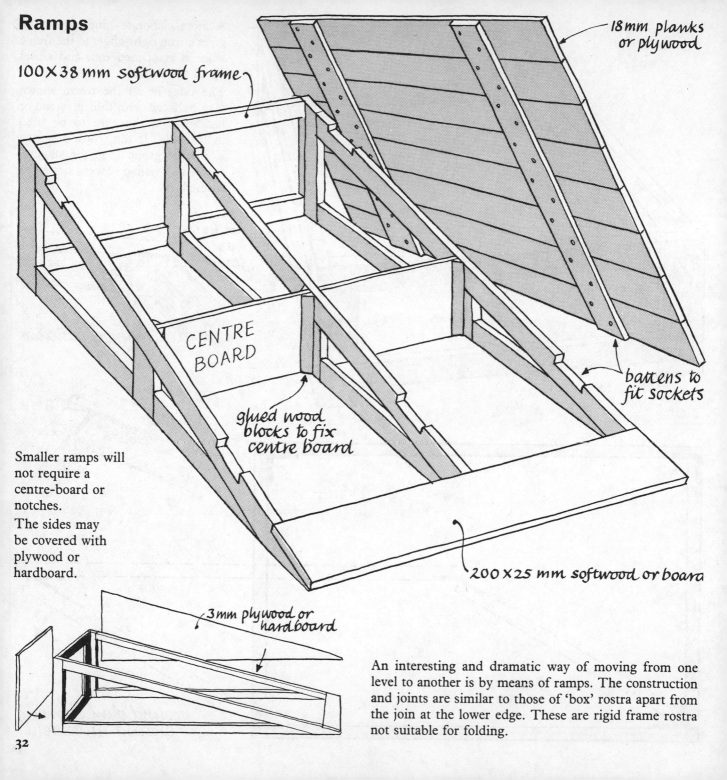

18mm planks or plywood

100×38 mm softwood frame

battens to fit sockets

CENTRE BOARD

glued wood blocks to fix centre board

Smaller ramps will not require a centre-board or notches.

The sides may be covered with plywood or hardboard.

200×25 mm softwood or board

3mm plywood or hardboard

An interesting and dramatic way of moving from one level to another is by means of ramps. The construction and joints are similar to those of 'box' rostra apart from the join at the lower edge. These are rigid frame rostra not suitable for folding.

32

Triangles and curves

Triangular rostrum: hinging is similar to that shown on page 29.

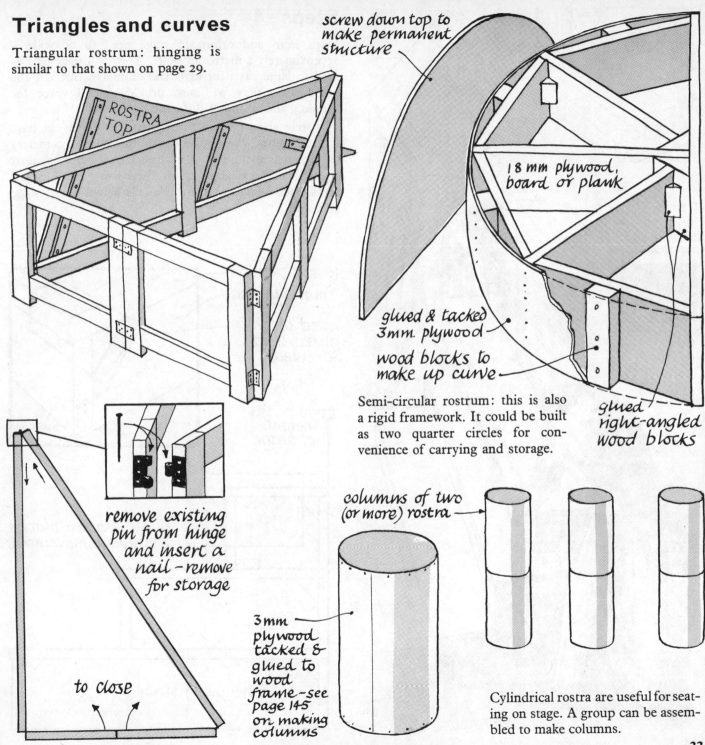

ROSTRA TOP

screw down top to make permanent structure

18 mm plywood, board or plank

glued & tacked 3mm. plywood

wood blocks to make up curve

glued right-angled wood blocks

Semi-circular rostrum: this is also a rigid framework. It could be built as two quarter circles for convenience of carrying and storage.

remove existing pin from hinge and insert a nail — remove for storage

to close

columns of two (or more) rostra

3mm plywood tacked & glued to wood frame — see page 145 on making columns

Cylindrical rostra are useful for seating on stage. A group can be assembled to make columns.

33

Steps – 1

Steps from auditorium to stage need to be wide – approximately 2 metres or more. They will then accommodate large casts for exits and entrances through the auditorium; they will also provide useful space for standing and sitting at different levels.

The steps shown are in three parts: the one at the base is 1 × 2 metres, the one in the middle 66 cm × 2 metres and the one at the top 33 cm × 2 metres. Placed against the front of the stage or apron, these rostra provide four steps, each being one quarter of the height of the stage or apron.

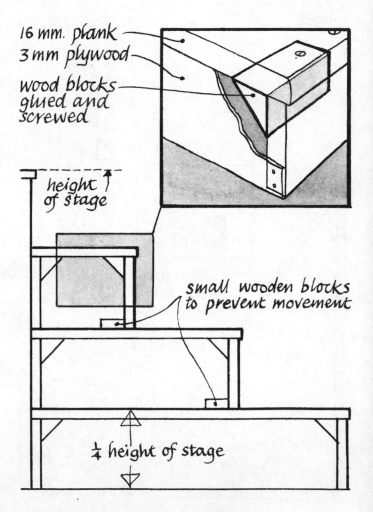

16 mm. plank
3 mm plywood
wood blocks glued and screwed

height of stage

small wooden blocks to prevent movement

¼ height of stage

Adaptable set of steps and rostrum

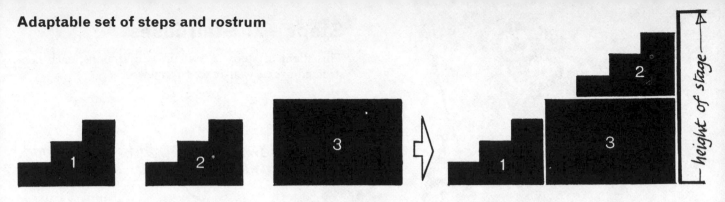

Two sets of treads and one small rostrum: the riser is 20 cm, the tread 30 cm, the rostrum 80 cm high × 120 × 120. This arrangement gives 8 steps if the last step on to the stage is included.

Some variations with the same equipment: variations 3, 4 and 5 will require an additional rostrum.

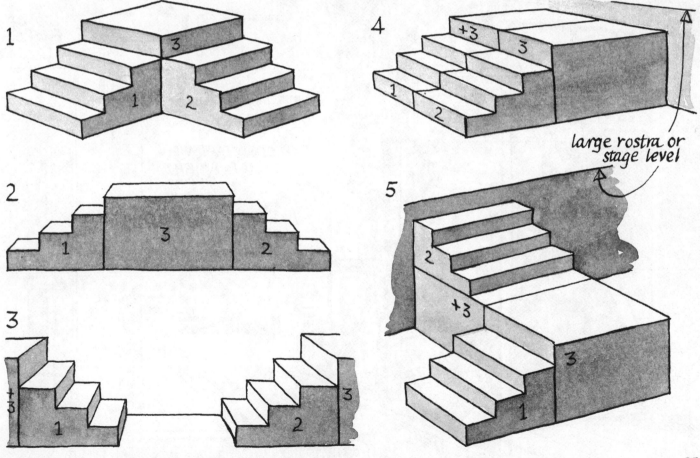

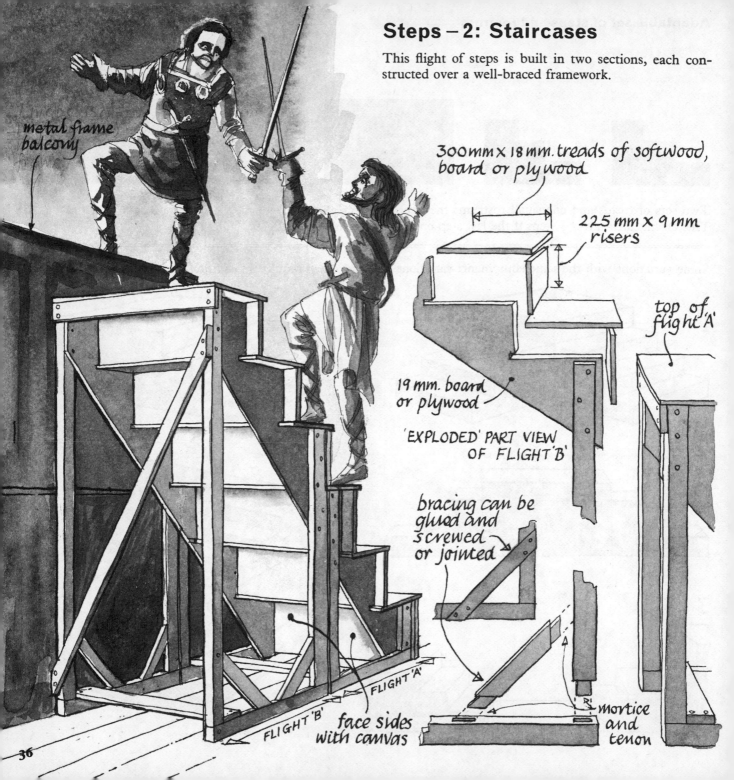

Steps – 2: Staircases

This flight of steps is built in two sections, each constructed over a well-braced framework.

metal frame balcony

300mm x 18mm. treads of softwood, board or plywood

225 mm x 9mm risers

19 mm. board or plywood

top of flight 'A'

'EXPLODED' PART VIEW OF FLIGHT 'B'

bracing can be glued and screwed or jointed

FLIGHT 'B' FLIGHT 'A'

face sides with canvas

mortice and tenon

Staircase with a landing

When more complex stair arrangements are required and a landing or balcony is to be the focal point of the scene, a construction similar to this may be attempted.

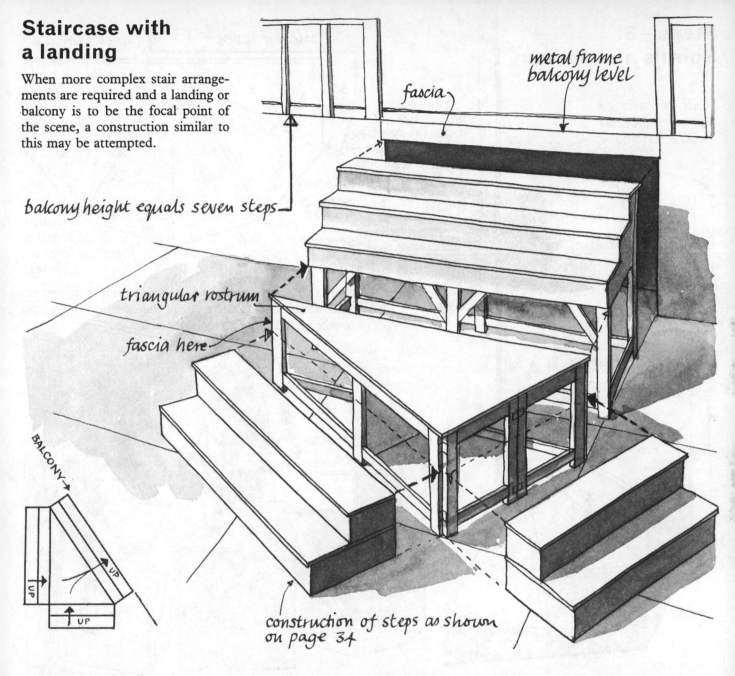

metal frame balcony level

fascia

balcony height equals seven steps

triangular rostrum

fascia here

BALCONY

UP UP UP

construction of steps as shown on page 34

This group of stairs shows two directions down from a balcony. The central triangular rostrum serves as a resting point and a possible change of direction. The smaller steps have solid sides of composition board. The risers are not weight-bearing and can be made from hardboard.

Photographs on pages 96–99 show one way of using this type of staircase in a setting.

Steps – 3: Spirals and curves

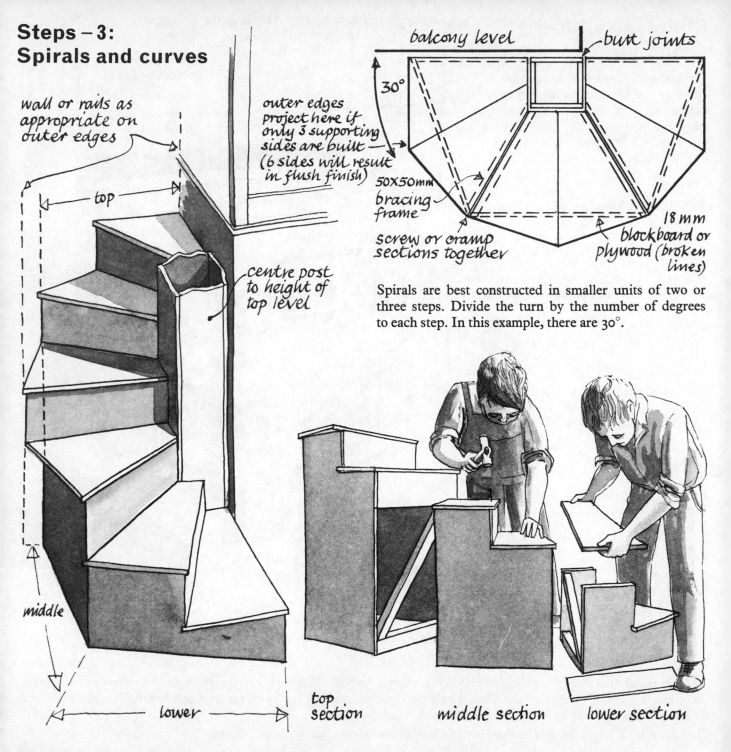

wall or rails as appropriate on outer edges

top

centre post to height of top level

outer edges project here if only 3 supporting sides are built — (6 sides will result in flush finish)

middle

lower

balcony level

butt joints

30°

50x50mm bracing frame

screw or cramp sections together

18 mm blockboard or plywood (broken lines)

Spirals are best constructed in smaller units of two or three steps. Divide the turn by the number of degrees to each step. In this example, there are 30°.

top section

middle section

lower section

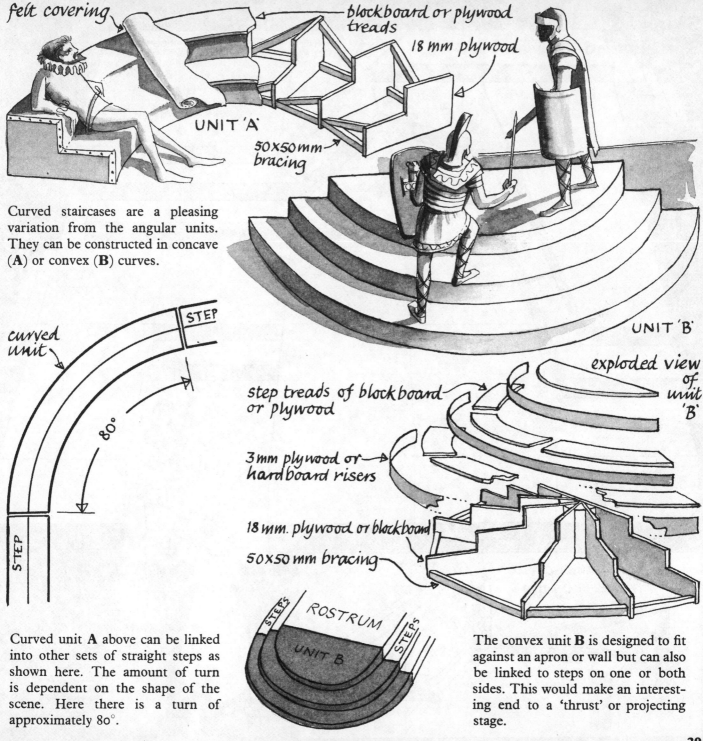

felt covering

blockboard or plywood treads

18 mm plywood

UNIT 'A'

50×50mm bracing

Curved staircases are a pleasing variation from the angular units. They can be constructed in concave (**A**) or convex (**B**) curves.

curved unit

STEP

80°

STEP

Curved unit **A** above can be linked into other sets of straight steps as shown here. The amount of turn is dependent on the shape of the scene. Here there is a turn of approximately 80°.

UNIT 'B'

exploded view of unit 'B'

step treads of blockboard or plywood

3 mm plywood or hardboard risers

18 mm. plywood or blockboard

50×50 mm bracing

STEPS ROSTRUM STEPS

UNIT B

The convex unit **B** is designed to fit against an apron or wall but can also be linked to steps on one or both sides. This would make an interesting end to a 'thrust' or projecting stage.

39

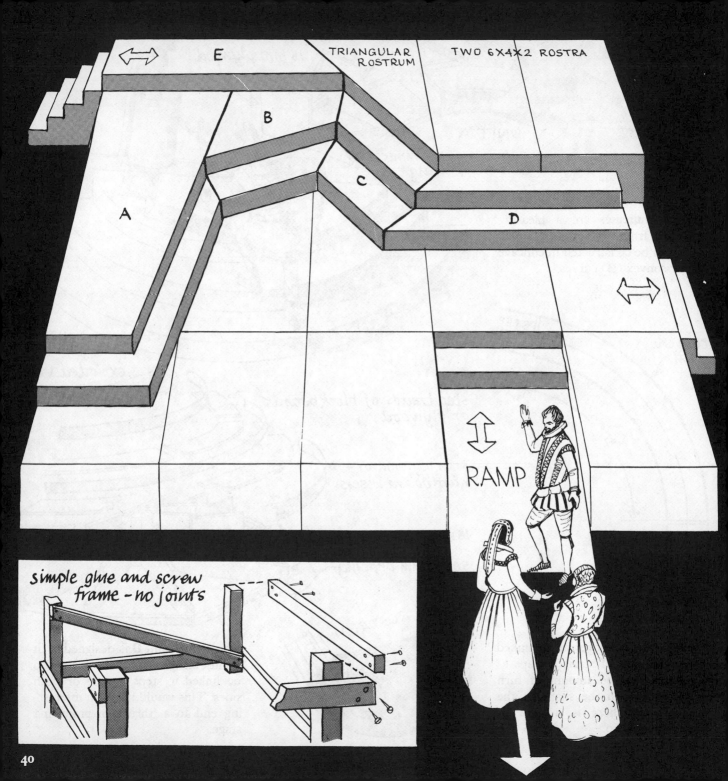

E

TRIANGULAR ROSTRUM

TWO 6X4X2 ROSTRA

B

C

A

D

RAMP

simple glue and screw frame - no joints

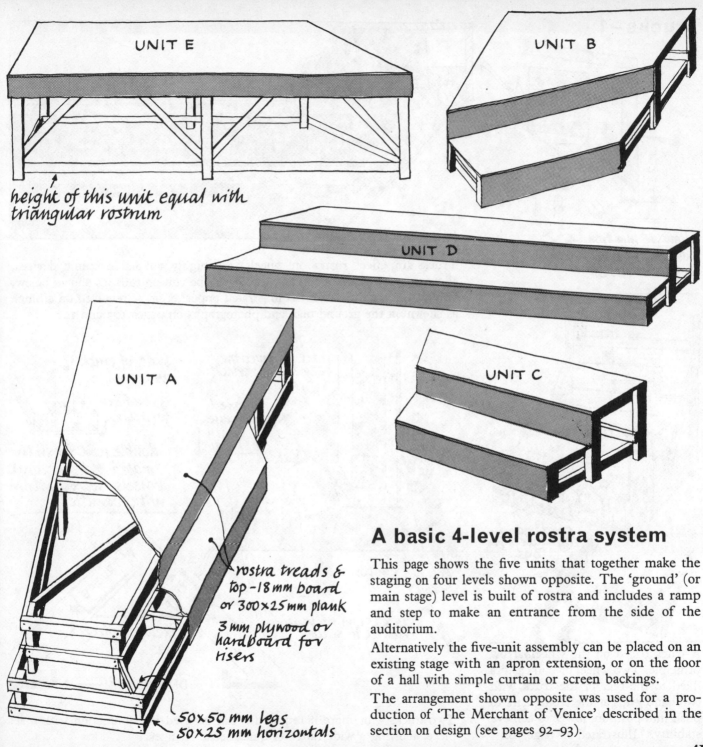

UNIT E

height of this unit equal with triangular rostrum

UNIT B

UNIT D

UNIT A

UNIT C

rostra treads &
top - 18 mm board
or 300×25 mm plank

3 mm plywood or
hardboard for
risers

50×50 mm legs
50×25 mm horizontals

A basic 4-level rostra system

This page shows the five units that together make the staging on four levels shown opposite. The 'ground' (or main stage) level is built of rostra and includes a ramp and step to make an entrance from the side of the auditorium.

Alternatively the five-unit assembly can be placed on an existing stage with an apron extension, or on the floor of a hall with simple curtain or screen backings.

The arrangement shown opposite was used for a production of 'The Merchant of Venice' described in the section on design (see pages 92–93).

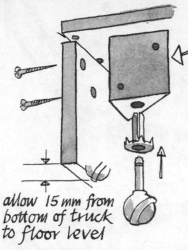

allow 15 mm from bottom of truck to floor level

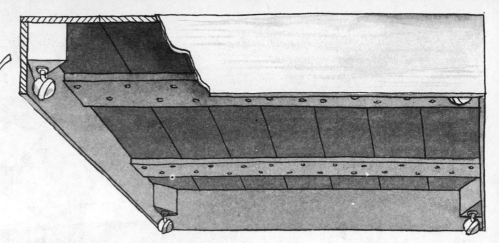

Trucks (in effect rostra on wheels) are highly adaptable scenic devices, allowing quick changes of scene. They can be run on rails, as shown below, be independent on castors, as illustrated opposite, or be revolved on a hinge as shown on the ground plan and photographs on pages 103 and 106.

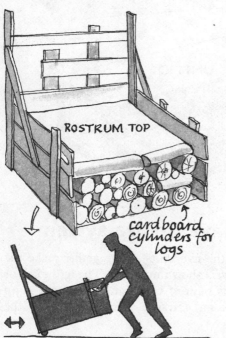

ROSTRUM TOP

cardboard cylinders for logs

A truck based on the wheelbarrow principle. Two wheel or ball castors fixed to the rear of the truck with two hand grips at the front. Lift to push into position, lower to achieve stability. Illustrated on page 70.

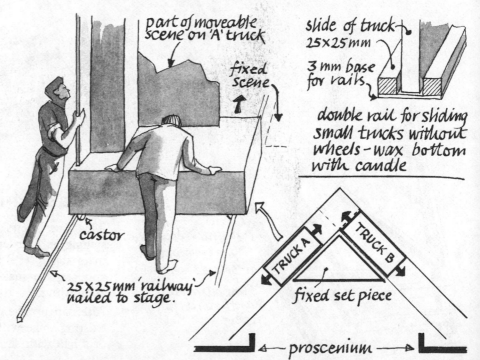

part of moveable scene on 'A' truck

fixed scene

castor

25 × 25 mm 'railway' nailed to stage.

slide of truck 25 × 25 mm

3 mm base for rails

double rail for sliding small trucks without wheels – wax bottom with candle

TRUCK A

TRUCK B

fixed set piece

proscenium

Two trucks – or more if required – can be used in conjunction with a set piece, allowing a wide range of quick scene changes.

truck unit A

truck unit B

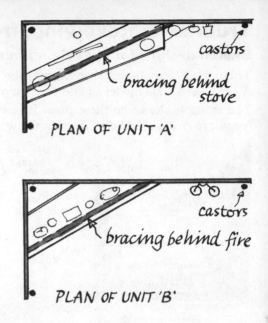

PLAN OF UNIT 'A'

castors

bracing behind stove

bracing behind fire

castors

PLAN OF UNIT 'B'

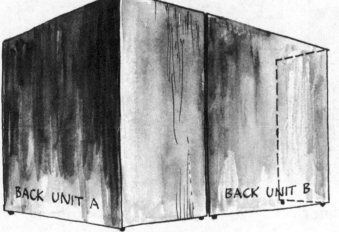

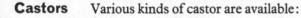

BACK UNIT A

BACK UNIT B

Two free-moving units

The two fireplaces shown above reveal, when reversed, either a long high wall or two smaller walls. Alternatively, another scene could be built and painted on the reverse sides. The fireplaces are made with thin plywood or hardboard on a 50 × 25 mm timber frame. See page 131 for an illustration showing 'wall' sides.

Castors   Various kinds of castor are available:

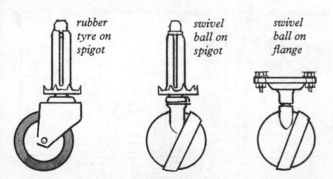

rubber tyre on spigot

swivel ball on spigot

swivel ball on flange

Small and medium-sized castors for revolving flats.

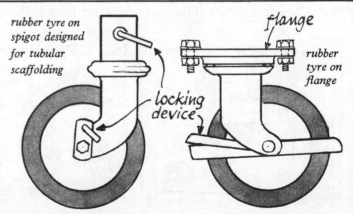

rubber tyre on spigot designed for tubular scaffolding

locking device

flange

rubber tyre on flange

Heavy-duty castors, suitable for trucks and large mobiles.

Trucks – 2: Revolving, free-turning

Sketch designs for a revolving truck

These small 'thumb-nail' sketches may serve as one method of thinking out an idea for scenic and constructional devices. A cardboard scale model should then be prepared to test the theory.

The example shown on these pages is based on a production of 'Romeo and Juliet' – see also the section on painting (page 129) for a method of treating the wall side of this mobile rostrum.

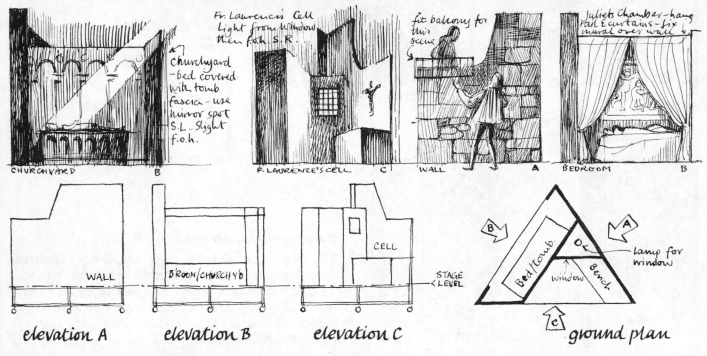

A small house for 'Fiddler on the Roof'.

A small house for 'Fiddler on the Roof'. These small sketches illustrate ideas for the numerous scenes demanded by the text. The construction of this large revolving truck is shown on page 46. Photographs on pages 26, 70 and 282.

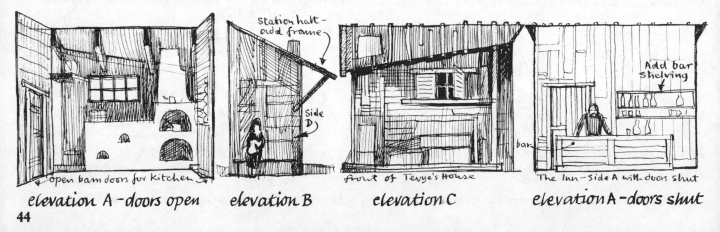

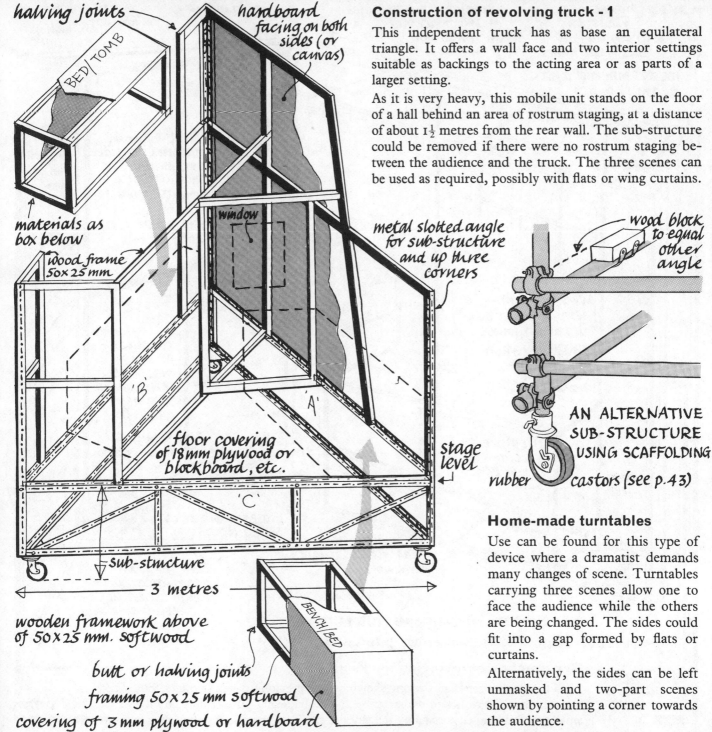

halving joints

hardboard facing on both sides (or canvas)

BED/TOMB

materials as box below

wood frame 50 × 25 mm

window

metal slotted angle for sub-structure and up three corners

'B'

'A'

floor covering of 18 mm plywood or blockboard, etc.

stage level

'C'

sub-structure

3 metres

wooden framework above of 50 × 25 mm. softwood

butt or halving joints

framing 50 × 25 mm softwood

covering of 3 mm plywood or hardboard

BENCH/BED

wood block to equal other angle

AN ALTERNATIVE SUB-STRUCTURE USING SCAFFOLDING

rubber castors (see p. 43)

Construction of revolving truck - 1

This independent truck has as base an equilateral triangle. It offers a wall face and two interior settings suitable as backings to the acting area or as parts of a larger setting.

As it is very heavy, this mobile unit stands on the floor of a hall behind an area of rostrum staging, at a distance of about $1\frac{1}{2}$ metres from the rear wall. The sub-structure could be removed if there were no rostrum staging between the audience and the truck. The three scenes can be used as required, possibly with flats or wing curtains.

Home-made turntables

Use can be found for this type of device where a dramatist demands many changes of scene. Turntables carrying three scenes allow one to face the audience while the others are being changed. The sides could fit into a gap formed by flats or curtains.

Alternatively, the sides can be left unmasked and two-part scenes shown by pointing a corner towards the audience.

45

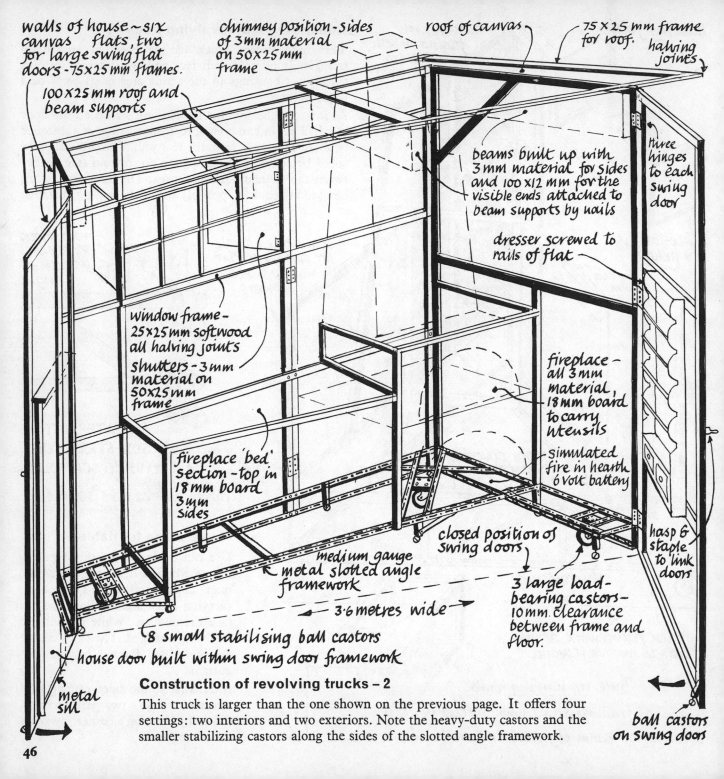

walls of house ~ six canvas flats, two for large swing flat doors - 75 × 25 mm frames.

chimney position - sides of 3 mm material on 50 × 25 mm frame

roof of canvas

75 × 25 mm frame for roof.

halving joints

100 × 25 mm roof and beam supports

beams built up with 3 mm material for sides and 100 × 12 mm for the visible ends attached to beam supports by nails

three hinges to each swing door

dresser screwed to rails of flat

window frame - 25 × 25 mm softwood all halving joints

shutters - 3 mm material on 50 × 25 mm frame

fireplace - all 3 mm material, 18 mm board to carry utensils

fireplace 'bed' section - top in 18 mm board 3 mm sides

simulated fire in hearth 6 volt battery

medium gauge metal slotted angle framework

closed position of swing doors

hasp & staple to link doors

3.6 metres wide

3 large load-bearing castors - 10 mm clearance between frame and floor.

8 small stabilising ball castors

house door built within swing door framework

metal sill

ball castors on swing doors

Construction of revolving trucks – 2

This truck is larger than the one shown on the previous page. It offers four settings: two interiors and two exteriors. Note the heavy-duty castors and the smaller stabilizing castors along the sides of the slotted angle framework.

Flats

3

CONSTRUCTION · GROUND ROWS AND CUT-OUTS · DOORS · WINDOWS · SCREENS

Flats and joints	48
Types of flat	50
Construction	52
Joining and bracing	54
Ground rows and cut-outs	58
Doors and windows	60
Screens	66
Softwood sections	68

FLATS

Stage scenery has traditionally been constructed from flats of varying shape and size. Their main function is to mask off the immediate back and sides of the stage, creating with the aid of paint and texture a new environment of mood and time. Although in some cases superseded by new materials and techniques, flats are – with curtains – still the most practical and versatile way of building height and width on the stage.

Flats consist of a wooden frame over which canvas is tightly stretched and tacked. The size of the frame is determined by hall ceilings and proscenium openings. The top of the frame should be level with the top of the borders in a proscenium theatre; this will be approximately 1 metre higher than the top of the proscenium arch – see lower illustration on page 16.

A wide selection of widths is desirable on a large stage for box sets (see pages 88–91) but for simple 'border and wing with curtains' a uniform width of about 1 metre is sufficient provided that the flats are correctly placed to mask the 'offstage' area (see page 17). For such a purpose, six wing flats will usually be enough, three for each side.

Canvas can be expensive. Hardboard can be substituted; it needs to be well glued and tacked and does, of course, add considerably to the total weight.

Variations on the basic unit and methods of securing flats to the stage are described on the following pages. The last few pages of this section deal with alternatives to cloths (screens and folding flats).

It is worth experimenting with a variety of materials on the surface of the basic unit: expanded polystrene, rag, torn and crumpled newspaper, plaster, etc. in order to achieve the required effect – see also the section on painting.

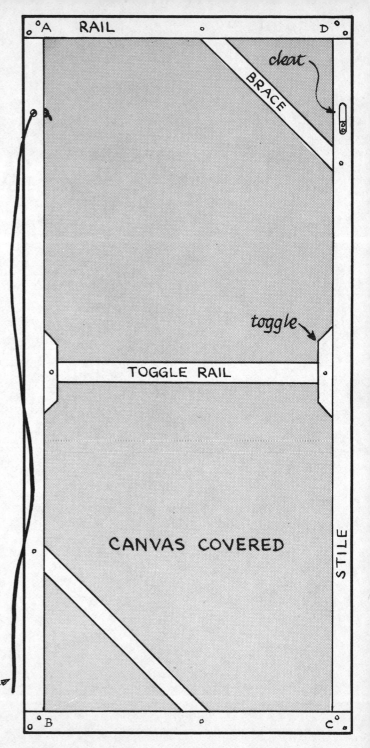

The joints

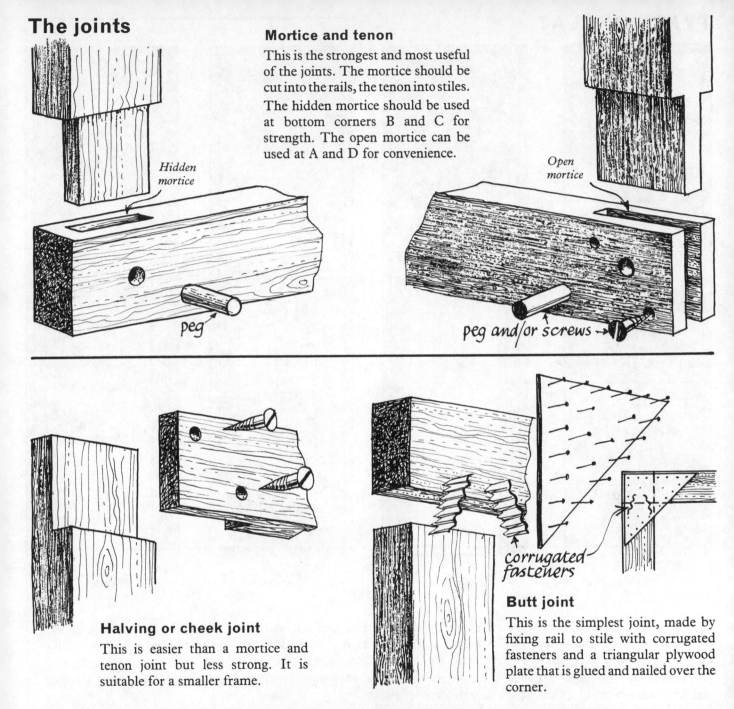

Mortice and tenon

This is the strongest and most useful of the joints. The mortice should be cut into the rails, the tenon into stiles.

The hidden mortice should be used at bottom corners B and C for strength. The open mortice can be used at A and D for convenience.

Hidden mortice

peg

Open mortice

peg and/or screws

corrugated fasteners

Halving or cheek joint

This is easier than a mortice and tenon joint but less strong. It is suitable for a smaller frame.

Butt joint

This is the simplest joint, made by fixing rail to stile with corrugated fasteners and a triangular plywood plate that is glued and nailed over the corner.

The halving and butt joints are quite adequate for most small frames, are quickly built and will withstand considerable use throughout a number of productions.

TYPES OF FLAT

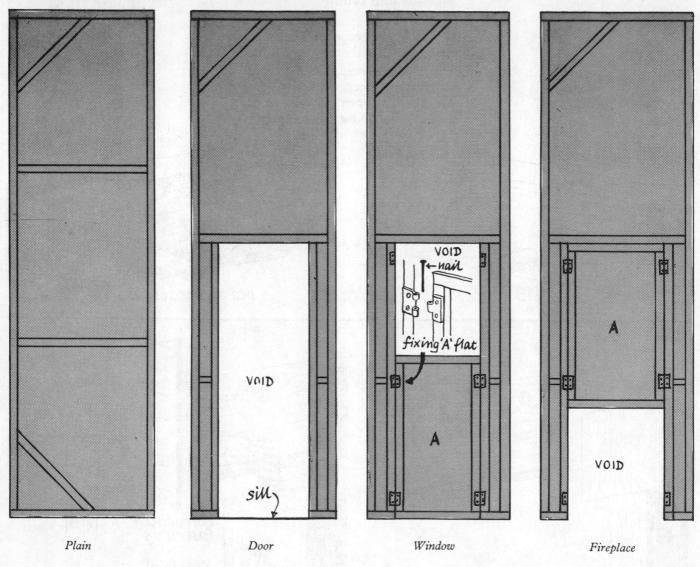

| *Plain* | *Door* | *Window* | *Fireplace* |

Flats can be divided into two main groups: those that are rectangular and are used chiefly for interiors or simple functional sets and those that have at least one irregular edge – sometimes two or three – and are used chiefly for exteriors. The latter are called 'cut-outs' and are illustrated on the opposite page.

Basic room flats are shown above with variations for door, window and fireplace. The door flat can be used for window and fireplace as well by placing part **A** in different positions.

Other rectangular flats are sometimes hinged together and are then called 'book flats'. More than two hinged together make a screen.

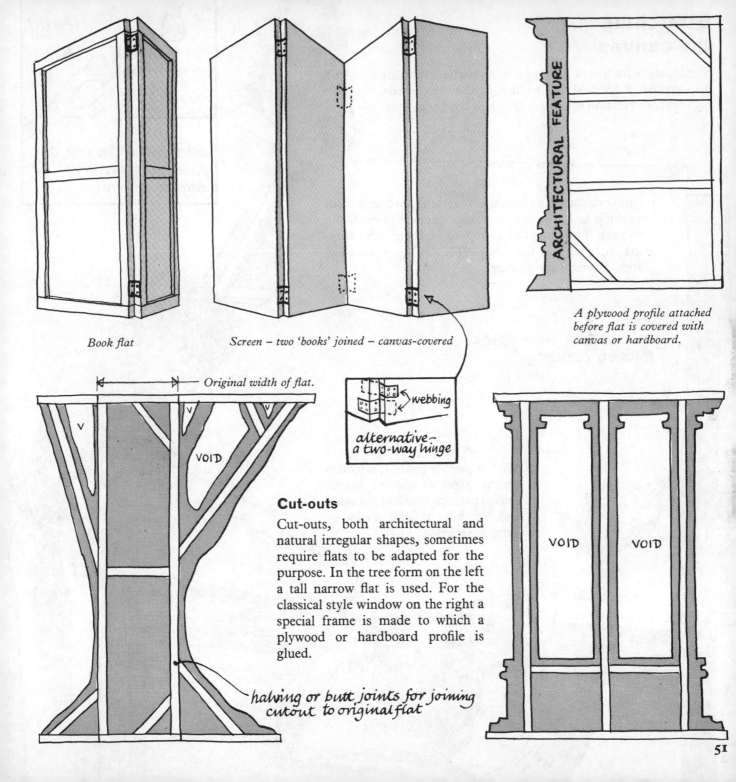

Book flat

Screen – two 'books' joined – canvas-covered

ARCHITECTURAL FEATURE

A plywood profile attached before flat is covered with canvas or hardboard.

← webbing

alternative – a two-way hinge

Original width of flat.

V

V

V

VOID

VOID VOID

Cut-outs

Cut-outs, both architectural and natural irregular shapes, sometimes require flats to be adapted for the purpose. In the tree form on the left a tall narrow flat is used. For the classical style window on the right a special frame is made to which a plywood or hardboard profile is glued.

halving or butt joints for joining cutout to original flat

Stretching the canvas

Scenic canvas, of flax or cotton duck, is purchased already fire-proofed in 36″ and 72″ widths (or their centimetre equivalents). Hessian is cheaper but does not last as long.

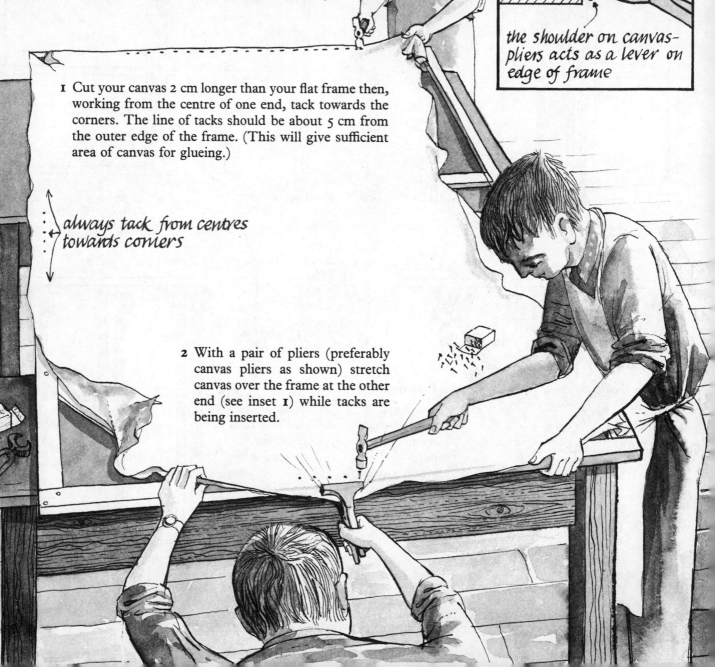

Inset 1.

canvas

the shoulder on canvas-pliers acts as a lever on edge of frame

1 Cut your canvas 2 cm longer than your flat frame then, working from the centre of one end, tack towards the corners. The line of tacks should be about 5 cm from the outer edge of the frame. (This will give sufficient area of canvas for glueing.)

always tack from centres towards corners

2 With a pair of pliers (preferably canvas pliers as shown) stretch canvas over the frame at the other end (see inset 1) while tacks are being inserted.

Glueing and trimming

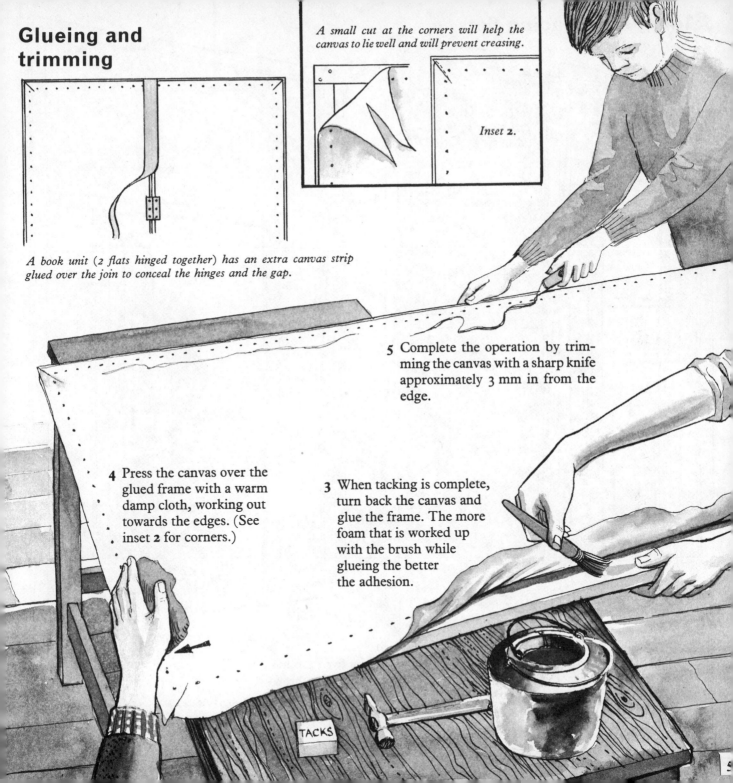

A book unit (2 flats hinged together) has an extra canvas strip glued over the join to conceal the hinges and the gap.

A small cut at the corners will help the canvas to lie well and will prevent creasing.

Inset 2.

5 Complete the operation by trimming the canvas with a sharp knife approximately 3 mm in from the edge.

4 Press the canvas over the glued frame with a warm damp cloth, working out towards the edges. (See inset **2** for corners.)

3 When tacking is complete, turn back the canvas and glue the frame. The more foam that is worked up with the brush while glueing the better the adhesion.

TACKS

Joining and bracing flats

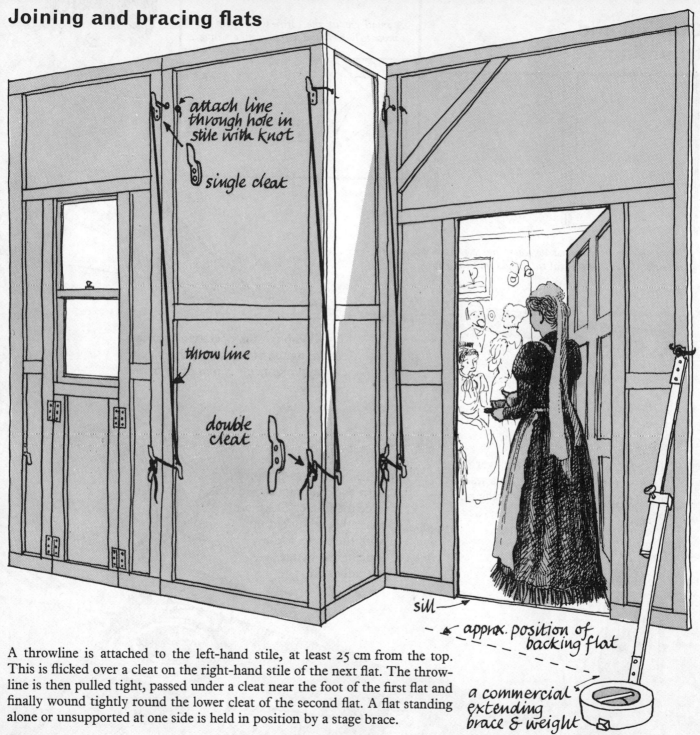

attach line through hole in stile with knot

single cleat

throw line

double cleat

sill

approx. position of backing flat

a commercial extending brace & weight

A throwline is attached to the left-hand stile, at least 25 cm from the top. This is flicked over a cleat on the right-hand stile of the next flat. The throwline is then pulled tight, passed under a cleat near the foot of the first flat and finally wound tightly round the lower cleat of the second flat. A flat standing alone or unsupported at one side is held in position by a stage brace.

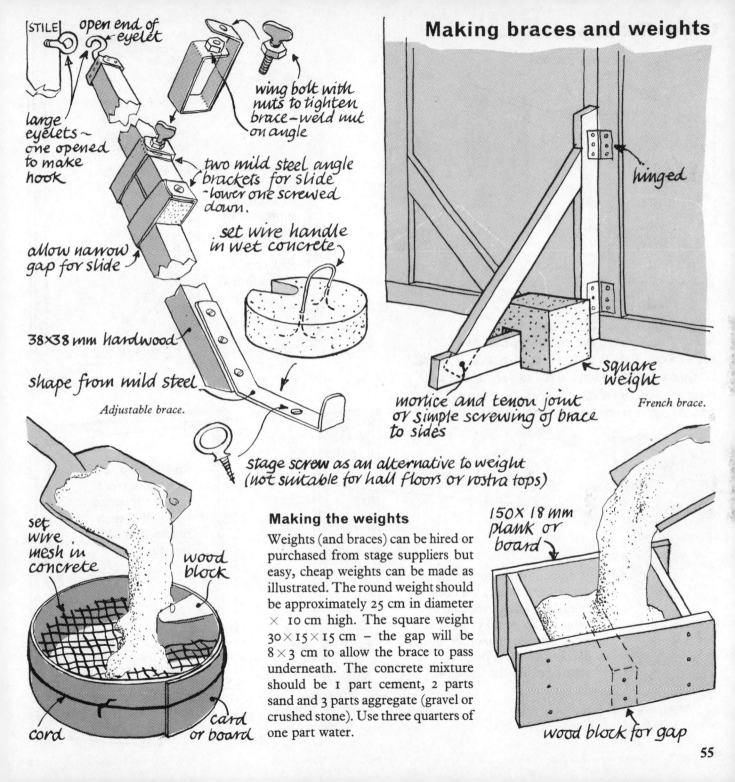

[STILE]

open end of eyelet

large eyelets — one opened to make hook

wing bolt with nuts to tighten brace — weld nut on angle

two mild steel angle brackets for slide — lower one screwed down.

allow narrow gap for slide

set wire handle in wet concrete

38×38 mm hardwood

shape from mild steel

Adjustable brace.

stage screw as an alternative to weight (not suitable for hall floors or rostra tops)

hinged

square weight

mortice and tenon joint or simple screwing of brace to sides

French brace.

set wire mesh in concrete

wood block

cord

card or board

Making the weights

Weights (and braces) can be hired or purchased from stage suppliers but easy, cheap weights can be made as illustrated. The round weight should be approximately 25 cm in diameter × 10 cm high. The square weight 30×15×15 cm – the gap will be 8×3 cm to allow the brace to pass underneath. The concrete mixture should be 1 part cement, 2 parts sand and 3 parts aggregate (gravel or crushed stone). Use three quarters of one part water.

150×18 mm plank or board

wood block for gap

55

Other flat supports . . .

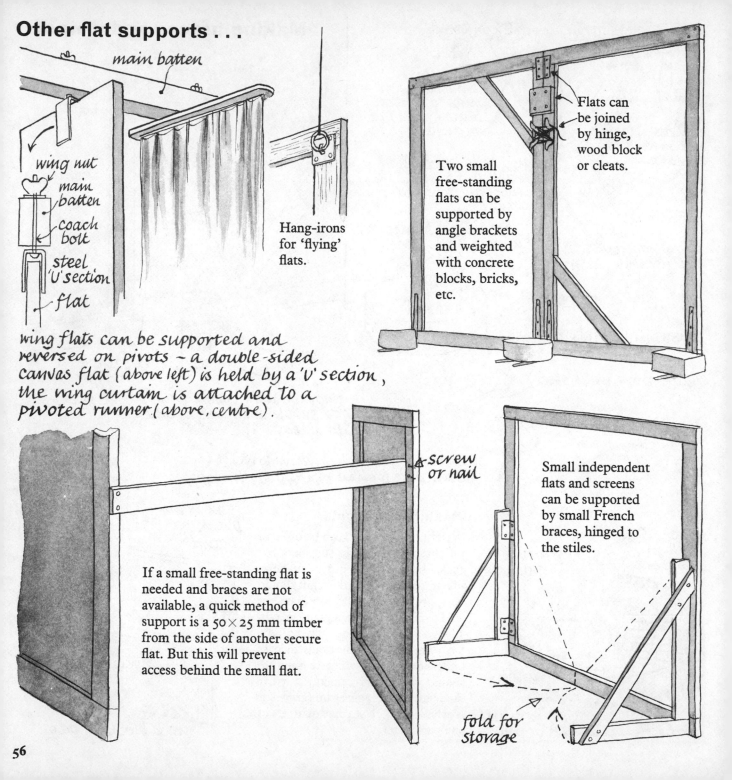

main batten

wing nut
main batten
coach bolt
steel 'U' section
flat

Hang-irons for 'flying' flats.

Flats can be joined by hinge, wood block or cleats.

Two small free-standing flats can be supported by angle brackets and weighted with concrete blocks, bricks, etc.

wing flats can be supported and reversed on pivots ~ a double-sided canvas flat (above left) is held by a 'V' section, the wing curtain is attached to a pivoted runner (above, centre).

screw or nail

If a small free-standing flat is needed and braces are not available, a quick method of support is a 50×25 mm timber from the side of another secure flat. But this will prevent access behind the small flat.

Small independent flats and screens can be supported by small French braces, hinged to the stiles.

fold for storage

A simple screen background consisting of three or four flats

To give maximum clearance between front and rear, the supports can be carried across the top rails as shown. The braces behind the back flats can be of the French or sliding brace type.

This kind of simple setting could be useful in a school hall as a screen for Nativity and Passion plays – see pages 240–242.

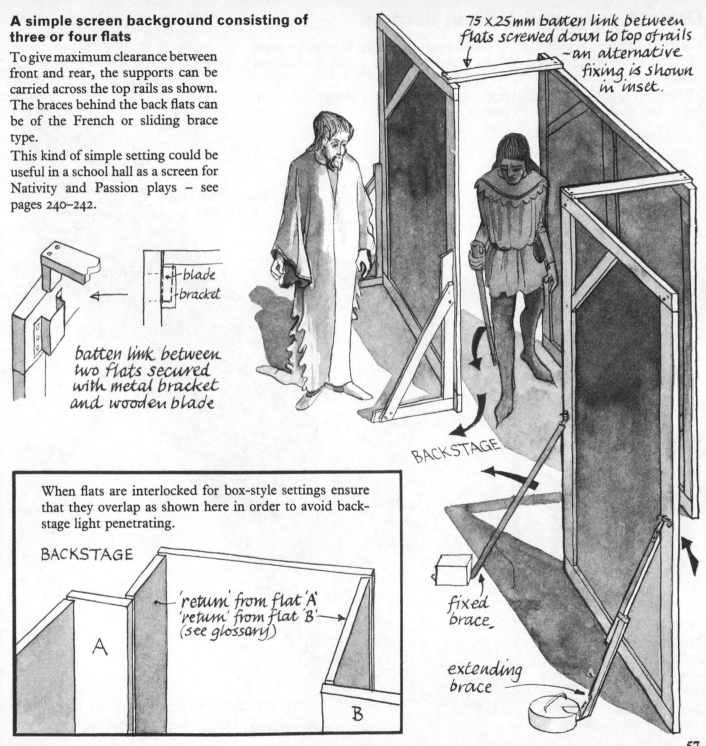

batten link between two flats secured with metal bracket and wooden blade

blade
bracket

75 × 25 mm batten link between flats screwed down to top of rails – an alternative fixing is shown in inset.

BACKSTAGE

fixed brace

extending brace

When flats are interlocked for box-style settings ensure that they overlap as shown here in order to avoid backstage light penetrating.

BACKSTAGE

'return' from flat 'A'
'return' from flat 'B'
(see glossary)

A

B

Ground-rows and cut-out borders

Large ground-rows are flats in a horizontal position on the floor of the stage with a profile of hills, trees, etc. cut out in plywood or hardboard and attached to the upper edge. See page 117 for an illustration.

The smaller ground-rows can be made entirely of plywood or hardboard with one or two strengtheners of 50×25 mm timber.

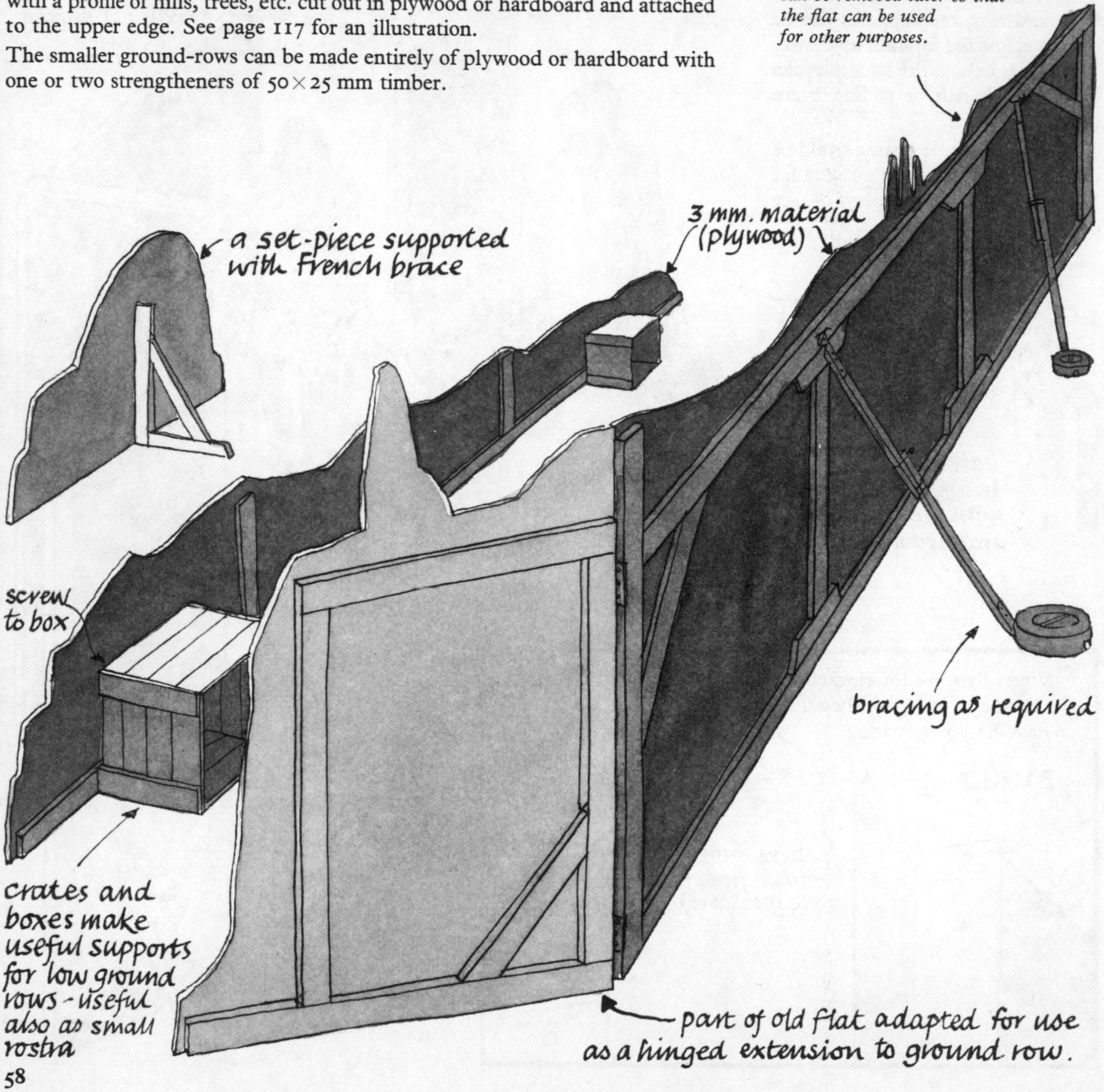

Thin plywood or hardboard tacked and glued to the top edge of the flat. This can be removed later so that the flat can be used for other purposes.

a set-piece supported with French brace

3 mm. material (plywood)

screw to box

bracing as required

crates and boxes make useful supports for low ground rows - useful also as small rostra

part of old flat adapted for use as a hinged extension to ground row.

58

tied to flies/battens

main battens

LIGHTING BATTEN

BORDER

cut-out borders

'leg' between wing and border

Cut-out borders are constructed in much the same way for wings and borders.
Cut-outs and ground-rows are ideal for pantomime and similar productions.

cut-out on wings

canvas cut-out using
gauze for large gaps

WING

ground row

footlights

hinged as book flat

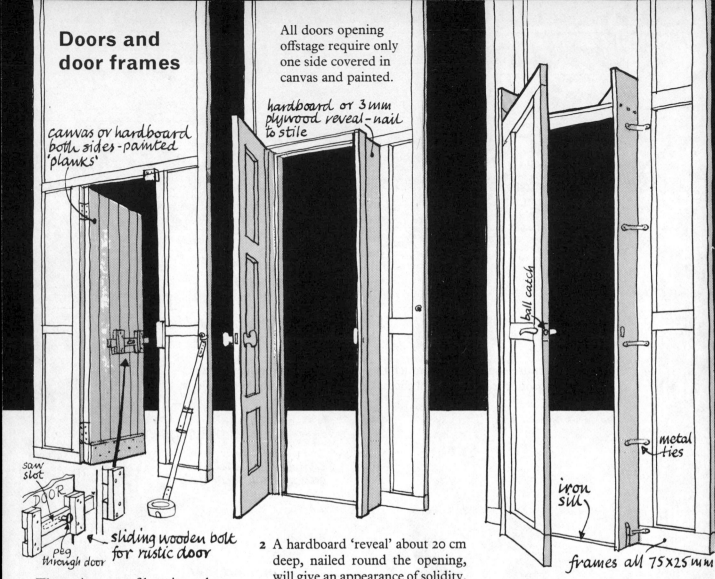

Doors and door frames

canvas or hardboard both sides - painted 'planks'

All doors opening offstage require only one side covered in canvas and painted.

hardboard or 3 mm plywood reveal - nail to stile

ball catch

metal ties

iron sill

saw slot

DOOR

peg through door

sliding wooden bolt for rustic door

frames all 75 × 25 mm

1 The easiest way of hanging a door is to hinge it direct to the flat opening – a strip of canvas behind the door will exclude backstage light.

2 A hardboard 'reveal' about 20 cm deep, nailed round the opening, will give an appearance of solidity. The back edges can be strengthened with 50 × 25 mm battens. Door stops or moulding (thin vertical 35 × 10 mm wood strips) will exclude light from backstage.

3 A more substantial version of **2**: the reveal is built of 20 × 2.5 cm planking and fastened to the flat with small metal brackets.

door stop →

Rear (backstage).

3mm moulding stop

Rear (backstage).

← 25 mm moulding ← door stop

Rear (backstage).

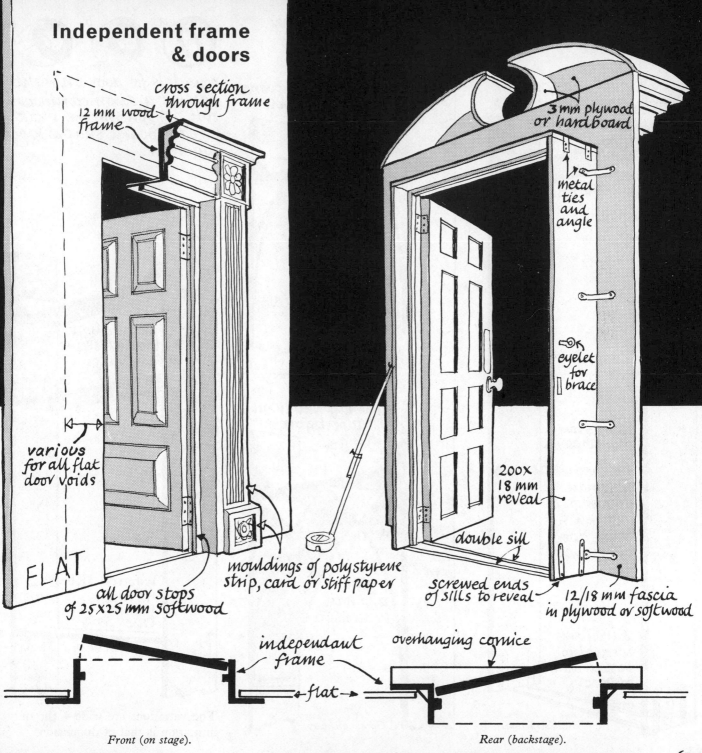

Independent frame & doors

cross section through frame

12 mm wood frame

various for all flat door voids

FLAT

all door stops of 25×25 mm softwood

mouldings of polystyrene strip, card or stiff paper

3 mm plywood or hardboard

metal ties and angle

eyelet for brace

200× 18 mm reveal

double sill

screwed ends of sills to reveal

12/18 mm fascia in plywood or softwood

independant frame

overhanging cornice

flat

Front (on stage).

Rear (backstage).

A frame for all purposes – door or window

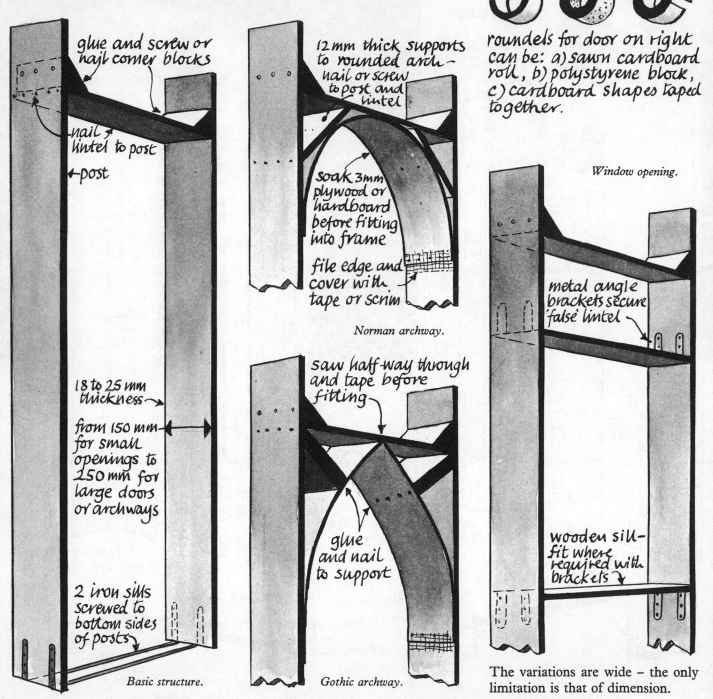

glue and screw or nail corner blocks

nail lintel to post

post

18 to 25 mm thickness

from 150 mm for small openings to 250 mm for large doors or archways

2 iron sills screwed to bottom sides of posts

Basic structure.

12 mm thick supports to rounded arch – nail or screw to post and lintel

soak 3mm plywood or hardboard before fitting into frame

file edge and cover with tape or scrim

Norman archway.

saw half-way through and tape before fitting

glue and nail to support

Gothic archway.

roundels for door on right can be: a) sawn cardboard roll, b) polystyrene block, c) cardboard shapes taped together.

Window opening.

metal angle brackets secure 'false' lintel

wooden sill fit where required with brackets

The variations are wide – the only limitation is that of dimension.

Gothic door with solid moulding.

arches shaped from 75 mm softwood pieces or 3mm ply shapes

French window.

if pulley system is attempted use 25mm thick frame and small pulley

25 x 25 mm wood frame

sash weights hidden behind flats to each side of window

Sash window.

parting bead - 25 x 12 mm.

A basic frame is useful if it has been designed to fit the door void of an existing flat. The change from one type of door or window to another is quite simple provided that care is taken with the means of attachment. A sash window, as illustrated on the right, would require four holes to carry sashes with weights. Since pulleys cannot conveniently be fitted into this type of frame, smooth grooves should be carefully made in the holes to carry the cords.

Windows

a This is an independent window with a frame designed to fit an existing window flat. The frame can be fitted with a casement, as shown, or with a sash (see previous page).

b A small window opening without frame or glass: it has been built into a modified existing stock flat, using a hardboard reveal and a 150×25 mm wood plank sill. A 50×25 mm batten under the front edge of the sill will eliminate the light crack.

c and **d** Two methods of creating leaded windows: painting lines on film or taping. Taping can be quicker and cheaper. The small inset in **d** shows the taping of a casement window, whereas the main illustration shows taping to the edge of the reveal where the window does not have to open.

e A small stained glass window.

Joints for the casement frame are illustrated below.

WINDOW VOID

moulding— 75×25 mm

a *The illustration shows a half-section through window-frame.*

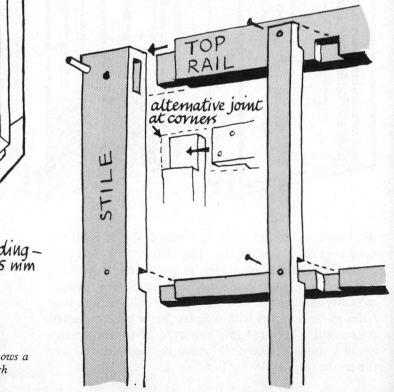

TOP RAIL

alternative joint at corners

STILE

64

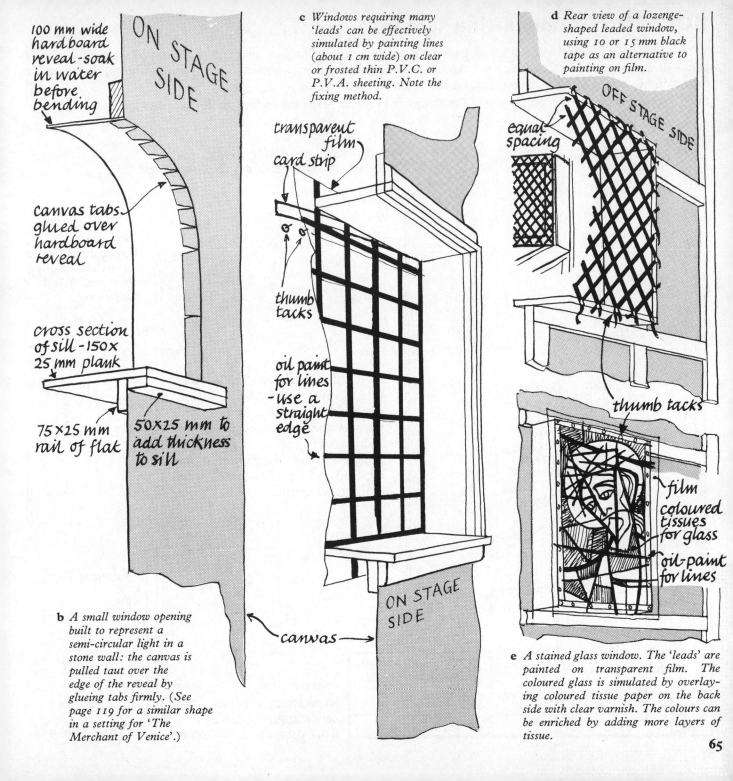

100 mm wide hardboard reveal - soak in water before bending

ON STAGE SIDE

canvas tabs glued over hardboard reveal

cross section of sill - 150 × 25 mm plank

75 × 25 mm rail of flat

50 × 25 mm to add thickness to sill

b *A small window opening built to represent a semi-circular light in a stone wall: the canvas is pulled taut over the edge of the reveal by glueing tabs firmly. (See page 119 for a similar shape in a setting for 'The Merchant of Venice'.)*

c *Windows requiring many 'leads' can be effectively simulated by painting lines (about 1 cm wide) on clear or frosted thin P.V.C. or P.V.A. sheeting. Note the fixing method.*

transparent film

card strip

thumb tacks

oil paint for lines - use a straight edge

ON STAGE SIDE

canvas

d *Rear view of a lozenge-shaped leaded window, using 10 or 15 mm black tape as an alternative to painting on film.*

OFF STAGE SIDE

equal spacing

thumb tacks

film

coloured tissues for glass

oil-paint for lines

e *A stained glass window. The 'leads' are painted on transparent film. The coloured glass is simulated by overlaying coloured tissue paper on the back side with clear varnish. The colours can be enriched by adding more layers of tissue.*

65

SCREENS: A concertina screen

Where funds or facilities will not allow backcloths and you are seeking an alternative method of scene-changing, a pair – or more – of book flats (page 51) can be used, hinged together as shown. This assembly shows, at one end, a firm fixing to a post by butt-hinges and, on the other, a French brace.

Such a screen is used in a production of 'She Stoops to Conquer' – see the section on design, page 97.

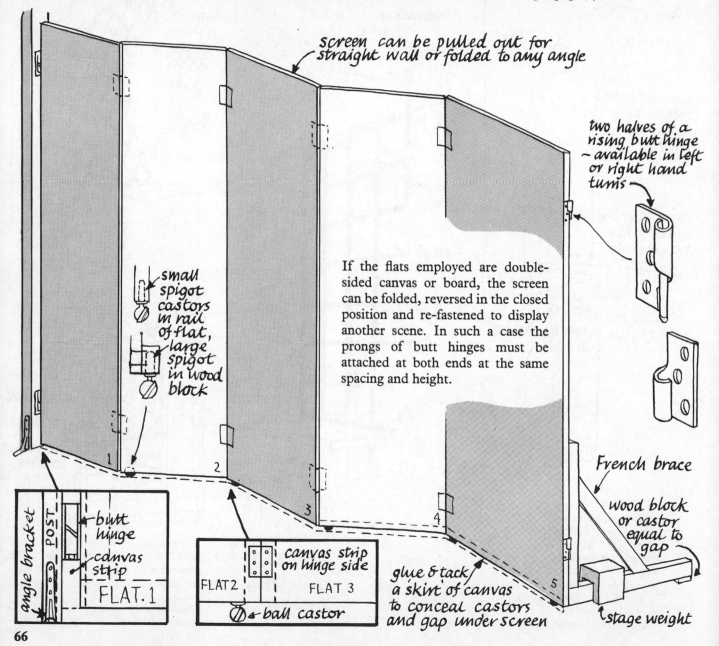

screen can be pulled out for straight wall or folded to any angle

two halves of a rising butt hinge – available in left or right hand turns

small spigot castors in rail of flat, large spigot in wood block

If the flats employed are double-sided canvas or board, the screen can be folded, reversed in the closed position and re-fastened to display another scene. In such a case the prongs of butt hinges must be attached at both ends at the same spacing and height.

French brace

wood block or castor equal to gap

angle bracket

POST

butt hinge

canvas strip

FLAT.1

FLAT 2   canvas strip on hinge side   FLAT 3

ball castor

glue & tack a skirt of canvas to conceal castors and gap under screen

stage weight

66

Arched screens

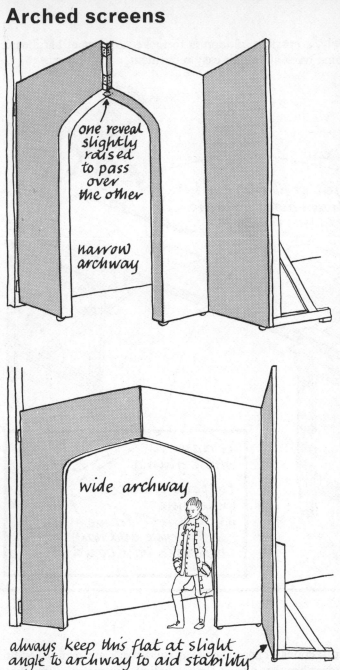

one reveal slightly raised to pass over the other

narrow archway

wide archway

always keep this flat at slight angle to archway to aid stability

The archway shown offers a wide range of shape by opening and closing the 'book'. A French brace hinged to the third flat ensures stability.

STEP LADDER

360° turn on flats by double webbing

This set of three flats includes a doorway and a window opening. Two flats can be easily folded through 90° to create a new spatial concept. The method of fixing to a vertical structure is again by rising butt hinges. An example of this type of screen can be noticed in the scenes and plan drawing for 'The Merchant of Venice', positioned upstage right – see pages 92–93. For a more detailed close-up of the painted surface turn to page 119.

Sliding screens

If curtains are not available, or backcloths are in short supply, a possible solution is to make up a set of hardboard screens. They can be made to any height and width. A running track allows for easy movement.

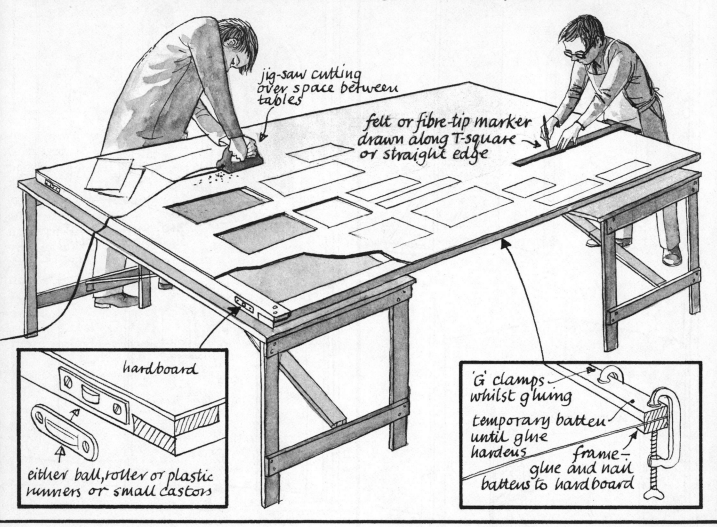

jig-saw cutting over space between tables

felt or fibre-tip marker drawn along T-square or straight edge

hardboard

either ball, roller or plastic runners or small castors

'G' clamps whilst gluing

temporary batten until glue hardens

frame - glue and nail battens to hardboard

SOFTWOOD SECTIONS

Listed right in diagrammatic layout are various metric wood sections. Those shown in solid black are mentioned on pages concerned with the manufacture of rostra and flats. Remember that planed timber will always measure less than sawn sizes (nominal sizes). Allowance should be made for this when calculating requirements. Plywood can be obtained in 3, 4, 6, 9, 12 and 18 mm thicknesses. Thicker sheets are not required. Dowelling is available in 3, 4, 6, 9, 12, 15, 18 and 22 mm diameters.

height of screens is determined by borders

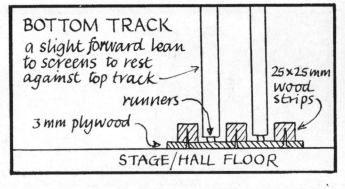

TOP TRACK

two 100 × 32 mm battens screwed to top plate

75 × 25 mm screen frame

hardboard

16 mm thick

This assembly shows a set of cut-out screens set out approximately 1 metre in front of the cyclorama or backcloth – used with strong back lighting. This method offers a variety of changes by means of a simple track system. When the screens are drawn back into the wings they reveal the scene painted on the backcloth or the cyclorama. Four, five or more can stretch over any width of stage provided that there is enough track for easy movement. The cut-outs may be varied to suit the needs of the play – this assembly was designed to show New York at night in a production of 'West Side Story' – see also the section on design, pages 105–106.

BOTTOM TRACK

a slight forward lean to screens to rest against top track

runners

3 mm plywood

25 × 25 mm wood strips

STAGE/HALL FLOOR

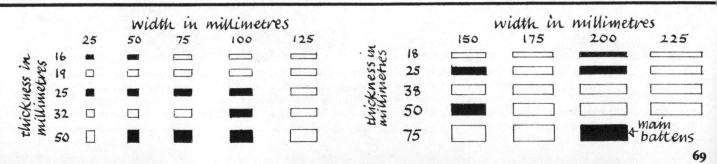

	width in millimetres				
thickness in millimetres	25	50	75	100	125
16	■	■	☐	☐	☐
19	☐	☐	☐	☐	☐
25	■	■	■	■	☐
32	☐	☐	☐	■	☐
50	☐	■	■	■	☐

	width in millimetres			
thickness in millimetres	150	175	200	225
18	☐	☐	■	☐
25	■	☐	■	☐
38	☐	☐	☐	☐
50	■	☐	☐	☐
75	☐	☐	■	☐ main battens

Scenes from 'Fiddler on the Roof'. Top: the kitchen of Tevye's house, the furniture removed to show more clearly the construction of the revolving truck (see page 46). Bottom left and right: the truck reversed to positions S.L. and S.R., offering exterior views of Tevye's house. In the yard scene on the left, fencing has been joined to the house to create a different silhouette effect – see page 149 for fencing. The scene on the right shows the house shape slightly modified by adding a rostrum truck – see page 42 – resembling a log pile against the wall. A ground row conceals the batten lighting for the cyclorama.

Design

4

PLANNING · MODELS · WORKING DRAWINGS · TYPES OF DESIGN

Basic notes	72
Planning the set	74
Sketch methods	75
Models	76
The working drawings (including useful symbols)	79
Types of stage design	82
Arena and theatre-in-the-round	82
Screen settings	85
Curtain sets	86
Wing and cloth sets	87
Box sets	88
Cyclorama sets	92
Composite settings	94
Permanent structures	96

SOME NOTES ON DESIGN

The planning and work required for any production depend on the time, energy and facilities available. Ideas may be simplified to meet a tight schedule. On the other hand, a very elaborate design is not necessarily more demanding (or rewarding) than a very simple one. The empty space that will become the acting area must always be considered in relation to good proportion within that space.

It is useful to consider a few approaches to the matter of design:

a If we think about the empty space, we begin to think in three dimensions, so that the setting and all the parts that go to make the setting will be conceived in 3-D.

b Balance must be achieved between the main planes (surfaces) and lines, the texture of the materials and the colour of paint and costumes.

c The placing of the parts and properties must always be related to the acting area and allow for the free movement of the actors.

It is important to stress the word 'balance' because this characteristic of good design can be overlooked if too much attention is given to detail or the less important parts of the setting. Always work from the whole concept – the large spatial areas and masses – and then develop the smaller details: the textural effects and colour within this framework.

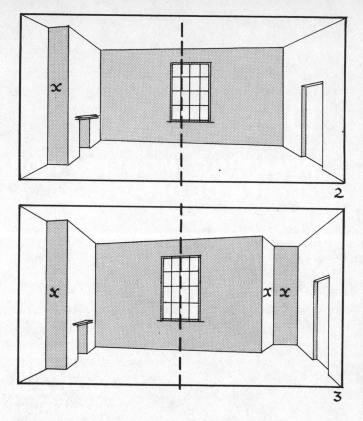

2

3

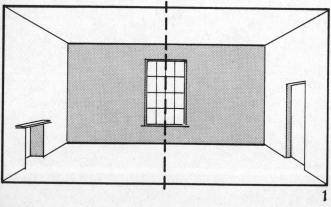

1

Balance should not be confused with symmetry, which is an exact correspondence of parts on either side of a centre line or axis – see **1** below.

In a simple setting with three walls, a floor and a ceiling (a box set) a completely symmetrical arrangement can be very dull and uninteresting.

A slight shift of emphasis from the central kind of balance can be achieved by moving the flats slightly, introducing a niche or chimney breast, for example, using quite narrow flats like **x** in **2** and **3**. This kind of balance offers much more variety to the eye. The sketch model on page 77 and perspective view on page 81 illustrate the point more clearly.

But symmetry does have a valuable part to play in many design ideas, especially in more elaborate, decorative settings. Provided that a wide variety of shape, pattern and tonal contrast are included, more or less symmetrical design can be quite satisfactory – see the setting on pages 84 and 85.

Some design terms

Certain terms used in design are introduced in this section:

Decorative design is related primarily to the painted scenery of backcloths, wings and borders; also to pattern and ornament within the setting.

Textural ideas relate to an interest in the surface appearance or 'feel' of the surfaces – often without the colour associated with more decorative designs.

The term *tonal* refers to the lightness or darkness of an area or surface, of whatever colour or texture, and is important when aiming for contrast or similarity between the parts of a setting.

The terms *decorative*, *textural* and *tonal* are usually related to the two-dimensional effects of painted canvas or the broken surfaces of paint.

When a design is more three-dimensional in concept, the term *structural* is used. This term expresses well the use of surfaces that suggest volume and solidity and where structures are erected and then covered with various materials. Settings of this kind can often employ new materials such as expanded polystyrene sheet and block, all kinds of metal foils and plasters. One major advantage of this type of scenery over the traditional painted scene is the range of possibilities it offers for imaginative lighting. When oblique lighting strikes across a built-up textural surface a much stronger sense of depth is achieved.

These terms apply equally to the section on painting (see pages 118–123 for surface painting, 128–131 for 3-D effects).

Reading, discussion and research

The design for a setting depends on a number of factors. It must meet the requirements of the text, the playwright's directions and the director's concept of the play.

To meet the demands of the text requires careful reading of the play and the stage directions, both at the beginning of each scene and throughout the text, so that the basic theme and the mood can be absorbed from scene to scene. The designer has then to develop and expand his own concept with the director.

Sometimes, when a playwright gives a detailed description of the setting, it can be more inhibiting than a simple word or phrase that describes only the location – 'the blasted heath', for example. Remember that your own concept, whilst being true to the playwright's needs, must not be submerged by too detailed a description. Always try to develop your own ideas round the main theme and location of the play.

Whatever the play, its location, time and period, it will always be necessary to do some research. Delve into background material from any source. You can use your local reference library, the museum, paintings, architectural features, costume books and personal recollections.

The director's understanding of the text must be discussed in detail and a common approach to all problems agreed. As the first sketches and notes are considered and discussed between director and designer, certain differences will become apparent – especially if the visual imagination of the two is not in accord. A design scheme has then to be developed to resolve any major differences.

Provided that the designer considers certain basic requirements of the acting area *before* sketching out his design the differences between designer and director are likely to be slight. The considerations are these:

Firstly, know your space. Are the exits and entrances in the right position for ideal movement of the cast, or will you have to introduce a new entrance? (See also the question of placing temporary stages – page 83.)

Secondly, the correct placing of the seating arrangements on stage and the careful positioning of properties and supports that could trip up the actors during certain moves.

Thirdly, considerable care to be exercised in the positions of lights – discussed in detail in the section on stage lighting.

Finally, think always of the basic limitations of the actual building. Is there sufficient headroom for a balcony? Will a large 'prop' fit within the narrow confines between the existing wings? Is there adequate dressing room space for quick changes of elaborate costumes?

Always plan carefully and relate visual concepts to the space and the facilities available.

PLANNING THE SET

There are as many approaches to planning a setting as there are designers, but a few methods are frequently used:

1 the sketch method; **2** notes and rough sketches; **3** the rough model; **4** settings in a model theatre. These methods may overlap but they will now, for convenience, be considered separately.

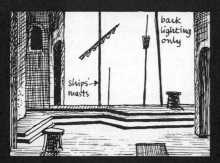

Presetting - Quayside

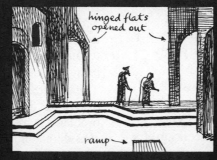

A1,S1 Street (or Quayside)
(use either pre-setting or this)

A1,S2 - Belmont

A2,S2 - Shylock's House - Street

A2,S4 - Another Street

A2,S7 - Casket scene - Belmont

A4,S1 - Court of Justice

A5,S1 - Avenue at Belmont

'The Merchant of Venice' – Shakespeare.

The eight sketches illustrate major scene and lighting changes.

This is an example of the first stage of planning the set using the sketch method. Three of the scenes based on these sketches are shown on pages 92 and 93.

1 The sketch method

Many designers prefer to draw a series of small sketches, usually executed in line or pen and wash, to show all the basic shape and structure and the effect of lighting on each scene.

The series of sketches on the opposite page are for the scene changes in a production of Shakespeare's 'Merchant of Venice'.

Executed in pen and ink only, the tonal effects are made by 'hatching' (a series of close lines) and help to show the director and lighting technician the basic concept of contrasts from scene to scene.

The sketches shown could as well have been executed in pen and wash or even with touches of colour – wash is quicker in application and gives a more 'fluid' effect.

Experiment with various media – pen, pen and wash, cut papers, watercolour and gouache or any other agreeable medium.

What must always be remembered is that the technique employed should suit the designer.

Notes in and around the sketches should give all necessary information on set changes and make clear the acting area.

2 Notes and rough sketches

Another method is to jot down everything that occurs to you as you read the text and talk with the director. This will make less demand on drawing ability and facilities but will require notes that are highly detailed – giving information to the director and all those concerned in the production.

Research should be undertaken and notes on colour, materials and lighting (together with samples) can be usefully attached to the main notes.

Very simple sketches of the elevation and plan view (explained on pages 79 and 81) will be helpful to clarify all written notes.

The quick sketch plan and elevation shown here with notes illustrate a starting point for planning a setting for Richard Rodney Bennett's 'All the King's Men'.

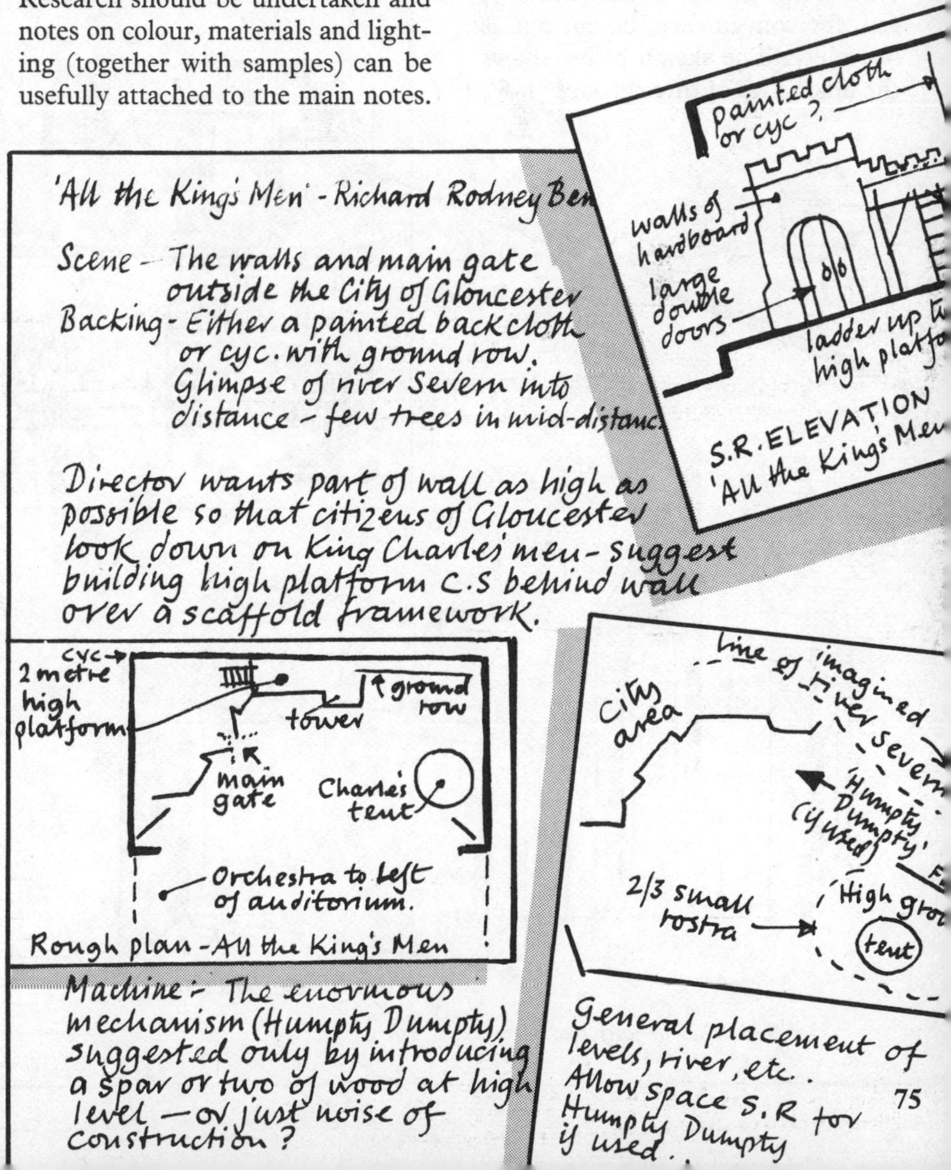

'All the King's Men' - Richard Rodney Ben[...]

Scene - The walls and main gate outside the City of Gloucester
Backing - Either a painted back cloth or cyc. with ground row.
Glimpse of river Severn into distance - few trees in mid-distance.

Director wants part of wall as high as possible so that citizens of Gloucester look down on King Charles' men - suggest building high platform C.S behind wall over a scaffold framework.

painted cloth or cyc?
walls of hardboard
large double doors
ladder up to high platform
S.R. ELEVATION 'All the King's Men'

cyc
2 metre high platform
tower
ground row
main gate
Charles' tent
Orchestra to left of auditorium.
Rough plan - All the King's Men

line of imagined river severn
City area
Humpty Dumpty (if used)
2/3 small rostra
High ground tent

Machine - The enormous mechanism (Humpty Dumpty) suggested only by introducing a spar or two of wood at high level – or just noise of construction?

General placement of levels, river, etc. Allow space S.R for Humpty Dumpty if used..

75

3 The rough model

Some designers prefer to draw a scale elevation of the setting on stiff paper or thin card, cutting out the parts with tabs and sticking to a base with some rough indications of colour.

Conventional box set

The illustration shows the scaled layout for making up a rough model. Draw up on thin card or stiff cartridge paper, colouring all parts *before* cutting to avoid the curling of the card.

Note that a group of flats (e.g. 3–5) can, for convenience, be cut out as one piece. The sketch below shows the linking up of three groups (1–8).

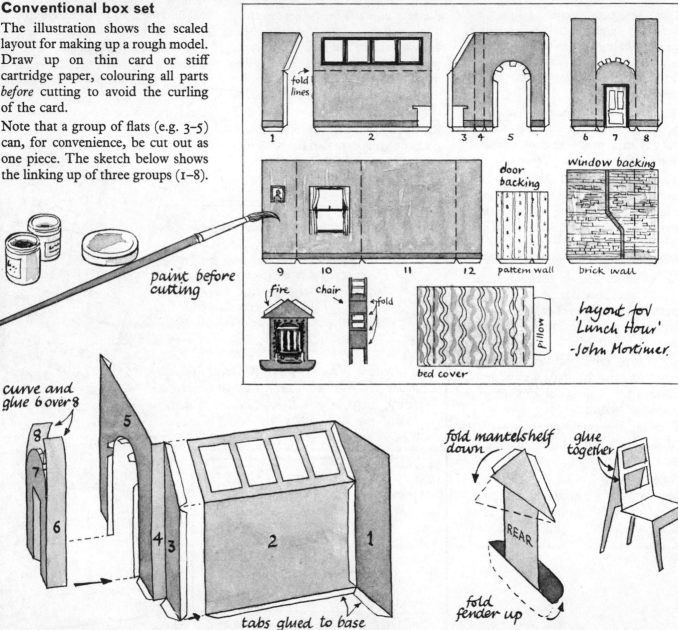

paint before cutting

fold lines

door backing

window backing

pattern wall

brick wall

fire   chair   fold

layout for 'Lunch Hour' -John Mortimer.

bed cover   Pillow

curve and glue 6 over 8

tabs glued to base

Rear view of flats 1 to 8.

fold mantelshelf down   glue together

REAR

fold fender up

Small props may be cut from thin pieces of card or balsa wood.

Prepare a piece of cardboard, thin plywood or hardboard for a base and draw out a ground plan showing positions for walls, etc. Place model scenery and props in position and colour floor, mats and other additions.

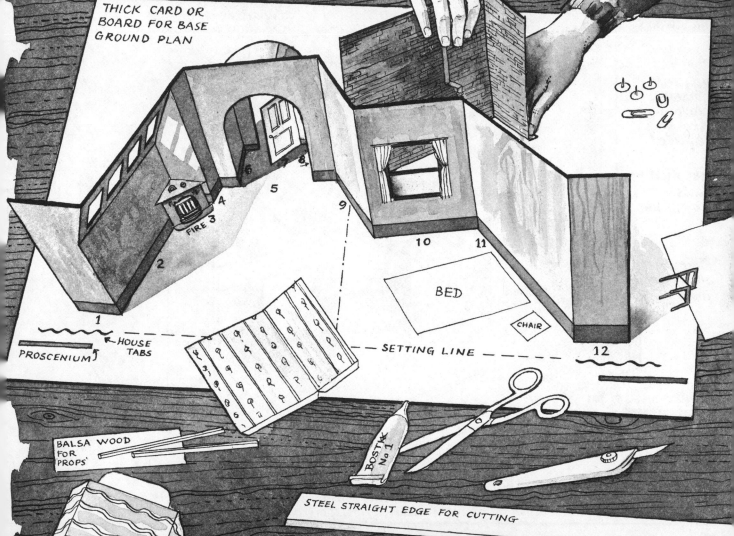

THICK CARD OR BOARD FOR BASE GROUND PLAN

FIRE 3

1 2 4 5 6 8 9 10 11 12

PROSCENIUM

HOUSE TABS

BED

CHAIR

SETTING LINE

BALSA WOOD FOR PROPS

BOSTIK No 1

STEEL STRAIGHT EDGE FOR CUTTING

4 Settings in a model theatre

The method most closely related to the actual stage setting is that using a scale model theatre – such models often have a lighting system based on a transformer and mains supply.

The setting within the scale model theatre shown below is a scene from 'Aladdin', showing the cave. A photograph of the setting and lighting effect is shown on page 87.

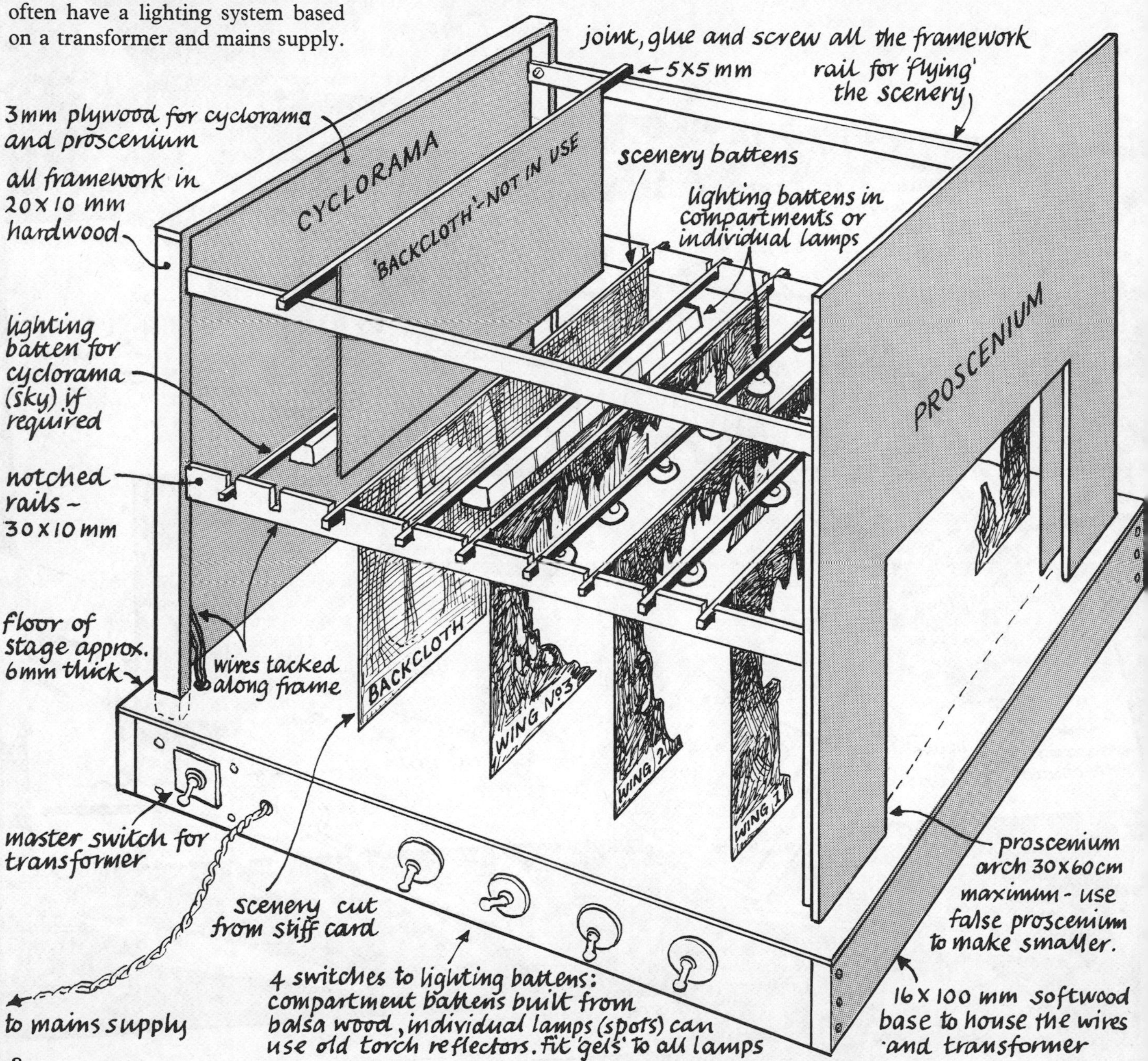

joint, glue and screw all the framework

5×5 mm

rail for 'flying' the scenery

3mm plywood for cyclorama and proscenium

CYCLORAMA

'BACKCLOTH'- NOT IN USE

scenery battens

lighting battens in compartments or individual lamps

all framework in 20×10 mm hardwood

PROSCENIUM

lighting batten for cyclorama (sky) if required

notched rails – 30×10 mm

floor of stage approx. 6mm thick

wires tacked along frame

BACKCLOTH

WING Nº3

WING 2

WING 1

master switch for transformer

scenery cut from stiff card

proscenium arch 30×60cm maximum – use false proscenium to make smaller

to mains supply

4 switches to lighting battens: compartment battens built from balsa wood, individual lamps (spots) can use old torch reflectors. Fit 'gels' to all lamps

16×100 mm softwood base to house the wires and transformer

THE WORKING DRAWINGS

Following the planning stage, it is useful to prepare working drawings before building complicated sets. (Simple cloth and border settings may not require such drawings.)

1 When one of the sketches or models has been agreed upon, the *ground-plan* is prepared.

The ground-plan is a top or bird's eye view of the floor of the stage showing all horizontal members of the parts of flats and other units. The plan will show the area of the stage, the position of the proscenium and of the cyclorama and the width of each flat. Also shown are the direction of door openings, curtains and exits.

2 To prepare your ground-plan, make sure that you have the correct measurements of the stage area. Note positions of all projections from walls, pillars or columns on the floor, girders overhead and anything else that juts into the stage area.

3 When all main dimensions are drawn on the plan in a scale of 4 cm to 1 m (1 : 25), plot the exact positions of the flats, rostra, cloths, curtains and other items relevant to the setting from the setting-line.

This line is related to the track-line of the front tabs. If front tabs are not being used, the setting line may be brought forward, on to the apron if there is one.

The important thing is to have a useful guide line. The centre-line (CL on the illustration below) makes a right-angle with the setting-line. Those concerned with the construction of the set can mark these lines on the stage itself – and work from them.

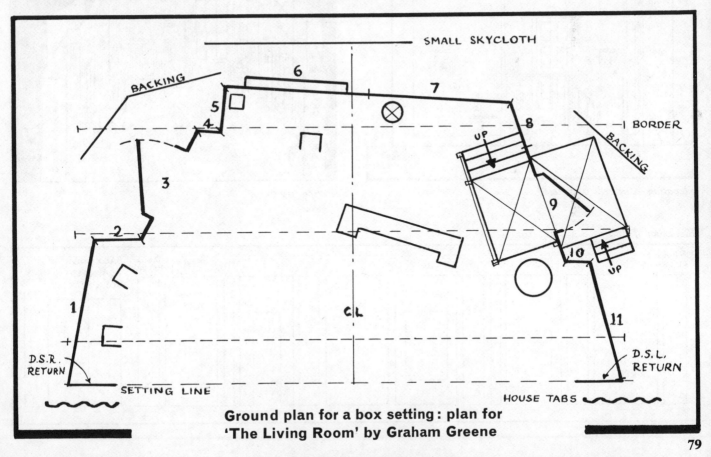

Ground plan for a box setting: plan for 'The Living Room' by Graham Greene

THE WORKING DRAWINGS
(continued)

4 The *elevation* or *section* drawings show the vertical and upright parts of your setting. The height of flats and rostra can be indicated to scale – widths are accurate, but it must be remembered that widths appear to vary, according to the angle from which they are viewed.

The elevation is taken through the centre-line of the stage (CL) as if sliced through the axis.

A *front* elevation can be useful in certain settings but more often a perspective view will, together with plan and elevation, provide better information, both to the director and to those involved in building the set.

5 Another useful drawing is one that offers elevation drawings of all the flats and units to be used. Each flat or unit is numbered to correspond with numbers marked on the ground-plan.

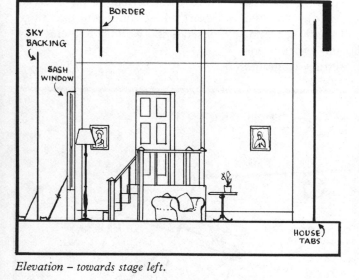

Elevation – towards stage left.

Perspective view.

Elevation of flats used in this setting.

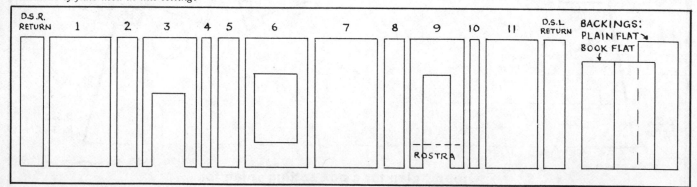

Useful symbols for plans

Working drawings showing a scaled plan need to show the flats, units and properties within the setting. If certain symbols are used (especially useful in box-sets containing much furniture) they will be helpful to the director and to those reponsible for placing properties.

Illustrated here are the conventional and essential symbols used on ground-plans and elevations. You may need to make up a few symbols of your own if unusual features are introduced, e.g. an outcrop of rock or a chariot.

The stage outline

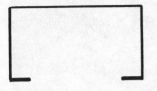

The plan view.

The elevation or section drawing.

Rostra

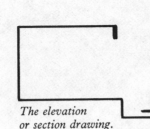

Two sizes of rostra (note diagonals to distinguish from tables).

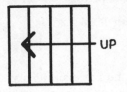

Steps – with an arrow and UP to indicate direction.

Cloths

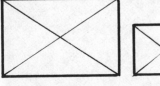

curtains (tabs)

backcloths

borders (items above stage level shown by dash)

Flats

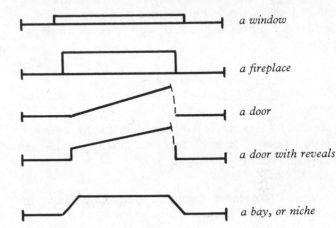

a single plain flat

wide and narrow together

flat with a cut-out (cut-out flat has no tick at end)

a window

a fireplace

a door

a door with reveals

a bay, or niche

a bay window

Properties

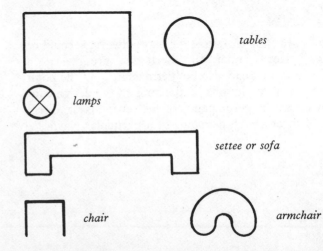

tables

lamps

settee or sofa

chair

armchair

81

TYPES OF STAGE DESIGN

Previous pages have been concerned with ways of planning a setting. The next pages in this section deal with different types of setting, from the simplest to the more elaborate.

It is hoped that these notes and illustrations will stimulate ideas and provide possible starting points for designer, director and others concerned with various backstage activities.

The types of setting can be conveniently grouped as follows:

1 *Arena* and *theatre-in-the-round* (including *open or thrust stages* – these stages are often portable or adaptable rostra-type staging.)

2 *Screen settings.*

3 *Curtain* – the most common, frequently found in school or college halls.

4 *Wing and cloth* – painted cloth sets.

5 *Box sets* – permanent or semi-permanent usually.

6 *Cyclorama* – where the skycloth plays an important part in the setting.

7 *Composite settings* – three or more confined acting areas in one setting, usually at different levels.

8 *Permanent or semi-permanent structures* – a 'built' set often of many levels with balcony, steps, etc.

It will be seen that certain of the plays illustrated could be suitably placed under an alternative group, e.g. a cyclorama setting can also be 'permanent', but the point to note is that 'cyclorama' is the spur to the design concept whereas the permanency of the setting is the direct result of meeting the demands of a particular play.

1 Arena and theatre-in-the-round

Perhaps the simplest of settings, certainly from the point of view of scenery, is the arena or theatre-in-the-round. The audience is grouped on three or on all sides, with the seating arranged higher than the stage or with the stage slightly above the level of the audience.

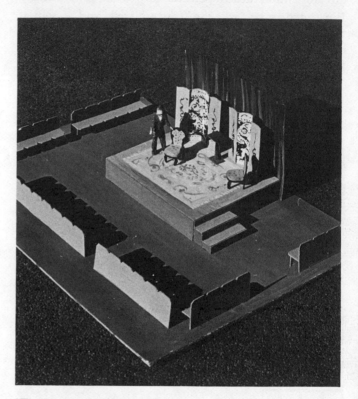

'*The Importance of Being Earnest*' by Oscar Wilde.

The model shown above illustrates the basic simplicity of the design – the only decorative feature being the two screens. The curtain (a screen or flats could have been used) is to hide players, sound and lighting equipment and for quick changing purposes.

The problem in this particular production of 'The Importance of Being Earnest' was to stage it in a long narrow hall for a one-night stand. This involved the transporting of the rostra stage, lighting equipment, curtains, screens and costumes.

The problem of making the production work in the narrow hall (15 × 6 m) can be seen from the small sketch-plan made on the site beforehand:

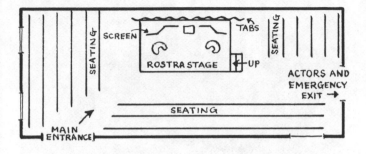

It was impossible to arrange the stage at either of the narrow ends because of the positions of the main entrance and emergency exit. The solution was to set the stage against the centre of the long wall facing the main entrance, leaving a minimum space backstage of half a metre and grouping the audience on three sides. (The method of fixing a curtain against the ceiling in a matter of minutes is shown on page 22.)

Two screens were used to give some sense of change to the scenes. They were painted on both sides, were interchangeable and could be used singly or not at all. The photograph below shows one of the screens, with the curtain fitted against the ceiling.

Thrust or open settings

Another simple basic setting can be the open rostra-and-steps stage backed by curtains, cloths or a simple cut-out screen – with curtained openings, entrances and exits.

The sketch plan shown here shows a typical thrust stage arrangement – the outer lines represent the confines of the hall.

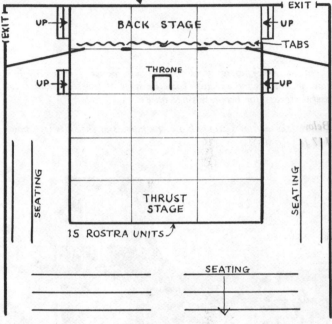

Sketch plan for 'Henry IV Part 1'.

The setting for 'Henry IV Part 1' is basically a protruding or thrust stage with an Elizabethan style of backing, built as a permanent structure from wood and hardboard. The openings are curtained in a patterned fabric printed by stencil (see page 122 for methods of stencilling.)

The problem of staging this production was the inconvenience of a comparatively low ceiling. So the upper storey shown in the illustrations on the next page had to be purely decorative in this particular hall. Obviously, if height allowed, the upper windows and balcony would be put to use, with a platform and steps behind the screen.

The use of lower rostra downstage left and right created another level for grouping the actors. The change of location was effected by banners and cut-outs raised in the centre upstage, between the 'walls' of the wood and hardboard structure.

A useful device to aid unity of design between upstage and downstage is shown in the relationship between the railings in the centre of the backing and the railings containing the lower rostra downstage.

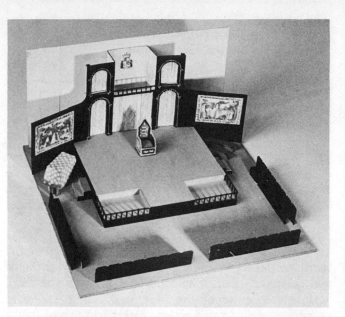

Right: a three-quarter view of the scale model showing the first row of seating and the aisles at the sides of the stage which are useful storage for properties not in use.

Below: the actual setting. Note the murals at the sides (see pages 117 for details).

Act III Scene 1: A room in Sir Peter Teazle's house ('The School for Scandal').
Another example of a symmetrical type of set using large movable screens with a fixed central false proscenium. The screens can be adapted from old flats.

Act IV Scene 1: The Picture Room.
All the same screens rearranged and the proscenium screen revealed to show an inset scene. The mirror over the fireplace alters the appearance and the pediment over the window is removed.

2 Screen settings

Where sufficient curtains, flats and other scenery are not readily available or where a quick-change method of scene changing is desirable, screens can fulfil the requirements.

Screens, in pairs, threes or fours can occasionally be found and be altered by re-covering and repainting. Where very large screens are needed book flats can be built up from existing flats.

With a screen on either side of the acting area, the back can be filled by simply building a wooden frame between the screens – usually rather higher to make a focal point. Either curtains or another screen can be fitted behind the frame giving the effect of a false proscenium. Or both curtains and screen can be used if a change of setting is required.

The two scenes shown here come from a production of 'The School for Scandal'. The two side screens are changed or switched and the curtains drawn back to alter the setting.

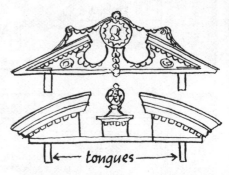

Further variations between scenes can be effected by interchanging pediments over the false proscenium. Tongues of wood are equally spaced on each pediment to slot into a pair of brackets behind the proscenium.

85

A

B

HALF CURTAIN
HALF CYCLORAMA
(BACK WALL)

ROSTRUM AND
STEPS

C

← PAINTED BACKCLOTH

D

CYCLORAMA
(OR BACKCLOTH)

CUT-OUT

GROUND ROW →

3 Curtain sets

Curtain setting is the most elementary and frequent type of existing setting.

It is found in most schools, colleges and church halls, serving as a general backing for assemblies of one kind or another and is ideal for this purpose.

Unfortunately, curtain settings are often the only backing for the annual play – and can be dull when no flats or rostra are available.

What can be done with curtains alone? Illustration **A** shows a curtain set typical of most schools, the traditional setting of three or sometimes four pairs of curtain wings, a back-curtain divided in the centre which can be drawn back and a pair of front tabs (curtains) set just within the proscenium frame. Three or four curtain borders correspond to the pairs of wings.

Try pushing back the upstage curtains into the wings and seeing what the back wall offers in the way of a cyclorama. Perhaps it is a clean, light and smooth surface and only needs a few lights to bring it to life. If this can be achieved, you have a cyclorama set with wing curtains.

Illustration **B** shows one half of the back curtain drawn back with a simple step and rostra.

A curtain set in conjunction with a painted backcloth can be most rewarding. If funds allow, two backcloths may be used, the back traverse tabs being drawn across while the cloths are changed. If there is no fly space above the stage, cloths can be rolled on a cylinder of wood (see page 23 for description). Illustration **C** shows this type of setting.

A curtain set combined with ground-rows or cut-outs and backcloth (or plain cyclorama) adds yet more variety. Cut-outs and ground-rows are described on pages 51 and 58 – small cut-outs that are low and not too wide can be attached to boxes or simple wooden brackets. Illustration **D** shows this arrangement.

If the wing curtains are on swivels (see pages 18 and 19), there can be a colour change on the reverse side.

4 Wing and cloth sets

Pantomime, revue, light operetta and all productions demanding a touch of fantasy benefit from the use of colourful decorative scenery. It is in this sphere of stage design that the painted canvas and occasionally gauze – the traditional wing and cloth setting – is most suitable. Little or no construction is required apart from the occasional rostra and at least two sets of steps or a simple staircase.

The scenes are conveyed in depth by means of plain or, more frequently, cut-out canvas wings and borders.

Gauze is used to support any large holes cut out of the canvas wings (see page 24 for the use of gauze on canvas). Each wing and border takes the eye back to the tour-de-force upstage – the painted backcloth. Very often a strong illusion of depth is achieved by these simple means.

The illustration below shows a scene from a scale model setting for Aladdin's cave. The only construction is a large treasure chest and a cut-out of a rock-like shape. (This scene is also shown in position within the model theatre on page 78.)

5 Box sets – 1

If the text of the play demands an interior setting with a strong sense of realism, then the box setting is ideal. Constructed from flats and usually with a 'ceiling' of suspended flats (although borders often replace the ceiling), the box set is only practical if a suitable quantity of flats is available. For example, the setting below would require between 20 and 30 depending on the widths used.

The playwright's directions for 'Look Back in Anger' are detailed and require careful study. The ceiling of the attic room has a marked slope: decisions have to be taken as to whether it is practical to build such a ceiling from flats. Borders may have to be substituted. But the dormer windows downstage right must be included to give the feel of an attic.

The lighting presents many interesting problems. A landing with a skylight seen through a long oblong window in the room is called for – this can be omitted but is worth aiming at. The lights for the dormers are essential and should be strongly lit.

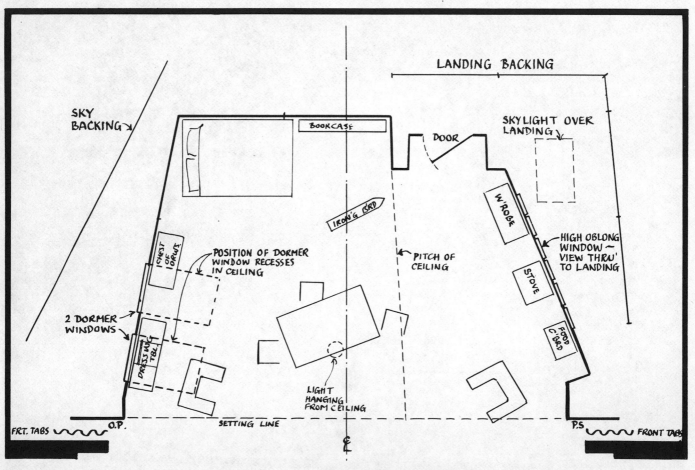

Ground plan for 'Look Back in Anger'

Look Back in Anger

The two illustrations on the right show the scale model setting. The ceiling plays a very prominent part in the design. Note how the shapes of each wall are affected by the long slope above – the back wall by its angle and the side walls by the marked contrast in height. Another interesting design feature is the shape made by the dormer windows into the ceiling area.

Note also that border batten lighting is useless in this type of setting – all light sources must be supplied from perches immediately behind the proscenium and from F.O.H. (front of house, the auditorium area). Intense local sources will be floods or concentrated spots behind the windows (see page 188 of the section on lighting).

In an old attic room one can imagine that the state of the ceiling and walls will have been neglected. Textural effects can be introduced to create the correct atmosphere (see pages 118–122 of the section on painting).

BOX SETTING for 'Look Back in Anger' by John Osborne. Act I Scene 1: Day.

Act II: Night.

Box sets – 2

Sometimes a play demanding realistic treatment needs two or more interiors. This gives an opportunity to build a box-within-a-box type of setting. Such is the case with 'Bernadette' by Noël Woolf and Sheila Buckley.

Three interiors are needed, all quite different in style and character: a disused prison room; a well-appointed study and an austere convent room.

The stage available was of average size and with plenty of space for 'flying' scenery – and there were plenty of flats available.

The ground plan and the three photographs show how three box sets were arranged, one inside another – the whole stage area being gradually revealed (rather like peeling away the skins of an onion). In another play, also requiring three scenes, this process might be reversed – adding a box within a box. And if all flats can be 'flown' the scenes can succeed each other in any order.

The ground plan, when related carefully to each of the three scenes, explains how each scene was pre-arranged at the start of the play. Three types of line have been used to make the plan clearer. Note how the wall on S.L. ('Stage Left' when facing the audience) was used in both Acts II and III but received a change of emphasis by the drape over the door and the pictures on the wall.

Act I: The cachot – a disused prison in Lourdes.

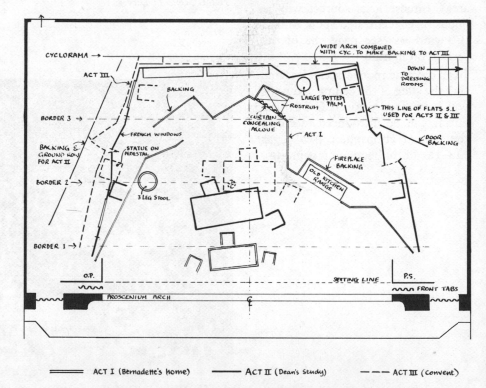

3-in-1 box set: ground plan for 'Bernadette'

Act II:
The Dean of Lourdes'
study –
note the drape on the
door S.L. and the
position of the wall S.L.

Ceiling flats were omitted in this production, black borders being used instead. Note how a wide range of lighting is employed to help create different localities. In Act I the light descends mainly from batten No. 1 S.L. In Act II the windows bring in intense light from a row of four 1000w floods. In Act III the ground-row lights pick out the cyclorama. (Ground-row refers to scenery and to lighting – see page 176 for lighting.)

Act III:
The convent at
Nevers –
note change of the S.L.
wall and the way it
ties in with the
new backing.

6 Cyclorama sets

A cyclorama set is basically a setting of curtain wings or wing flats, with the upstage area entirely backed by the skycloth – which sometimes curves downstage at the sides. The whole acting space can be framed by the proscenium arch but the concept of a large open sky area and wings is quite valid without the use of a proscenium provided that the 'sky' is itself framed.

The scenic constructions most suitable for cyclorama settings are rather skeletal – the more 'bones' or linear structure, the more interesting the silhouettes. It is immediately evident how important this type of setting is in the scenes shown here from 'The Merchant of Venice'.

Note how the setting has been deliberately opened out, pushing the architecture to both sides of the stage but tying them together by the use of steps enveloping the whole stage area.

In the opening scene the harbour is achieved by the use of three verticals and a cross-piece to indicate ships and a rather stumpy cylinder for a capstan.

The importance of the cyclorama to set off this scene can be clearly seen.

Act I Scene I: The harbour scene from 'The Merchant of Venice'.

In the ground plan below note the use of a wide variety of mobile pivoted flats to achieve maximum variety between the various scenes. The mobile screen marked 'A' on the ground plan is shown on page 67 of the section on flats.

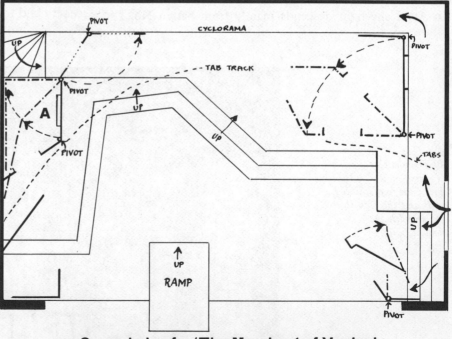

Ground plan for 'The Merchant of Venice'
A cyclorama set with mobile pivoted flats

Both scenes here rely strongly upon the cyclorama, only the court scene making use of the softening effect of curtains for an interior. Note how the canvas frame arcade (illustration right) links the two sides of the setting.

Note the use of a ramp in this rostra-stage setting – it allows the cast to use the auditorium gangways for their entrances and exits, which can greatly enliven the movement of the players.

Right: Act V Scene 1: The garden scene, Belmont. Note the small half-arch at one end of the arcade in relation to the previous scene.

Below: Act IV Scene 1: A court of justice.

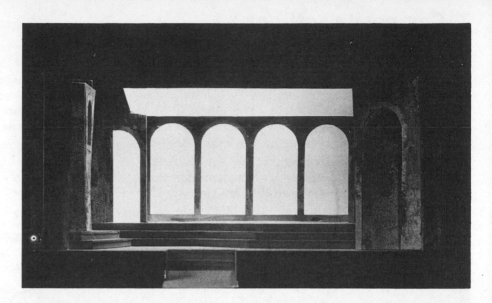

See page 127 for curtain printing, page 153 for throne construction, pages 40–41 for steps.

7 Composite settings

Settings requiring two or more rooms or other locations simultaneously are termed composite sets. Such acting areas are sometimes used together, at other times separately. Areas not in use are usually blacked out or masked by gauzes. For example, 'The Diary of Anne Frank' and 'Five Finger Exercise' require rooms only; 'Under Milk Wood' requires rooms and exterior locations.

Another play requiring a composite set is Arthur Miller's 'Death of a Salesman' which demands three rooms and a surrounding, dream-like, exterior.

The illustrations here show the different levels required; it will be noticed that plenty of height is needed to carry the linear 2-dimensional framework of the house. If the acting area is low, the design will have to be considered horizontally rather than vertically – perhaps the upper bedroom could rise by three rather than eight steps.

Of course, if rostra and building materials are not available to construct higher levels, the stage floor can be used. Nothing need prevent the ingenuity of the designer from finding a solution!

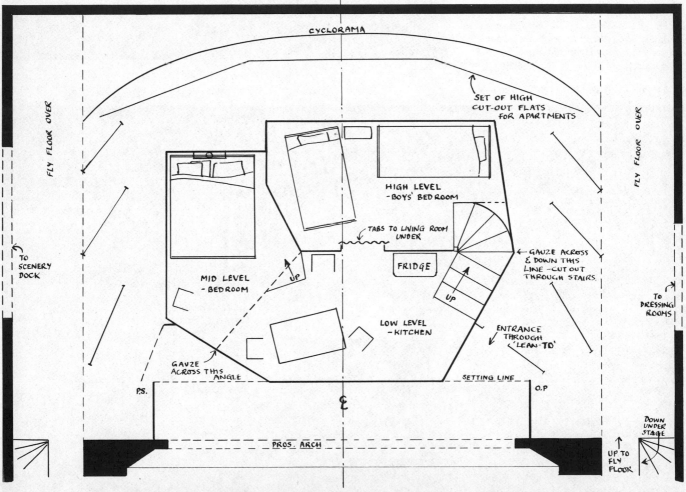

A composite setting: ground plan for 'Death of a Salesman'

Above: the general setting.

Right: evening, the kitchen area.
Lighting is concentrated downstage centre.

This particular play is most suitably played against and behind gauzes to achieve some of the dream quality required by the author. Funds will not always extend to this, but very well placed lighting for each room can achieve a reasonable substitute for gauzes.

8 Permanent settings – 1: She Stoops to Conquer

Sometimes there is an opportunity to stage a play that will run for a week or longer, giving the designer a chance to try a more expansive or elaborate setting, using a structural framework.

The next few pages show three examples of this type of setting where tubular scaffolding or the newer slotted angle alloy frameworks have been used.

The text of Oliver Goldsmith's 'She Stoops to Conquer' demands a permanent set with two short scenes played before a cloth.

The illustrations and ground plan show a very naturalistic setting with a variety of acting levels.

The major problem for this setting was a lack of headroom in which to roll or 'fly' a cloth for the two short scenes (the Three Pigeons inn and the garden of the house). The solution was to make use of a concertina screen (see page 66 for details) painted on both sides and reversible by means of a simple hooking device.

The ground plan and the lower photograph from the page opposite show the position of the screen when closed and the effect when open for the Three Pigeons scene. (The garden scene is not shown here.)

An example of a working drawing where an elevation is necessary to help those constructing the set to understand the plan view more clearly.

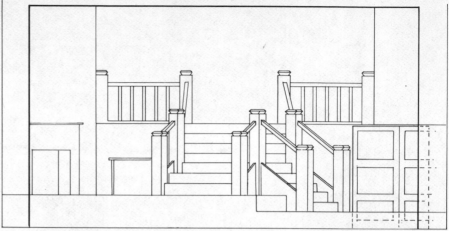

Elevation drawing for 'She Stoops to Conquer'

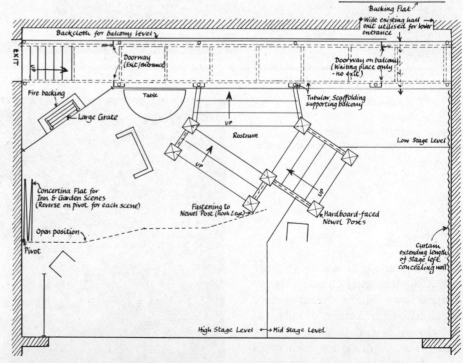

Ground plan for 'She Stoops to Conquer'

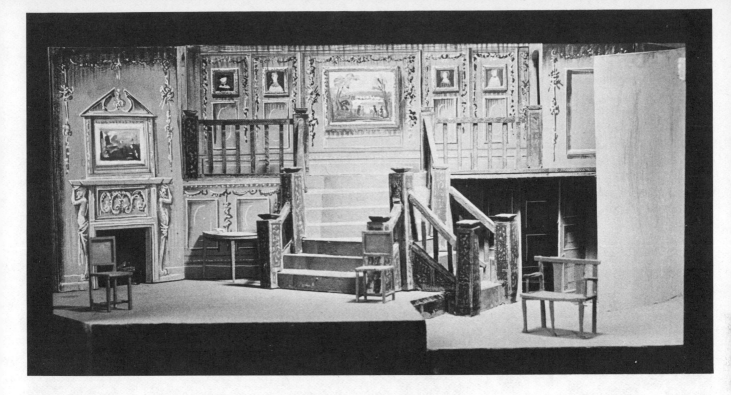

Two scenes from a scale model: Above: Mr. Hardcastle's house – the main setting.

Below: The Three Pigeons – a short scene using mobile screens that are reversible for the garden scene on the back.

The stair arrangement which may at first glance appear complicated was in fact made up of central rostra with three sets of steps arranged round them (more details on page 37 of the section on rostra).

The balcony, constructed with tubular scaffolding, is shown at different stages of construction in the setting on page 99.

The completed set for 'She Stoops to Conquer' is shown overleaf.

She Stoops to Conquer

The close-up photograph below illustrates some of the details in this kind of naturalistic setting. The properties department needs to be rather busy accumulating pieces of furniture as much in the eighteenth-century period as possible. The framed pictures shown here were painted with the setting but many cheap second-hand pictures can be obtained. Some large department stores and antique dealers are prepared to loan reproductions and furniture if given credit in the programmes.

The animal heads are less easy to find but are not essential to the setting. The candle-sticks are battery-operated (their manufacture is described on page 139 of the section on properties). A gun replica may be obtained or the gun be made – see page 223 of the section on arms and armour. The panelling on the walls and fireplace was all painted – see details on page 132 of the section on painting.

Lighting for the play was concentrated at F.O.H. with another group of Fresnel spots on batten No. 1 for the inn and garden scenes – all other lighting was off in order to black out S.L. behind the concertina screen.

Building a permanent setting

The illustrations show the building of rostra staging, steps and balcony for a production of 'She Stoops to Conquer' in a school hall – described on pages 96 and 97.

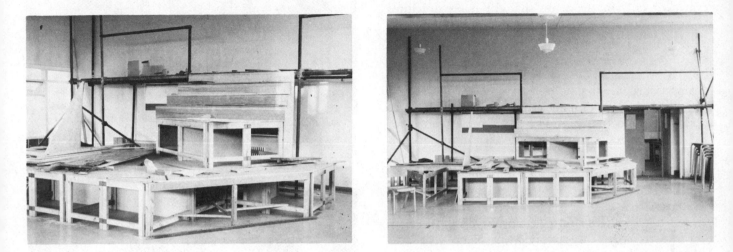

Above: Two views of tubular scaffolding balcony showing framework and open sides of rostra. See pages 28 and 29 for rostra construction, pages 10 and 11 for types of scaffolding.

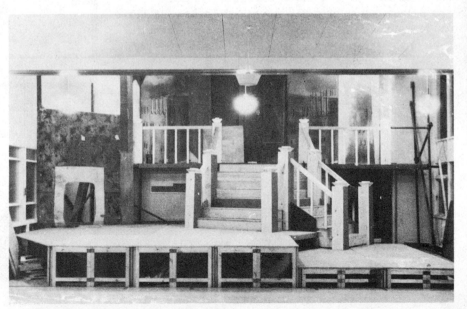

Right: The completed carpentry work before putting up the flats and stage front, and before lighting.

Note the hall lights which were later removed and replaced by F.O.H. lighting.

Permanent settings – 2: Twelfth Night

The setting shown on this and the next two pages is permanent only in the sense that the main structures (consisting of central rostra, steps and ramp) remain unchanged from scene to scene. All changes of locality and sense of time are achieved through lighting and properties.

This particular production posed a problem: it was first to be staged on a traditional proscenium stage and later to be transferred to a large hall as an arena production with the audience on three sides. The setting had to allow for the change.

The preliminary sketches on the right show one possible solution to this problem. The set is built up from rostra and steps with a skeletal frame – the steps being quite low and open underneath to avoid obscuring the view from the sides in the arena arrangement. The two sketches also illustrate the ways of using a strong lighting change on a cyclorama – giving a complete reversal of silhouette from dark to light.

Although it may appear to be a very large undertaking to build this set again in new surroundings, the assembly can in fact be done in a matter of four or five hours with a large team of helpers. All fixing has to be carefully planned but it is not too difficult if measurements are accurate and all the jointing sound in construction.

Right: three sketches for Shakespeare's 'Twelfth Night'. Above, with cyclorama lit; centre, with forestage lit; below, with drapes across central arches and general lighting.

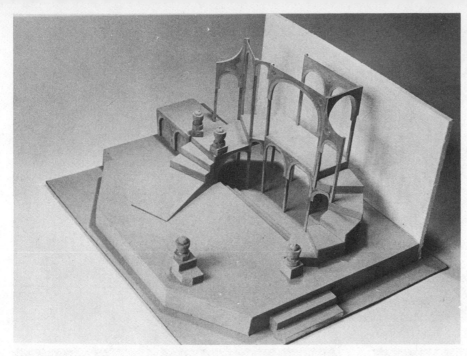

The scale model as an independent setting for an arena production.

Twelfth Night

The pictures on this page show how the idea of an adaptable setting was developed from ground plan into scale model. The rostra stage has a sunken area in centre-stage to allow a passageway under the balcony – this creates another acting level. It is always useful to make a number of different levels for Shakespearean productions because of the many scenes. Certain areas can then be turned into small 'insets', e.g. the curtained space under the balcony indicates a separate room.

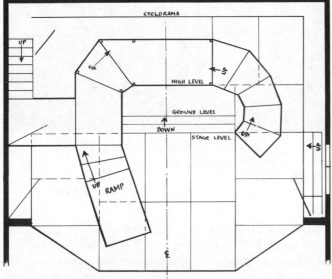

Ground plan for 'Twelfth Night' - a step and rostra setting with cyclorama

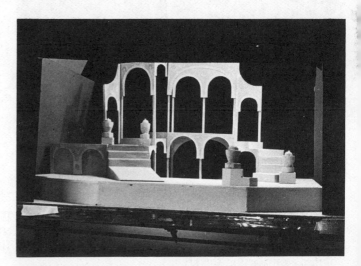

The same scale model as above fitted within the proscenium model theatre.

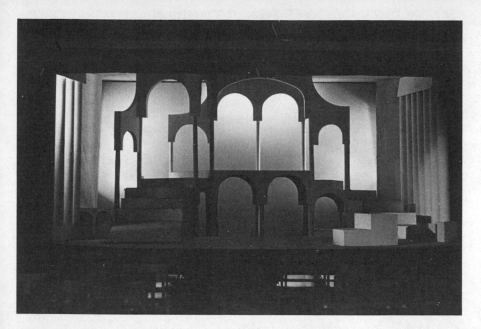

Three scenes from 'Twelfth Night' – all within the proscenium setting.

Left: with cyclorama and S.R. lighting behind the row of columns. (Compare with the original sketch at the top of page 100.)

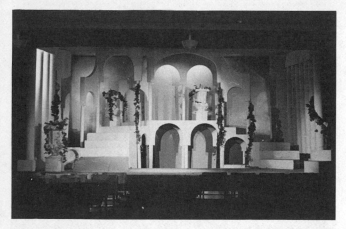

With more general centre stage lighting, foliage and urns for the garden settings. (See page 142 for making urns and similar garden properties.)

The lower arches hung with decorated curtains for an interior scene – decorating was done by the batik method described on page 125.

The construction of columns

The two rows of columns (pillars) S.L. and S.R. were made from old cardboard cylinders discarded by paper and textile firms. The columns were linked together by glued scrim and paper and secured on the off-stage side by pieces of slotted angle bolted together. They formed a useful function as wings and helped to create a unity of design with the columns supporting the arches.

The C.S. columns were constructed from stiff paper shaped and glued round a dummy cylinder. When dry, the paper cylinders were removed and fitted round the metal framework supporting the hardboard arches.

Permanent settings – 3: West Side Story

The illustrations on this and the next three pages show scenes from a production of 'West Side Story'. It uses as a basis a semi-permanent setting. The set consists of a permanent construction – in this case, the archway – with various mobile, revolving and inset pieces of scenery to make frequent changes of location. The variety of scenery, with carefully placed and controlled lighting, produces an effective range of mood, place and time.

It is essential when designing sets for musicals to understand the special requirements of dance routines and movement. The cast is usually large and needs to move freely over the stage area.

The designer must offer the maximum in clear stage space and must avoid cluttering up this space with props or other design features during those scenes that require a dance number.

It will be seen from the sketch and ground plan that this production made use of a wide archway over the floor of a hall, giving a clear floor area and a certain sense of claustrophobia and menace appropriate to the location and mood of 'West Side Story'.

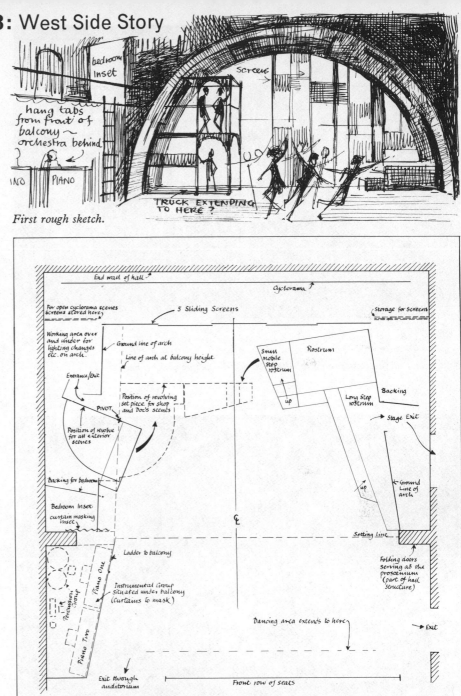

First rough sketch.

Ground plan for 'West Side Story'

Two views of the construction of the arch – from above and below.

West Side Story

The construction of the arch is shown on the left. A slotted angle frame was built from floor level to form a large angular tent across the hall with gangways behind.

Attached to the frame at regular intervals were wooden spacers to carry battens across the depth of the archway.

When the wooden frame was completed large sheets of hardboard were fastened by screws to form a wide semi-circle. The illustrations on the left show a number of sheets in position.

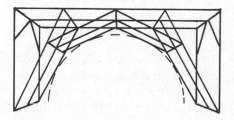

The metal frame.

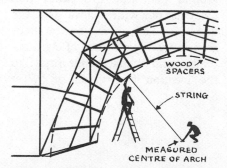

The wooden frame attached to the metal frame. The radius of the arch is found by using a length of string from a point marked on the floor below the centre of the archway.

A view from below: note the wooden spacers which carry the battens. The battens, properly adjusted, form an accurate semi-circle.

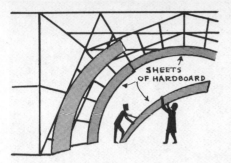

Sheets of hardboard screwed to the spaced battens complete the archway. Spaces for exits and small gaps for archway lighting are left open.

The frequent changes of scene (15) and the ten different locations demanded by the synopsis were achieved by the use of large pierced screens drawn across upstage behind the archway, arranged in a variety of ways (see pages 68 and 69 for the construction of this type of screen).

Another device was a mobile structure pivoted centre S.R. ('stage right' when looking towards the audience) to the side of the arch – a large hole being allowed to accommodate its return. This structure served both as the bridal shop interior and as the drugstore.

A balcony downstage right led into an inset within the top front of the archway for the two bedroom scenes – see the illustration on the next page.

The space below the balcony provided limited room for the orchestra – see the ground plan on page 103 for details.

The audience was seated on tiered rostra to assist the view of those at the rear. This type of seating arrangement can be seen on page 7.

Above: under the highway. Holes pierced in the roof of the arch allowed archway lamp lighting through the holes.

Below: the 'neighbourhood'. One screen was used at the back.

Above: the bridal shop. The mobile was pulled out from the arch.

Below: bedroom 'inset' scene with the street below.

Painting and printing 5

MATERIALS · PREPARATION · 2 AND 3 DIMENSIONAL EFFECTS

The working space 108
Brushes and painting aids 109
Scenic colour 110
Dyes, metal colours and fixing agents . . . 111
Preparation of size and colour 112
Colour mixing and matching; priming . . . 113
Scaling-up 114
Naturalistic painting 116
Surface painting and treatment 118
Painted textures 119
Patterned surfaces (including stencils, blocks, batik, screen printing) 122
Painting gauzes 127
3-dimensional surfaces 128
Lining 132

THE WORKING SPACE

A large high workshop or hall is the ideal studio for scenic painting. The importance of height is apparent when flats of 3 metres or more need painting side by side to create a unified wall surface.

Some schools and amateur dramatic societies may well lack sufficient space in a workshop but may have free use of the stage for painting purposes. This arrangement can be even more satisfactory with the flats assembled in their correct positions – but ensure that sufficient light is available, whether daylight or general lighting from stage floods or 'house' lighting.

If space is not available, then the flats must be painted in horizontal positions, perhaps flat on the floor or leaning against the wall. The floor position is tiring and trestles or benches will make a good working height.

Ensure that plenty of working top area is at hand for materials, or use a trolley as illustrated below. Note also that water and heating are easily accessible.

Right: a painting trolley can be built or adapted from an old card table with an under-shelf and castors. It will hold most of the necessary materials. It will not, however, be suitable on a raked stage unless castors are omitted or braking blocks are used.

Below: examples of suitable heating – a a gas ring, b electric hot-plates and c a camping gas stove.

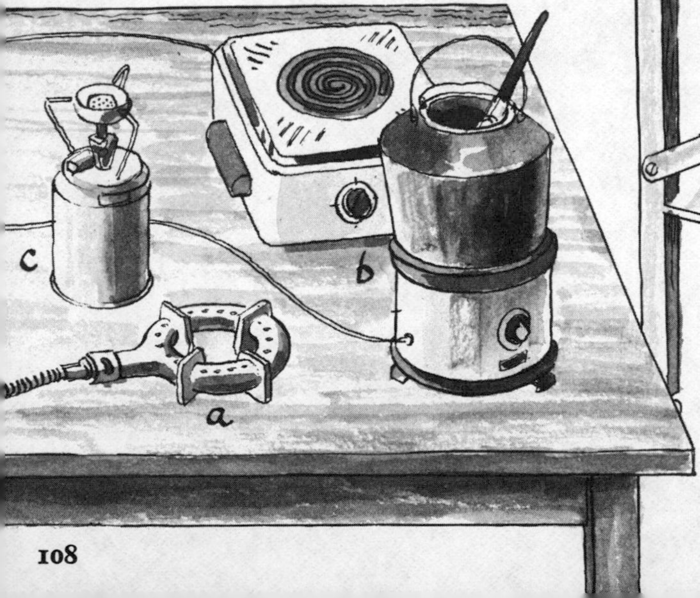

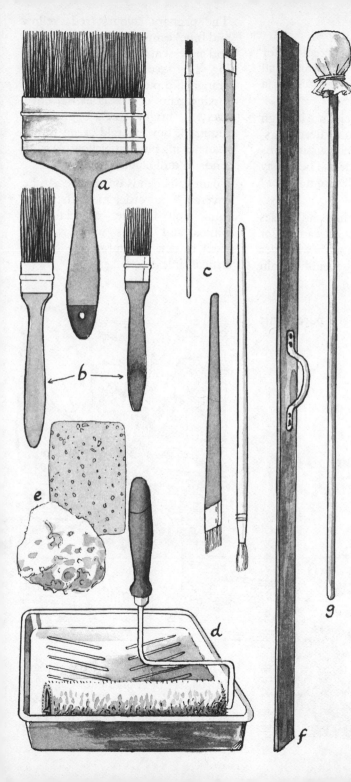

BRUSHES AND PAINTING AIDS

A wide assortment of good quality paint-brushes is essential for satisfactory scenic painting.

The most useful are:

a a 15–20 cm pure bristle brush for 'laying in' (the covering of large surfaces);

b an assorted range of 25, 50, 75 and 100 mm pure or mixed bristle brushes for finer work;

c small fitches (detail scenery brushes): round, square and cut-angle (cutting-in brushes) – brushes for detailed work and lining (the drawing of lines);

d a paint roller and tray for other kinds of wall painting and printing block techniques;

e sponges and rags for specialised textures;

f a straight-edge for lining, fitted with an old door handle;

g a painter's mahl-stick – useful for resting the arm when painting details on a vertical surface;

h a range of buckets, large tins with handles and other containers for paint – a wire handle inserted through smaller tins can be helpful.

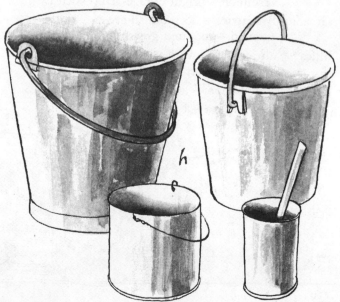

SCENIC COLOUR

The pigment colours are in powder form and are the basic ingredient for all kinds of paint. Added to this pigment is a fixing agent which binds all the particles together. The fixing agent used in scenic painting is 'size', a glue powder that dissolves in hot water.

Available in about sixty colours, the pigments are sold by weight. Although many of the primary and earth colours can be obtained in some decorators' shops and paint shops under the general term of 'decorators' colour' it seems to be increasingly difficult to obtain the variety of colour needed. There may be good stocks in certain places; otherwise it is advisable to order from scenery suppliers – firms are listed on page 276.

All the colours are, of course, intermixable and hundreds of tints and shades can be obtained by selecting from the lists on suppliers' colour cards. For practical purposes only a limited range of colours will be required: whatever colours you choose for a particular production there will be only certain basic colours needed for all scenery.

I have found the following colours the most useful:

White: powdered 'whiting' for general priming and tinting, and pure scenic white for intense colour (usually zinc white).

Black: vegetable 'lamp' black or 'dense' scenery black.

Yellows: lemon – a pale cool yellow,
chrome – a warm strong yellow (mid-colour),
ochre – warm deep earthy yellow.

Reds: crimson – deep cool red,
red ochre – dark red earth,
vermilion – bright orange-red (expensive).

Greens: Brunswick – deep bluish green,
emerald – cool mid-green.

Blues: ultramarine – very deep intense cold blue,
Prussian – a strong blue, tinged with green.

Browns: Raw Umber – a yellow brown,
Raw Sienna – a reddish brown,
Vandyke – very dark.

The primary colours (red, yellow and blue) cannot be made by mixing and are essential for good clear painting. The secondary colours (green, orange and purple) can be made by mixing pairs of primaries. If, however, a bright intense green is required, buy emerald green rather than mixing blue and yellow. Mixing tends to dull colours slightly.

Quantity depends on the area to be covered – but order more than you think you require, especially of whites and blacks which always seem to run uncomfortably low at critical times!

The powder colours are usually sold in paper or polythene bags but should be transferred to more substantial containers. Label clearly and secure with lids for storage.

Dyes and metal colours

Cloths, curtains, transparent gauzes and other fabrics are all textiles that can be dyed. These materials (with certain exceptions to be explained later) are not suitable for general painting and require aniline dye treatment. (Dye is permanent and cannot be washed out.)

Dyes have the advantage of staining the material without the thickening quality of paint and give intense and brilliant surface effects to costume and curtaining.

Available in about 20 colours and sold by weight, they are fixed with a salt known as Glauber Salts. Mixing instructions are available from the suppliers (page 276).

Many new dyeing techniques have been developed. Write to suppliers for information – see page 276.

Metallic colours

Bronze powders are available in a wide range of metallic colours: pale, medium and deep gold and silver, and nickel (a dull silver).

Aluminium powders are sold in greens, purples, blues and reds – these mix well with the bronzes.

All these metal powders can be fixed with 'gold' size (a thin varnish), shellac (glue in methylated spirit), P.V.A. medium and even thickened size water. Each fixative depends on the use. Gold size, shellac and P.V.A. are for properties; thinned P.V.A. for costumes; size water for scenery and some textiles. Experiment on various scrap materials to achieve the desired effect.

Lacquer, enamel and emulsion paint

Where hard brilliant shine is required on furniture or properties, a Chinese lacquer is suitable. Enamel paints can also be used but take longer to dry.

Although relatively expensive compared with a powder colour and size mixture, emulsion paints can be useful for certain scenery work and require no fixing agent. Emulsion is also waterproof and can be painted over without the sullying effect of an under-painting accidentally spoiling the new brushwork. A disadvantage, however, is that repeated painting of scenery cannot be removed as with powder colours.

Paint sprays

All enamel and metallic colours are now available in aerosol tins. Although quick and easy to use, the spray method of painting tends to be indiscriminate and wasteful unless large areas are to be covered. Some interesting effects can be obtained by using paint sprays with stencils.

Fixing Agents

Size powder is obtainable in small or bulk quantities according to need. A half-kilogramme packet will make about 5 litres of size water.

Animal glues in 'pearl' crystals or flake or as a size powder are useful for thickening colours, sticking down card, canvas and paper, adding montage/collage surfaces before painting. (A wide range of adhesives for various needs is listed on pages 273-5.)

Shellac This is glue in methylated spirit which is useful for metallic colours. It is sold in flake or powder form to which methylated spirit must be added. It can also be purchased in liquid form. The clear shellac is the most suitable.

Assorted pigments, powders and liquids used in scenic painting.

PREPARATION: Size . . .

Put 1 part of size into a bucket, add about another part of cold water and allow to soak for a short time.

Pour seven parts of boiling water to make up a bucketful of hot size water, stirring well until completely dissolved.

If large areas of scenery need to be covered in a short time, make up a further bucketful.

Left-over size water can be stored for a short time but must be reheated each time that colour is made up.

. . . and powder colour

Half fill a large bucket with whiting and add cold water just to cover the powder.

Soak and break up any lumps. Leave overnight to allow good blending of the powder and water.

This white will be your basic primer for preparing canvas.

Half fill a smaller bucket with black powder colour if you require dark backings and dark areas for the setting. Again, mix with cold water to a thick paste.

Prepare these and all the other colours you require (by matching as closely as possible the colours on rough sketches or scale models) and mix to a consistency of thick paste.

Mixing size and colour

The proportion of hot size to prepared colour should be about 50 : 50. Pour the size slowly into the colour, stirring all the time. Test the covering capacity of the mixture, taking care not to add too much size water.

To sum up: make all your powders into a paste with cold water and then into a thin cream with hot size.

The covering power (opacity) of colour can be tested by dipping a piece of card into the mixture – if the strength of colour remains and the colour stays fixed, the mixture will be suitable. No under surface should be seen through the paint.

Colour mixing and matching

Select and mix your colours taking care to match the colours to sketches or scale model.

Scenic colours always dry lighter than expected, so prepare your colours accordingly by making each colour a shade or two deeper.

To test the shade of colour, paint an area on a scrap of card or board and hold over heat for a few moments.

When dry, test the colour against the scheme required. If too light add more dark mixed pigment, or vice versa.

When satisfied with the mixture, brush outside of container. Liquid colour changes on cooling so headaches will be avoided if you can identify the contents quickly when the colour is next required.

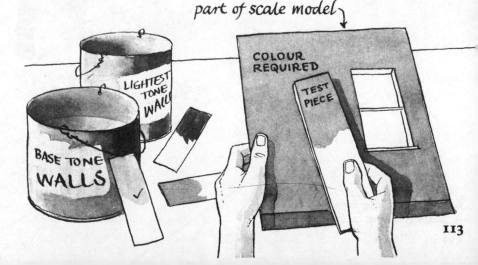

Priming

Whether of canvas, board or other material and whether new or old, the surface must first be prepared for painting. (In certain cases an un-primed hardboard can be painted without first priming but this is an exception.)

This preparatory priming coat ('lay-ing in') is applied with the largest brush or roller. If the setting is to be in rather a light colour use the bucket of prepared whiting.

Settings with a strong dominant colour scheme can benefit if the priming coat has some of that colour added – this will make a suitable base for working on.

Avoid overworking the priming coat on old painted canvases or the previous layer of paint will sully the work – quick lively brush work will always give good results. On canvas covered by many layers of paint, wash and scrape off the surface before re-priming.

SCALING-UP

To enlarge a scale-model or roughly sketched scene to full size requires a simple scaling-up method. Any detailed work on a backcloth, very large flats or other cloths will require a working method.

If, for example, you make a grid of 1 or 2 cm squares on your 1 : 25 scale model backcloth, you can prepare a grid on a backcloth with 25 cm or 50 cm (0.5 m) squares. The large squares will do for general layout, the 25 cm squares are helpful for any detailed areas.

If you wish to preserve for display purposes sketches or scale model from being marked with grid lines, rule the 1 or 2 cm squares in ink or pencil on tracing paper on top. Mark out the 25 cm or 50 cm lines on the sides of the flat or backcloth. Rub a piece of cord with chalk (for dark backgrounds) or charcoal (for light backgrounds). Hold the cord taut between the marks on the sides of the flats, pull the string away from the surface at the centre and let go with a sharp snap. A clear line should be deposited.

Chalking lines, working across the surface in 50 cm grid lines on large cloths.

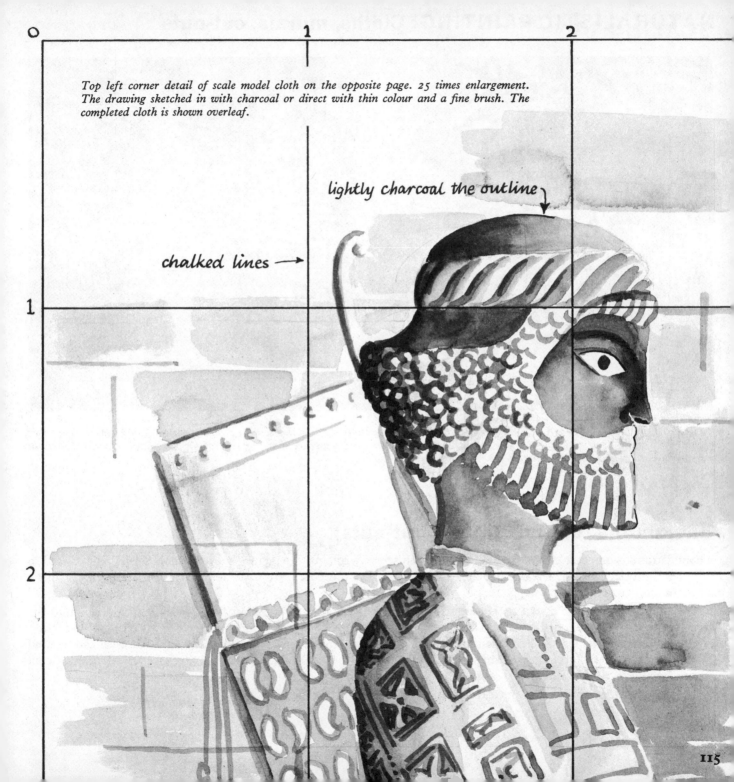

Top left corner detail of scale model cloth on the opposite page. 25 times enlargement. The drawing sketched in with charcoal or direct with thin colour and a fine brush. The completed cloth is shown overleaf.

lightly charcoal the outline

chalked lines →

115

NATURALISTIC PAINTING: Cloths, murals, cut-outs

The Gardens of Babylon scene from 'Adventure Story' by Terence Rattigan. For this scene a realistic backcloth and flats were painted with broad brushes using rather dry colour on the 'bricks'. For the same scene, see also page 166 of the section on properties. Note the canvas cut-out cloth (a 'leg') hanging on the right of the photograph above.

Backcloths (or background cut-outs)

The illustrations on these two pages aim at realism in scenic terms. In the picture above a whole setting is designed to represent an oriental garden. On the facing page the painted 'tapestries' are used more as properties to help evoke a mood in one area only of the stage setting.

Necessary to this realistic approach is research into costume, architecture, painting and sculpture, and also into the social aspects of the period. Research is, of course, needed for all types of design, but here most of all. If particular pieces of sculpture or ceramic are to be represented by painting, the scaling-up method described overleaf can be used in the design. Care should be taken when recreating a mood or place to avoid slavish copying; shape, colour and detail should be selective and simplified.

Remember that form and colour must blend into an overall concept of the play.

Cloth cut-outs

Always paint cut-outs before cutting to avoid curling. Additional layer of canvas or, better, an area of gauze should be glued behind to strengthen and to prevent curling.

Right: Juliet's bedroom from 'Romeo and Juliet' – showing a mural (wall-painting) and some panelling. These transform the 'tomb' part of the setting shown on page 129. The iron gates are replaced by net curtains and the back wall is covered by the mural.

Below left: one of the two mediaeval hunting scenes used as a decorative foil to the walls on either side of the setting for 'Henry IV Part 1' shown on page 84 (the border is done by stencil – see page 122).

Below right: example of a cut-out – showing a rather free and fluid use of the brush.

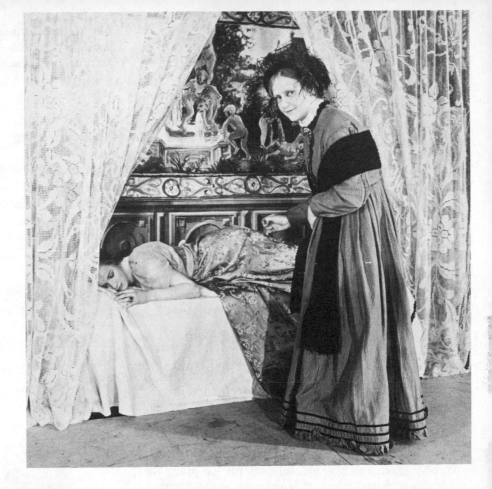

SURFACE PAINTING

All painted surfaces need a variety of treatment, from simple colour washes to more complex textures.

Look carefully at a 'plain' wall, free of all decoration. At first glance it may appear uniform but a light source falling across it will throw a more intense light on one part and make other parts 'fade' away or perhaps make a shadow.

This awareness of gradations, of tone on flat surfaces, is essential to scenic painting if variety and interest are to be achieved.

So whatever base or background colour, always have one or two colours close in tone and hue for adding to the base colour. These will be helpful in some of the methods described here.

(Definitions of some terms used in painting and design are included in the section on design – pages 72–73.)

Backgrounds

'Grounds' or background colours can be either the priming coat (the 'laying-in' coat mentioned earlier), or a colour wash on top of the primer. Large backcloths, borders and legs can be built up with a large brush or broom using two or three metal trays of related colours – blue, blue/green and emerald, for example – dipping the brush freely from colour to colour or using separate brushes. Atmosphere and mood will be evoked if the brushwork is free in application – avoid too flat an appearance on large areas.

SURFACE TREATMENT

To give interest and variety to any surface (apart from straightforward brushwork), a number of texture techniques can be tried. Four techniques are in frequent use in the theatre:

1 spatter and splash
2 scumbling and drybrush
3 stippling and daubing
4 ragroll and paint roller

Also to be described are methods of patterning a wall or textile, giving the effect of wallpaper or similar surface decoration. These methods fall into four groups:

1 stencils
2 block prints
3 batik printing
4 screen printing

There is also a small section on painting gauzes.

Finally, one can create surfaces that stand out in a third dimension – built up on flats or rostra to achieve a more solid effect. Many traditional materials are used but new materials are also introduced:

1 wood debris – sawdust, chippings and shavings
2 plaster
3 expanded polystyrene sheet of varying thicknesses
4 scrap material; newspaper, metal foil, old canvas, etc.

Each surface will be illustrated in turn.

an alternative position– working on the floor from centre to edges

← trays of related background tones

Painting a cloth or group of flats with two or more related colour tones. Large decorator's brushes or brooms can be used, the colours are contained in wide trays or buckets.

Painted textures – 1

1 Spatter and splash

This is a flicking method with a brush, producing much mess unless the floor and other surfaces are well protected by old newspapers. It is most effective in breaking up a uniform even surface and for producing gradation from light to dark. Using two or more tones of colour on a base colour or other textured surface, a wide variety of effects can be obtained. The paint should be of a creamy consistency.

2 Scumbling and drybrush

With the scumbling method, the brush is 'worried' or twisted about with strong wrist work to produce an uneven swirling surface texture. The paint needs to be slightly thickened. Drybrush painting requires fairly thick colour which is dragged lightly across the surface producing a broken colour with the under-painting revealed below.

Two or more shades of colour will make a richer surface texture.

Both methods are applied with the intention of combining top and under-painting effects.

A scene from 'The Merchant of Venice' showing two of the textures described on this page: the background is dark, the stones are scumbled in and spatter work is applied on some parts over the scumbling.

Spatter – knock against the other arm to produce spray.

Scumbling – active twist to the wrist – not much pressure.

Drybrush – drag lightly across the surface.

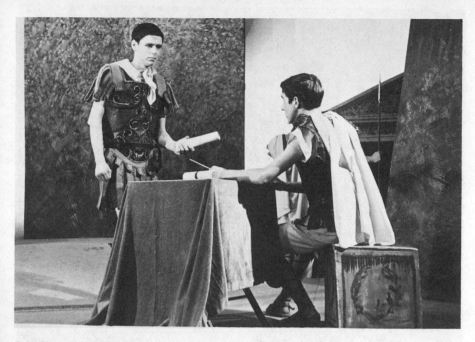

Stippling with a large brush. The square flat upstage is stippled in three tones of ochre and yellow. (Scene from 'Julius Caesar').

Painted Textures - 2

3 Stippling and daubing

Use an old well-worn bristle brush with fairly dry colour for stippling textures. Dab the brush at the surface to produce a variety of dot or spotted areas. Use different pressures and do not overload the brush with paint – only a small amount is required at a time. A small sponge (with open pores) is also very effective for more concentrated masses.

4 Ragroll

Two techniques can be used with rag textures.

a roll the rag over the wet painted surface to spread and break down the uniformity.

b wrap the rag round a paint roller (it can be secured with string). Apply a fairly creamy paint from paint tray and roll in all directions for a lively and agitated surface, or vertically only for a more restful and calm effect.

The latter effect can make a successful backing for block, screen or stencil work. (See photograph right.)

A close-up of a ragroll used on a wet paint surface.

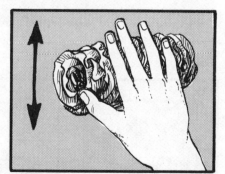

Above left: ragroll used alone.
Below left: stippling with short, quick dabs.

Roller texture

A paint roller using rather dry colours and applied without too much pressure can be a useful aid to surface treatment. Placed with care it can reproduce a stone wall, both in the scale of actual stones and the roughness of the stone surface. Variations in the size of each stone block can be achieved by careful use of the roller, in direction and in pressure. (See small illustration below.)

Stone blocks – the narrow blocks are produced by turning the roller in a vertical direction.

The rag roller pulls gently down the flat without hurry – the rag will slip if rushed.

A flat with a rag-roll surface looking like patterned fabric.

Note the four roller widths, using a rag-roll in one tone of background texture.

The use of rag wrapped round the roller can be effective for producing an interesting backing to various kinds of overlaid pattern. The illustration on the left shows a vertical rolling technique together with a few drybrush lines. On top there is a block pattern in lighter colour. The method of block printing is described overleaf.

Patterned surfaces

Apart from cost, the use of actual wallpaper for stage interiors is not suitable or desirable – the designs are usually too small and, from a practical point of view, the paper would be difficult to stick to rough canvas or to remove when the flats are required again.

1 Stencils

To simulate a large patterned wall surface the most useful method is the stencil. Make the stencil from prepared waterproof stencil paper; otherwise use stiff paper or thin card and treat the surface with shellac or any quick-drying paint after the pattern has been cut out.

Waterproofing the stencil will avoid the curling of edges. If you have a large area to cover it is advisable to have an extra stencil in reserve as they have to take a lot of rough treatment and can break down with too much use.

To be effective from a distance, the pattern should not be too small. A minimum of 30 cm for the stencil will give a reasonable-sized pattern from the back of the auditorium.

Your design may consist of one, two or even three parts. Cut your stencil on a smooth surface with a sharp knife and make a register mark at the sides and/or at the top and bottom to ensure that the pattern can be repeated successfully. Apply colour by stippling with a short stiff bristle, dipping only lightly into paint and stippling off the surplus on to scrap material – never use much paint on the bristle as it may overflow behind the stencil. Paint running down the canvas (or board) after the stencil has been removed can be very aggravating!

A sponge may be used as an alternative to a bristle. Sprayed paint can also be used but some preliminary attempts should be made and the surface to be printed masked where necessary.

As an alternative to colouring through a cut stencil, a design can be 'pricked' through the stencil with a nail and then pounced through with a charcoal bag. The design is then lightly indicated and may be developed in a freer style with a paint brush. This method is only suitable on smooth surfaces.

A double stencil pattern – two shades of colour on a light ground.

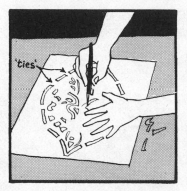

Cutting the stencil – to ensure that no loose pieces drop out leave 'ties' across.

Stippling through stencil – a faint vertical line in charcoal ensures accurate positioning.

2 Block prints

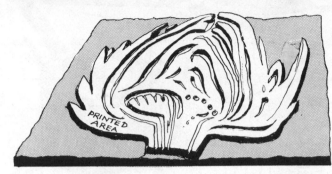

The block illustrated on the left was used over the ragroll surface on page 121.

The printing technique requires pressure to be applied to the printed surface. Most canvas flats are therefore unsuitable for this treatment unless very taut indeed. It is however an interesting method on hard surfaces, such as hardboard, and can make attractive texture patterns on a large scale.

This block and the 'brick' block below were both made from expanded polystyrene sheet of 25 mm and 15 mm thicknesses respectively. The method of making the blocks is as follows:

1 *Glue a sheet of hardboard or pin-board to the back of the polystyrene sheet with P.V.A.-based glue. Apply pressure and leave to harden. This will prevent breakage.*

2 *Paint the design on the polystyrene with thick creamy paint.*

3 *While still wet, pass the design quickly across a candle flame so that all unpainted parts will shrink back.*

4 *The block is ready for printing. Roll over the design with thick paint and press firmly down.*

If 'realistic' brick walling is required, a very quick and effective method is to combine a block print with brush and spatter work.

Below: seven courses of bricks printed at once! The diagram shows how the block printing slots together. The block was prepared as described above. The slightly broken surface of expanded polystyrene gives realism to the whole wall surface. Spatter on top and mix the shades of colour.

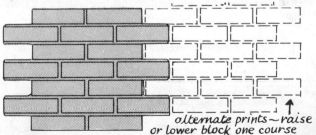

alternate prints~raise or lower block one course

Right: close-up of the block and the printed image – part of the brick arch for 'West Side Story' – see pages 104 and 105.

3 Batik printing

Another way of printing fabrics, offering a much wider variety of texture and colour, is *batik*. A craft originating in Java and Indonesia and now popular the world over, it is ideal for costume and for special concentrated colour spots within a stage setting.

Batik is a form of resist printing, using hot wax. The pattern or image is applied with special tools dipped in the wax and worked over the fabric. The fabric is then dyed – the areas untouched by the wax take the colour. Cold water dyes are used most frequently to prevent the wax from melting. After dyeing the wax is boiled off and the cloth washed and ironed.

Materials and equipment:

A heater – gas ring, electric hotplate, etc.

A form of double boiler – glue pot or tins within a saucepan.

A collection of tins (with holes punched in the sides) that can contain small night-lights or shortened candles – used as miniature heaters when a large group is working in batik.

A non-metallic bowl or bath for dye.

A liquid measure.

Rubber gloves.

Storage and mixing jars.

Plenty of newspapers.

Some plastic spoons.

The most suitable materials for dyeing are cotton, calico and linen.

Candles or blocks of paraffin wax.

Resin or beeswax.

The tools – tjanting for fine lines and dots, brushes for spreading wide areas.

Some of the equipment.

Method of application

Cut up the candles or paraffin wax into small pieces and put into small tins within a saucepan of water. Boil the water over the heater.

If a large group is working distribute hot wax in small individual tins and tin-heaters. Return the wax to the main heater occasionally if it cools off.

A small quantity (approximately 1 : 5) of beeswax or resin will make the wax less brittle and easier to work.

Spread a number of layers of newspaper on a flat surface. Stretch fabric over a frame and pin; alternatively, pin the fabric over the edges of a table, inserting strips of wood all round the top surface of the table to prevent the fabric touching the newspaper and depositing wax on it.

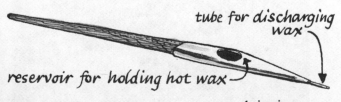

A tjanting.

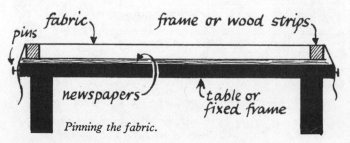

Pinning the fabric.

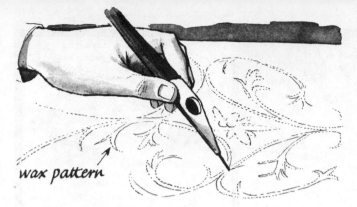

wax pattern

The tjanting in use making a linear kind of pattern. See result on curtains (right).

Blocks for batik printing

Blocks for printing quite large patterns can be made from scrap materials: corks, tubes of various sizes, all kinds of scrap metal provided that the printing surface is flat. The 'block' is dipped into a wide tin lid of hot wax and then pressed down firmly on the fabric surface.

The dyes

These must be suitable for cold water application. Ideal for this purpose are Dylon dyes, but many other brand names are available.

A number of other resist methods are used today. For detailed information on a variety of printing methods, some of the books in the book list on page 277 can be recommended.

A set of curtains using the batik process – within a stage setting for 'Twelfth Night' (see also page 101 for further scenes of the same production).

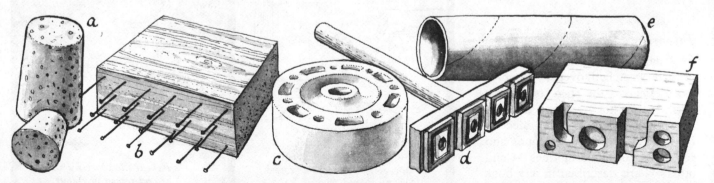

*Batik blocks: **a** cork; **b** wooden block with pins – only the pins are dipped; **c** a plaster mould block (see page 134 on making moulds) – the top must be smoothed to a flat surface; **d** a home-made stamp block using a dowel rod for the handle – scrap metal is soldered or nailed to the base; **e** cardboard tube; **f** balsa wood with a carved base.*

4 Screen printing and dyeing textiles

Curtains, costumes and other soft furnishings (including stage tapestries made from hessian) are best coloured with dye. Scenic paints give a very stiff quality to the material and can crack badly if applied thickly – though they can strengthen the colour effects if used with care.

Aniline dyes are sold in powder or crystal form: the former is dissolved in cold water, the latter in hot. Each needs to be 'fixed' with a salt called Glauber Salts. (See list of suppliers on page 276.)

When a large pattern is required on a textile, the silkscreen technique can be a quick and effective method. Using a panel of silk, cut-out paper stencils and aniline dye mixed with a polycell water paste, an area measuring 10 m × 4 m can be covered within a day. It is an advantage if the textile to be printed has already been dyed – it gives greater colour and textural effect. If the under-dyeing is uneven the overall appearance of the drapes will be enhanced.

Tapestries

Free painting with aniline dyes on hessian stretched over a frame is most effective for stage tapestries. Batik (using hot wax) and tie-and-dye methods can also be effective for large sun-spot backgrounds and costumes. Both techniques – and others – are described in any book about the dyeing of textiles. (See book list on page 277.)

126

1 *Use tacks or a staple-gun to fix a piece of silk to a prepared wooden frame.*

2 *Cut out a paper stencil – the dimensions to fit inside the silk frame.*

3 *Lay the stencil inside the frame against the silk and seal off all edges with sticky tape. Repeat the whole process for any second colour stencil.*

4 *Pour liquid dye into the polycell paste and stir well. Prepare a second colour of dye if needed. Use a rubber blade or 'squeegee' of the right width for the frame.*

5 *Pull squeegee over the stencil using a generous amount of colour. Use downward pressure over all parts of the stencil. (A car window squeegee can be used for small stencils.)*

6 *Repeat the process with a second stencil or colour if desired.*

PAINTING GAUZES

Since it is used primarily for atmospheric effects (see page 24 on the lighting of gauzes) a gauze must retain its transparent quality when coloured. Dyes are the obvious solution as the gauze is then stained and not clogged with paint.

For more 'solid' (opaque) effects, e.g. walls or various silhouettes, thin or thick paint can be dragged across the gauze. Lit obliquely from the front a strong shape or silhouette will stand out, fading only if a light is brought up behind and the front light dimmed out.

Left: detail showing part of a curtain with the screen design described in the diagrams. This design can be seen in a setting on page 93.

Right: a gauze with front lighting only – picture of a woman.

Far right: the same gauze in the workshop with back lighting only.

3-Dimensional surfaces – 1

Many other textural surfaces can be created by means of collage or by building up the surfaces with a variety of materials. Such surfaces have the slight advantage over the painted texture that they will all stand out well with oblique stage lighting over them, giving a strong three-dimensional appearance.

1 WOOD DEBRIS: sawdust, shavings and chippings

Sawdust and other debris can be sprinkled on a glued or thickly sized surface, or mixed with paint before the paint is applied to the surface. The photograph on the right shows the quality of surface achieved by such means.

2 PLASTERING

Layers of plaster are trowelled on to the canvas before painting. Swirled around freely (whiting having been added to the mixture) it is slow-drying and will stand working on for some hours.

This sort of surface can add variety to a large wall. The plaster can have dye added or can be painted over when dry.

Sawdust

Wood chippings

Plaster with finger pattern texture.

Plaster as surface texture – note the oblique lighting.

Wood shavings

A setting using geometrical shapes, with walls covered in expanded polystyrene sheets and areas of paint. (Churchyard scene from 'Romeo and Juliet') A close-up on page 117 shows the inset tomb scene transformed into a bedchamber.

3 EXPANDED POLYSTYRENE

New materials are worth experimenting with in theatre design. One of the most versatile is expanded polystyrene. In massive form it can be sculpted with hot wire (see also page 147 of the section on properties) and in sheet form it can be used as a printing block (page 123) or, as in the illustration above, as a wall surface.

In a rather austere design for 'Romeo and Juliet' it was decided to give the walls more of a three-dimensional effect by adding a surface with varying sizes of sheet. The wall behind the plaster and wire crucifix was covered with a mixture of small and medium pieces with a few painted squares. The large tomb entrance at the centre and stage left used much larger tiles and revolved to show further wall coverings (see page 45 for mobile rostra and page 144 for crucifix).

3-Dimensional surfaces – 2

The back wall: a close-up of textures. The tree prop and milestone (rather out of focus) are for a daytime setting – see page 155 for the two props.

Scrap material: newspaper, metal foil, etc.

These two views of a setting for the musical 'Oliver' show a variety of 'solid' texture and illustrate the point that lighting creates a strong feeling of three dimensions.

Newspapers, brown wrapping paper and all papers that fold and crumple easily make a material for these effects. Soak in size water for a few minutes and gently press against old flats or other backings not required for repainting.

Left: a complex of three-dimensional textures – newspaper swinging across the lower part of the wall, pieces of plastic and narrow strips of plywood separating tones into near-vertical sections.

The design intention was to create a mood of seediness and dirt in a poor part of Dickensian London. Some of the mould and pollution associated with dank, moist dockland were also in mind.

Right: a wider view of the same setting with a few changes of props and mobile flats together with a new direction of lighting to create a more sinister mood. The high relief of shadow is well in evidence here.

This setting embodies most of the painted and built-up textures described in this section of the book. Note the two large mobile trucks – see page 43 for their construction.

LINING

Care should be taken in measuring and marking out panelling for an interior set. When sketching or using chalked line as described on page 114 and a plumb line always measure from the stage level and not from tops of flats and cloths – this will ensure equal height throughout a series of flats and rostra. For long walls use the chalked line as described on page 114 and a plumb line for main verticals.

Using one of the fitch liners (10 mm, 15 mm or 20 mm as appropriate) loaded with a highlight colour, run across the straight-edge. Complete all highlights, noting carefully your source of light so that edges of the panelling catch the light correctly.

Repeat the process for the shadow lines. Ensure that you prepare sufficient colour for each shadow line and that shadow lines are all tonally related to the base colour. Where a softened effect is needed to suggest a curved or cylindrical surface, use a clean wet brush to blend the still moist colours together.

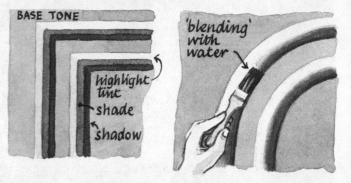

A scene showing the technique of lining. The panelling and wood 'relief' together with the moulding on the banister newel posts are all painted. (Scene from 'She Stoops to Conquer' – a more detailed view of the setting is on page 98.)

Blending edges

To avoid an abrupt contrast at the top of flats between the painted surface of the flats and the curtain borders above, soften off the top of the flats by dragging a dry brush dipped in black or another suitable dark colour to match tone of the borders. Start with pressure on the top edge and gently lift the brush away from the surface. This technique can also be used on vertical edges where a similar softening is required. (See the setting for 'Bernadette' on pages 90–91 as an example.)

Properties

6

LIGHTING PROPS · SCULPTURE · THRONES · OUTDOOR PROPS · FOOD AND DRINK

The working area and materials 134
Lamps and lanterns (including fires) . . . 135
Monumental sculpture 140
Sculptural reliefs 146
Rocks 148
Railings and balustrades 149
Thrones 150
Street furniture 154
Trees, shrubs and flowers 156
Frames (pictures and mirrors) 158
Clocks 159
Drinking vessels 160
Jugs and pitchers 164
Musical instruments 166
The box (boxes and chests of all kinds) . . . 168
Paper props (scrolls, money, etc.) 170
Quills and inkwells 171
Food and kitchen ware 172

THE WORKING AREA

Reasonable facilities for working are required for the making of properties. Some items, such as small goblets, require little space, whereas a large throne needs considerably more.

Conditions for working will obviously vary from place to place but an ordered arrangement should always be the aim, whether in a cramped classroom or the ideal workshop.

Each differing process of manufacture requires a clearly defined working area, especially where large groups of people are working as teams. One should aim at three or four areas at least.

If, for example, paper pulp is being used at the same time as varnish, shellac glue and enamel paint, try to avoid any overlapping in the use of the materials. Then the likelihood of spoiling a well-prepared 'prop' can be eliminated.

Another essential for smooth progress at all stages of manufacture is good storage.

The storage area needs plenty of cupboard and shelf space with all necessary items well labelled and, if possible, arranged in well defined groups. *Adhesives* will include every type of glue, contact adhesives and sticky tapes; *fastening and fixing* all screws, nails, tacks, staples, etc. *Containers* are well worth collecting: metal tins from tobacco to biscuit size are the most useful (especially the smaller ones); many kinds of plastic pots and small buckets, often with clip-on lids – handy for liquids and glues and also for mixing paint.

Always carry a large stock of newspapers and rags. Newsprint is still the most versatile of materials: it can be used for cleaning, protecting working surfaces and making pulp and mâché.

THE MATERIALS

A complete list of necessary tools and materials is shown on pages 274 and 275. Not all are essential and certain items will seldom be required. It is only necessary to experiment to discover what is most suitable for one's needs. However, mention should be made here of one important source of materials – the scrap yard.

Collect scrap of all kinds: factories produce a vast amount of industrial waste and the retail trade discards many kinds of containers. A request to almost any retailer to save certain kinds of refuse will bring many useful items. The author has frequently made great savings on expanded polystyrene, cardboard, hardboard, string, wire, metal foil and scrap sheet metal by such means – thus reserving funds for more durable and expensive items, such as a new spotlight or flood.

Galvanised wire and wire mesh are, with wood, the most essential materials for property making. Keep a stock of thick, medium, and thin wire for the various structures. If space allows, keep a few tea-chests in a back room, cellar or under a bench to store scrap. If each chest is reserved for particular types of thing (plastic containers, tubes and rolls, string and wire, etc.) a large, comprehensive and accessible supply will soon be available.

Occasionally, a new way of making a prop will be suggested by the shape of a scrap item.

Cardboard is always a useful and versatile material for props. The stiff, firm card used in the footwear and clothing trades for containers is excellent. Corrugated card is used in industry for packing purposes: it is pliable and ideal for many curved surfaces.

Note: most of the props illustrated by photographs in this and other sections were constructed and painted by schoolchildren.

Wire and wire mesh

To avoid cluttering the illustrations with excessive labelling in this section, galvanised plain wire and galvanised wire netting (known also as chicken wire) are simplified to 'wire' and 'wire mesh' respectively.

When purchasing these items the correct description for heavy, medium and fine wire is 10 gauge, 12 gauge and 16 gauge galvanised plain wire (note that the higher the number, the finer the wire).

Large, medium and fine wire mesh is sold as galvanised wire netting 25 mm, 18 mm and 13 mm respectively (the measurement refers to the hole size).

LAMPS AND LANTERNS

Lights on stage, such as standard lamps or table lamps, are readily available on hire – or on loan from members of the cast.

Antique lamps, street lamps and fires can be built up from thin wood strip, papier mâché, wire and tissue. The illumination of the smaller lights (hand lanterns, torches) can be achieved by using $4\frac{1}{2}$ volt batteries and torch bulbs, controlled either by switch or by turning the bulb gently in its socket. In the case of candles, the bulbs can be lightly glued and covered with tissue torn to a flame shape – giving quite a realistic effect when lit.

Larger street lamps can be effectively lit by 40 or 60 watt bulbs controlled from the switchboard – the number of tissue layers used will determine the amount of light visible. Old, dirty glass can be effectively suggested by layers of varnish.

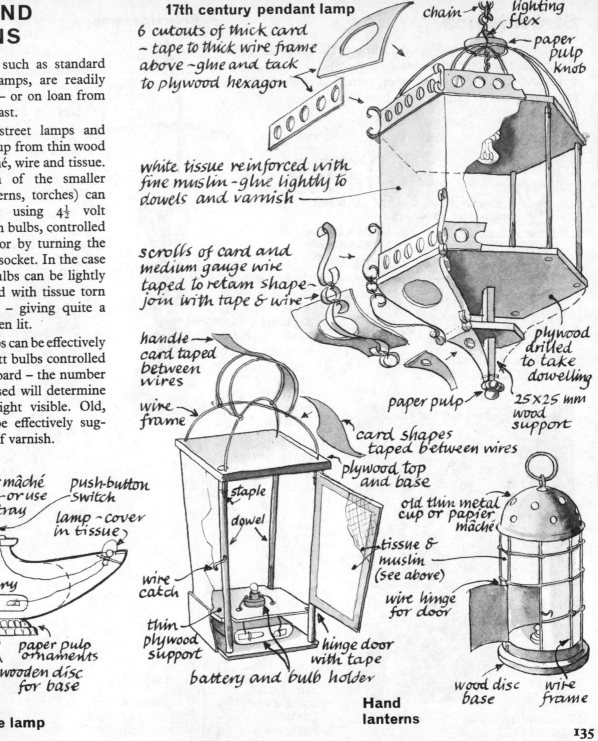

17th century pendant lamp

6 cutouts of thick card – tape to thick wire frame above – glue and tack to plywood hexagon

chain — lighting flex

paper pulp knob

white tissue reinforced with fine muslin – glue lightly to dowels and varnish

scrolls of card and medium gauge wire taped to retain shape – join with tape & wire

plywood drilled to take dowelling

paper pulp

25×25 mm wood support

handle – card taped between wires

wire frame

card shapes taped between wires

plywood top and base

staple

dowel

old thin metal cup or papier mâché

tissue & muslin (see above)

wire hinge for door

wire catch

thin plywood support

hinge door with tape

battery and bulb holder

wood disc base

wire frame

Hand lanterns

body of papier mâché on wire frame – or use old metal ashtray

push-button switch

lamp – cover in tissue

battery

heavy gauge wire frame wired and taped to body

paper pulp ornaments

wooden disc for base

Antique lamp

Street lamps

Constructed over a rigid wooden support the lamps are given shape and character with various materials. Use wire, wood strips and stiffened felt for frames, varnished tissue or muslin for glass. Paint to simulate weathered look.

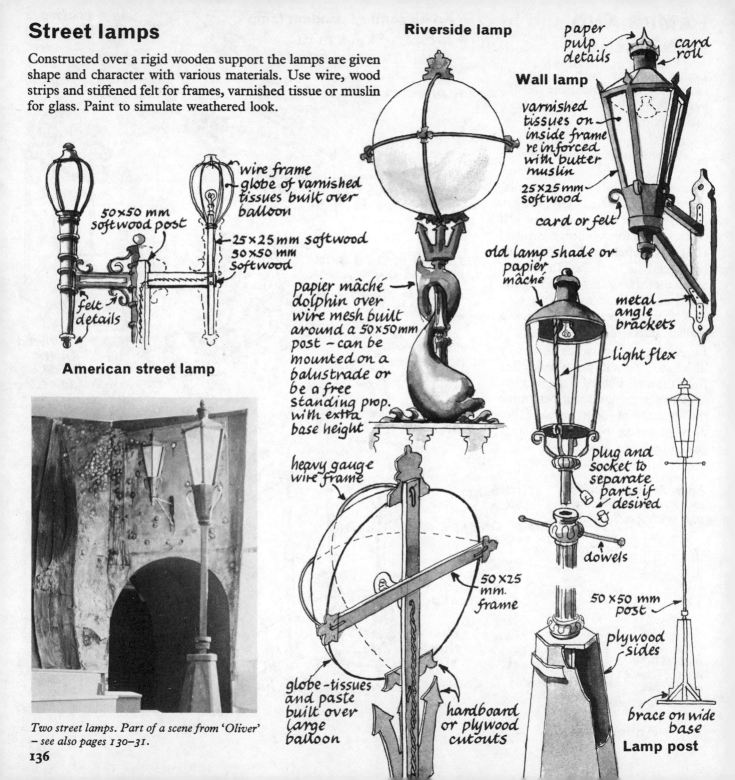

Riverside lamp

paper pulp details

card roll

Wall lamp

wire frame globe of varnished tissues built over balloon

50×50 mm softwood post

25×25 mm softwood
50×50 mm softwood

felt details

varnished tissues on inside frame reinforced with butter muslin

25×25 mm softwood

card or felt

old lamp shade or papier mâché

metal angle brackets

papier mâché dolphin over wire mesh built around a 50×50 mm post – can be mounted on a balustrade or be a free standing prop. with extra base height

light flex

plug and socket to separate parts if desired

dowels

American street lamp

heavy gauge wire frame

50×25 mm. frame

Two street lamps. Part of a scene from 'Oliver' – see also pages 130–31.

globe-tissues and paste built over large balloon

hardboard or plywood cutouts

50×50 mm post

plywood sides

brace on wide base

Lamp post

136

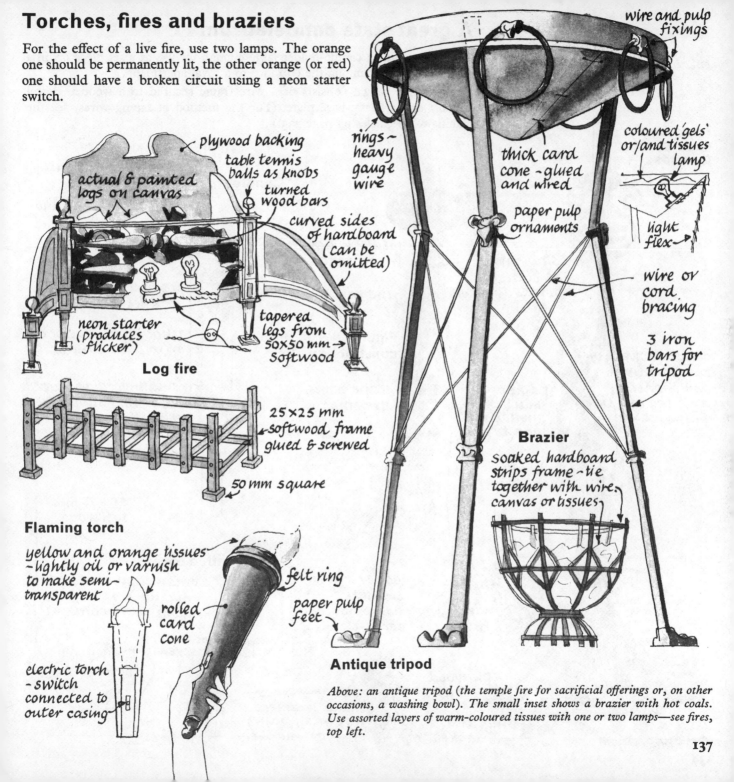

Torches, fires and braziers

For the effect of a live fire, use two lamps. The orange one should be permanently lit, the other orange (or red) one should have a broken circuit using a neon starter switch.

wire and pulp fixings

Log fire

plywood backing

actual & painted logs on canvas

table tennis balls as knobs

turned wood bars

curved sides of hardboard (can be omitted)

neon starter (produces flicker)

tapered legs from 50×50 mm softwood

rings ~ heavy gauge wire

thick card cone ~ glued and wired

paper pulp ornaments

coloured 'gels' or/and tissues lamp

light flex

wire or cord bracing

3 iron bars for tripod

25×25 mm softwood frame glued & screwed

50 mm square

Brazier

soaked hardboard strips frame ~ tie together with wire. canvas or tissues

Flaming torch

yellow and orange tissues ~ lightly oil or varnish to make semi-transparent

felt ring

rolled card cone

paper pulp feet

electric torch ~ switch connected to outer casing

Antique tripod

Above: an antique tripod (the temple fire for sacrificial offerings or, on other occasions, a washing bowl). The small inset shows a brazier with hot coals. Use assorted layers of warm-coloured tissues with one or two lamps—see fires, top left.

A great state candelabrum

This page shows a candle-holder large enough for use as a set piece or, in a pair, suitable for flanking the entrance to a royal apartment.

The example shown consists of a wire frame secured to a wooden dowel support and a heavy base plate. (For the method of taping wires, see the making of spectacles on page 233.)

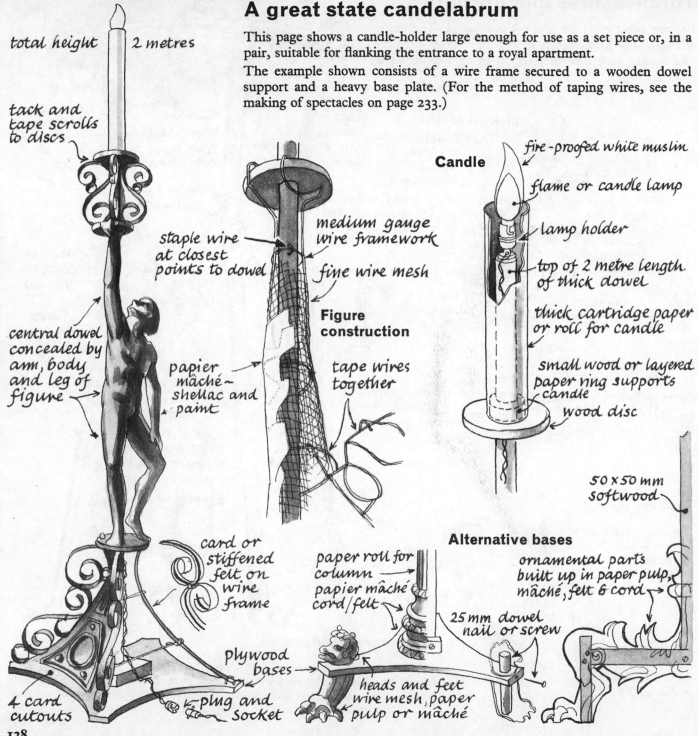

total height 2 metres

tack and tape scrolls to discs

staple wire at closest points to dowel

medium gauge wire framework

fine wire mesh

Figure construction

central dowel concealed by arm, body and leg of figure

papier mâché - shellac and paint

tape wires together

Candle

fire-proofed white muslin

flame or candle lamp

lamp holder

top of 2 metre length of thick dowel

thick cartridge paper or roll for candle

small wood or layered paper ring supports candle

wood disc

card or stiffened felt on wire frame

50 x 50 mm softwood

Alternative bases

paper roll for column papier mâché cord/felt

ornamental parts built up in paper pulp, mâché, felt & cord

25 mm dowel nail or screw

plywood bases

4 card cutouts

plug and socket

heads and feet wire mesh, paper pulp or mâché

138

Candlesticks

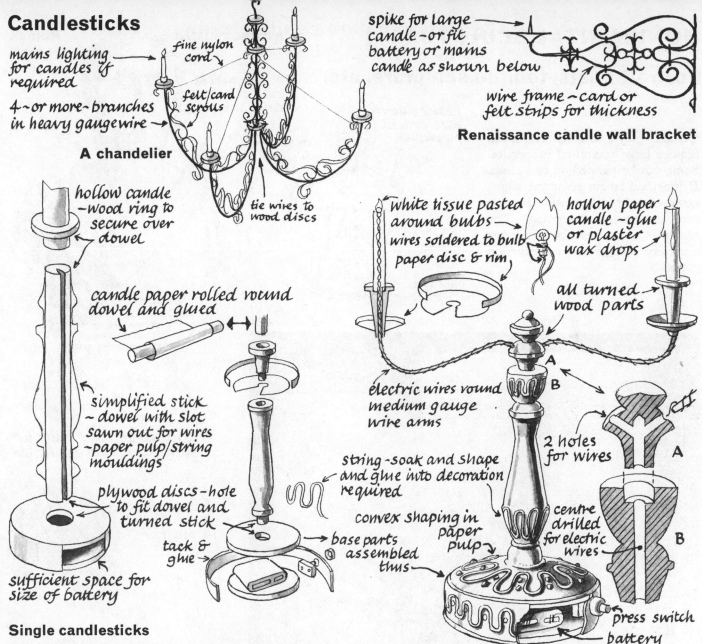

mains lighting for candles if required

4~or more~branches in heavy gauge wire →

fine nylon cord

felt/card scrolls

A chandelier

tie wires to wood discs

spike for large candle~or fit battery or mains candle as shown below

wire frame~card or felt strips for thickness

Renaissance candle wall bracket

hollow candle ~wood ring to secure over dowel

candle paper rolled round dowel and glued

simplified stick ~ dowel with slot sawn out for wires ~paper pulp/string mouldings

plywood discs~hole to fit dowel and turned stick

tack & glue →

sufficient space for size of battery

white tissue pasted around bulbs~ wires soldered to bulb paper disc & rim

hollow paper candle~glue or plaster wax drops

all turned wood parts

A

B

electric wires round medium gauge wire arms

string~soak and shape and glue into decoration required

convex shaping in paper pulp

base parts assembled thus

2 holes for wires

centre drilled for electric wires

A

B

press switch battery

Single candlesticks

Two methods of building a candlestick: left – using a piece of dowel rod, ail mouldings built up with glue and pulp or plastic wood; right – a lathe-turned candlestick (if the height is 25–35 cm it can be turned in one piece – larger ones should be made in parts as shown, to facilitate drilling through centres).

Two-branch Georgian candlestick

(properties in a scene from 'She Stoops to Conquer' – page 98)

Decorative features are built up with papier mâché, pulp and string. The under-painting is black, the finish silver.

139

MONUMENTAL SCULPTURE – 1

Portrait busts, temple sculpture, etc.

Certain plays, usually historical, require large sculptural properties. Some can be painted on to a cloth. If time and labour resources allow, however, a three-dimensional sculpture is worth attempting. The examples on the next few pages give a variety of type and construction methods.

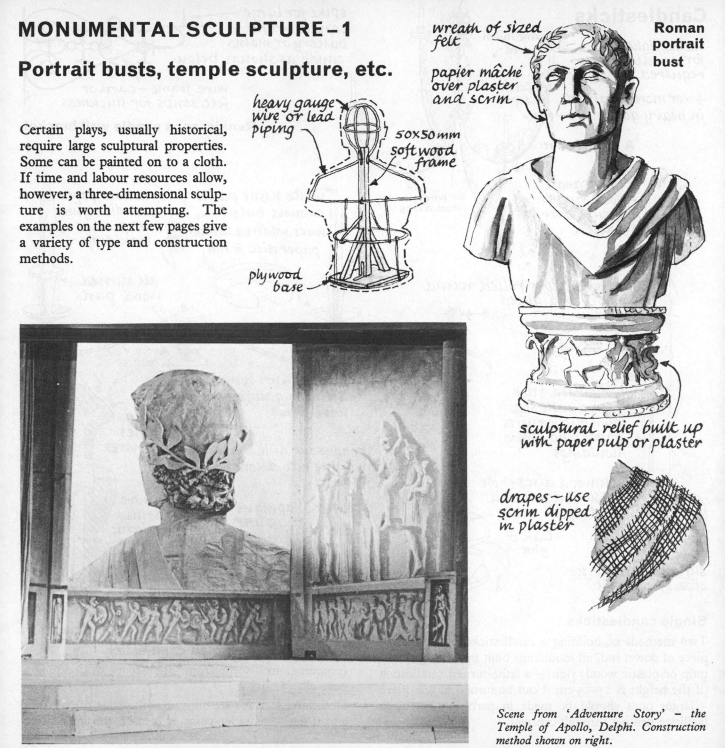

heavy gauge wire or lead piping

50×50 mm soft wood frame

plywood base

wreath of sized felt

papier mâché over plaster and scrim

sculptural relief built up with paper pulp or plaster

drapes – use scrim dipped in plaster

Scene from 'Adventure Story' – the Temple of Apollo, Delphi. Construction method shown on right.

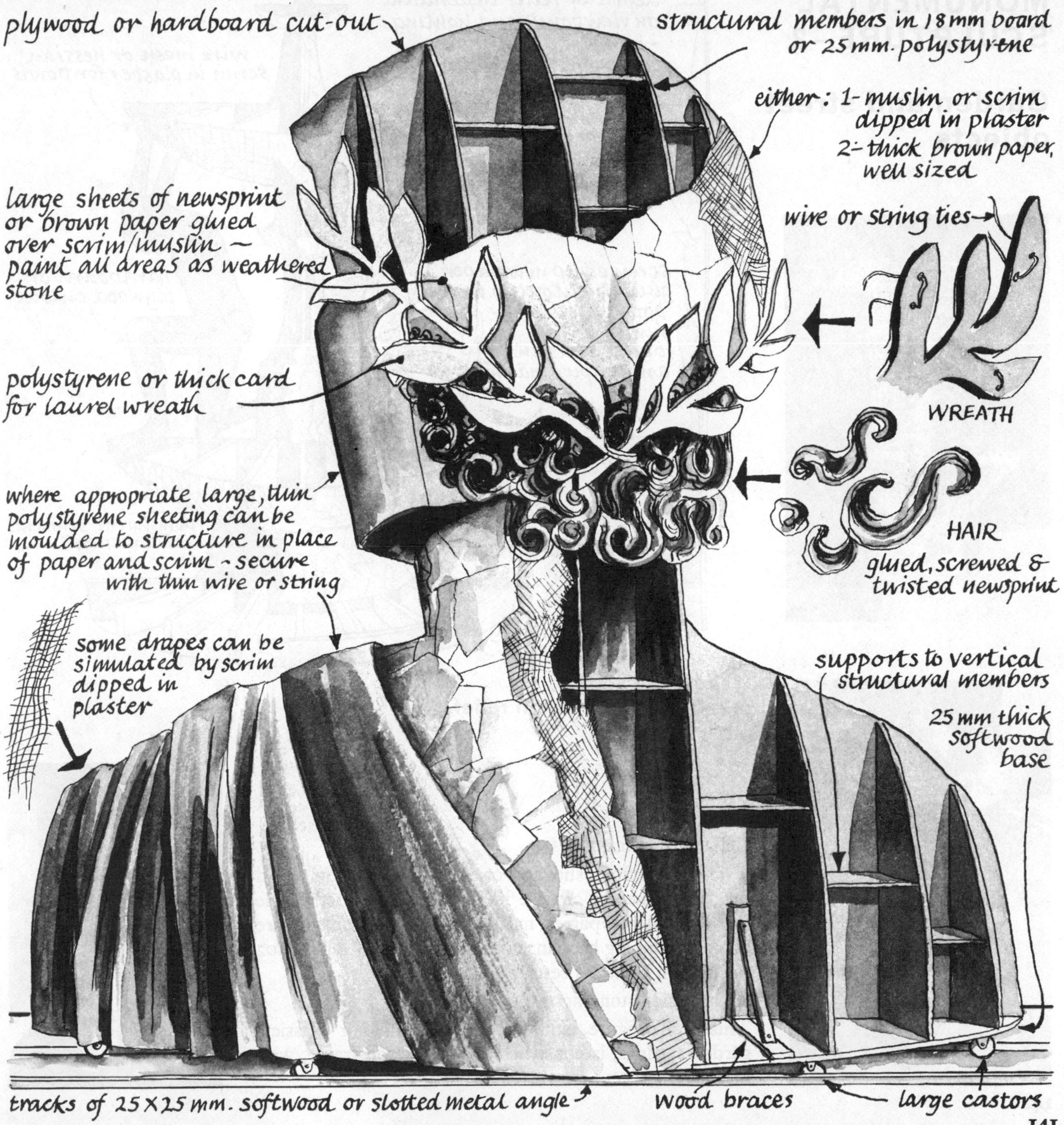

plywood or hardboard cut-out

structural members in 18 mm board or 25 mm. polystyrene

either: 1- muslin or scrim dipped in plaster
2- thick brown paper, well sized

wire or string ties

large sheets of newsprint or brown paper glued over scrim/muslin — paint all areas as weathered stone

WREATH

polystyrene or thick card for laurel wreath

HAIR
glued, screwed & twisted newsprint

where appropriate large, thin polystyrene sheeting can be moulded to structure in place of paper and scrim — secure with thin wire or string

supports to vertical structural members

25 mm thick softwood base

some drapes can be simulated by scrim dipped in plaster

tracks of 25 × 25 mm. softwood or slotted metal angle

Wood braces

large castors

141

MONUMENTAL SCULPTURE – 2

Garden and street objects

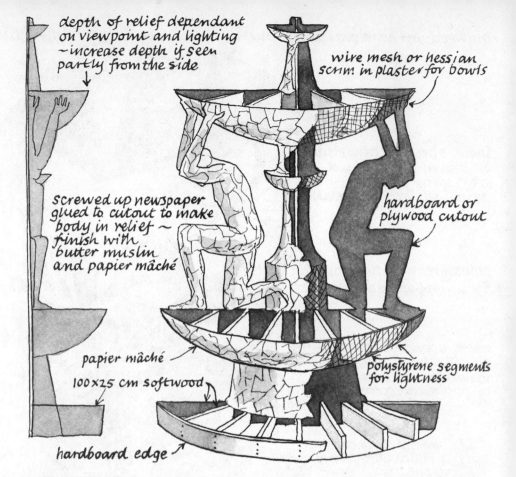

depth of relief dependant on viewpoint and lighting ~ increase depth if seen partly from the side

wire mesh or hessian scrim in plaster for bowls

screwed up newspaper glued to cutout to make body in relief ~ finish with butter muslin and papier mâché

hardboard or plywood cutout

papier mâché

100 × 25 cm softwood

polystyrene segments for lightness

hardboard edge

Street fountain in relief

Urn

Left: garden urn.

Two photographs showing construction and completed urn. Note the use of wire mesh round the wood frame before applying papier mâché. The 'swag' shapes are made by dipping hessian scrim into plaster. See page 102 for urns in a garden setting.

Right: small stone figures.

This stone figure, suitable for fountains or classical garden settings, is constructed with a wood frame, wire mesh and plaster.

The fountain, whose construction is shown on the left, as it appeared in a scene from 'The Merchant of Venice' – other scenes are shown on pages 92–93.

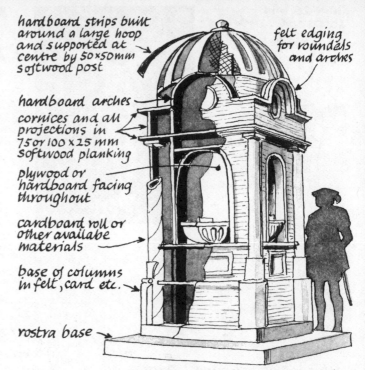

hardboard strips built around a large hoop and supported at centre by 50×50mm softwood post

felt edging for roundels and arches

hardboard arches

cornices and all projections in 75 or 100×25 mm softwood planking

plywood or hardboard facing throughout

cardboard roll or other available materials

base of columns in felt, card etc.

rostra base

Market place drinking fountain

Occasionally a market place, courtyard or garden scene can be enhanced by a major property in the central area of the stage. The drinking fountain shown above is built with three sides, if set square to the setting line. Only two sides need be completed if set at 45 degrees.

An octagonal step fountain is shown below with a stone figure, suitable for a courtyard scene. An arcaded backing with or without rostra steps would make a suitable acting area.

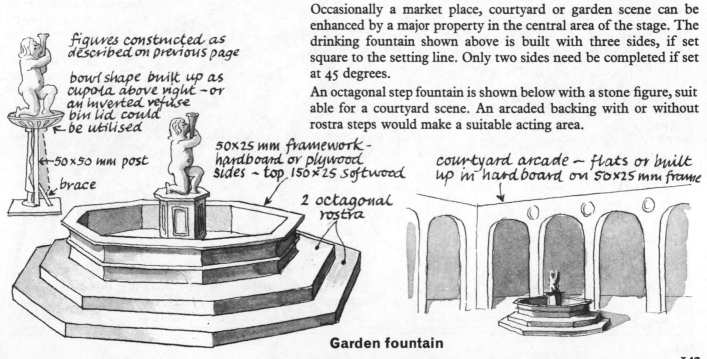

figures constructed as described on previous page

bowl shape built up as cupola above right – or an inverted refuse bin lid could be utilised

← 50×50 mm post

brace

50×25 mm framework – hardboard or plywood sides – top 150×25 softwood

2 octagonal rostra

courtyard arcade – flats or built up in hardboard on 50×25 mm frame

Garden fountain

Architectural detail and structure

200×25 mm
softwood

fine
wire
mesh

screwed
25×25 mm
softwood
frame

large nails

Crucifix

Left: crucifix constructed with a wood frame and wire mesh. The modelling can be built up with scrim dipped in plaster for a small crucifix. Any large example would be built up with papier mâché because of weight problems – see page 129 ('Romeo and Juliet').

Below: tympanum. Medieval doorways, especially to churches and chapels, can be enhanced by a sculptured tympanum above. Built over a prepared wooden former, strengthened with galvanised wire, the modelling can be done with wire mesh and finished with papier mâché. If on a small scale, the whole tympanum could be modelled in expanded polystyrene sheet (approximately 3 cm thick) cut with a hot wire – see page 147.

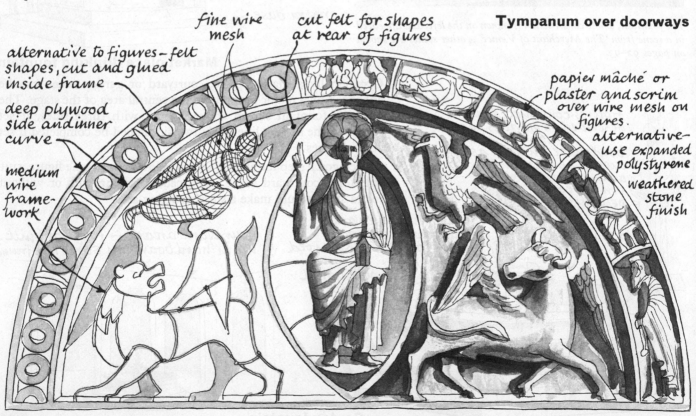

fine wire
mesh

cut felt for shapes
at rear of figures

Tympanum over doorways

alternative to figures – felt
shapes, cut and glued
inside frame

deep plywood
side and inner
curve

medium
wire frame-
work

papier mâché or
plaster and scrim
over wire mesh on
figures.
alternative –
use expanded
polystyrene

weathered
stone
finish

144

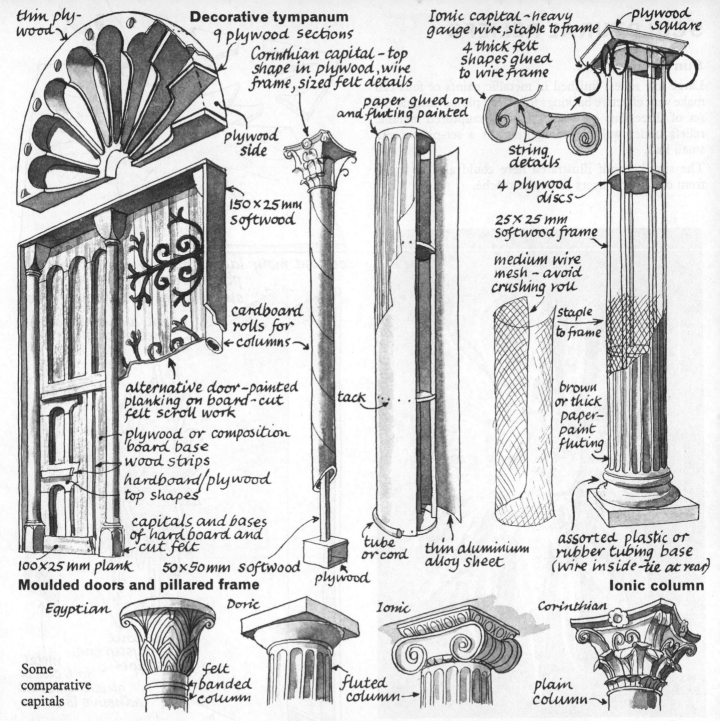

thin ply-wood

Decorative tympanum
9 plywood sections

Corinthian capital – top shape in plywood, wire frame, sized felt details

plywood side

150 × 25 mm softwood

cardboard rolls for columns

alternative door – painted planking on board – cut felt scroll work

plywood or composition board base
wood strips

hardboard/plywood top shapes

capitals and bases of hardboard and cut felt

100 × 25 mm plank

50 × 50 mm softwood

Moulded doors and pillared frame

paper glued on and fluting painted

tack

tube or cord

plywood

thin aluminium alloy sheet

Ionic capital – heavy gauge wire, staple to frame

4 thick felt shapes glued to wire frame

string details

4 plywood discs

25 × 25 mm softwood frame

medium wire mesh – avoid crushing roll

staple to frame

brown or thick paper – paint fluting

assorted plastic or rubber tubing base (wire inside – tie at rear)

plywood square

Ionic column

Some comparative capitals

Egyptian
felt banded column

Doric
fluted column

Ionic
plain column

Corinthian

Columns can be constructed as shown or be simply assembled by using cardboard rolls – see page 102 for details.

145

SCULPTURAL RELIEFS

Sun motif

Large low reliefs finished in metallic paints or foils can make very effective backings to history plays. Imagine the set of three flats on page 57, with sculptured metallic reliefs under well-placed lighting, as a set-piece for a small hall.

The simple motif illustrated here could also be made from cardboard layers or papier mâché.

The finished relief, constructed as shown on the right. Finish in varying layers of metallic paper, foil and paint.

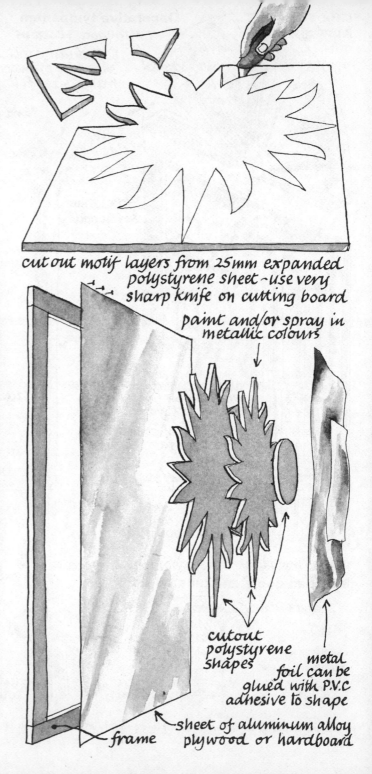

cut out motif layers from 25mm expanded polystyrene sheet ~ use very sharp knife on cutting board

paint and/or spray in metallic colours

cutout polystyrene shapes

metal foil can be glued with P.V.C adhesive to shape

frame

sheet of aluminium alloy plywood or hardboard

symbols without a backing can be made from felt cutouts and glued to flats or panels

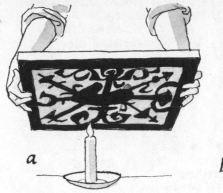

a

b

a – burning out trophy by moving quickly across flame ~ painted areas resist heat

b – using an electric wire cutter ~ both methods use 25 mm expanded polystyrene

battery or transformer

Trophies, symbols and architectural frieze

An alternative to painted decoration and ornaments on architectural scenery and properties is 3-dimensional relief. Reliefs are useful for architectural features such as pilasters to which lighting will give a feeling of added depth.

rectangular trophy using polystyrene on backing of plywood or hardboard

symbol in felt or polystyrene on a roundel of plywood

cut felt symbol

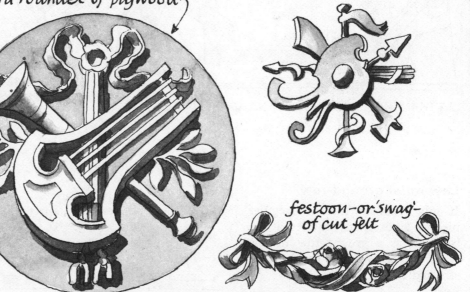

festoon ~ or 'swag' ~ of cut felt

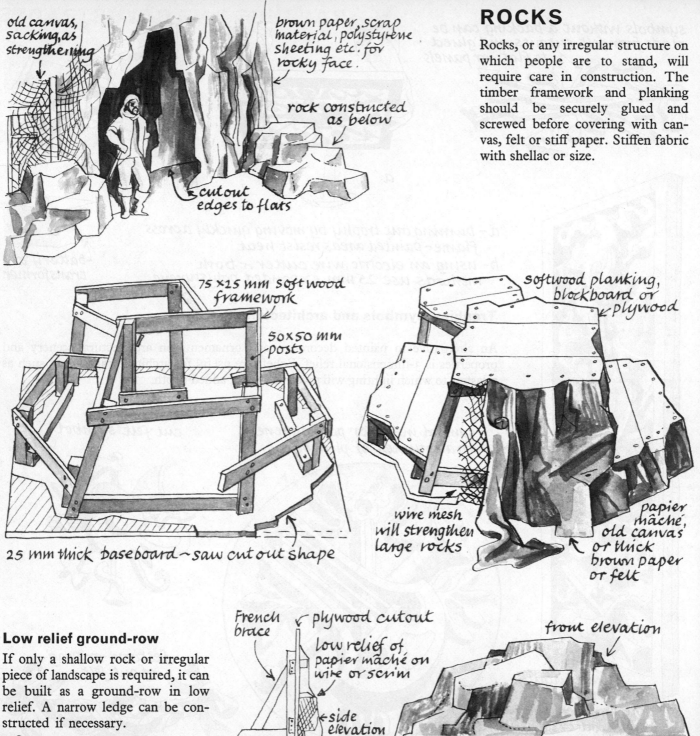

old canvas, sacking, as strengthening

brown paper, scrap material, polystyrene sheeting etc. for rocky face.

rock constructed as below

cutout edges to flats

ROCKS

Rocks, or any irregular structure on which people are to stand, will require care in construction. The timber framework and planking should be securely glued and screwed before covering with canvas, felt or stiff paper. Stiffen fabric with shellac or size.

75 × 25 mm soft wood framework

50 × 50 mm posts

25 mm thick baseboard ~ saw cut out shape

softwood planking, blockboard or plywood

wire mesh will strengthen large rocks

papier mâché, old canvas or thick brown paper or felt

Low relief ground-row

If only a shallow rock or irregular piece of landscape is required, it can be built as a ground-row in low relief. A narrow ledge can be constructed if necessary.

148

French brace

plywood cutout

low relief of papier mâché on wire or scrim

side elevation

front elevation

RAILINGS AND BALUSTRADES

Exterior settings occasionally need dividing with walls or railings. Classical exteriors need balustrades and country scenes a fence. A narrow, shallow stage can be given a new sense of depth by these means.

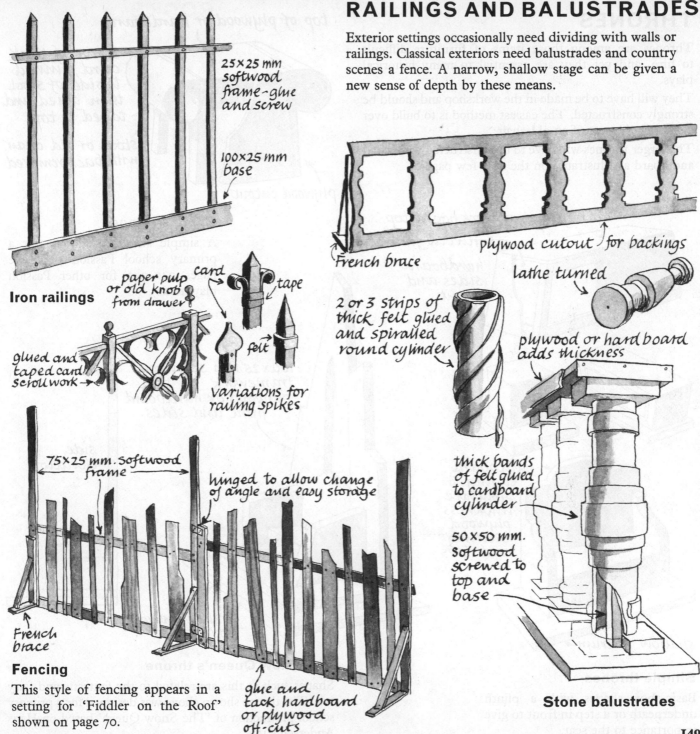

25 × 25 mm softwood frame-glue and screw

100 × 25 mm base

Iron railings

paper pulp or old knob from drawer

card

tape

glued and taped card scroll work

felt

variations for railing spikes

French brace

plywood cutout for backings

lathe turned

2 or 3 strips of thick felt glued and spiralled round cylinder

plywood or hard board adds thickness

75 × 25 mm. softwood frame

hinged to allow change of angle and easy storage

thick bands of felt glued to cardboard cylinder

50 × 50 mm. softwood screwed to top and base

French brace

Fencing

This style of fencing appears in a setting for 'Fiddler on the Roof' shown on page 70.

glue and tack hardboard or plywood off-cuts

Stone balustrades

149

THRONES

Thrones are among those items of furniture difficult to hire, and yet they are essential to many historical plays.

They will have to be made in the workshop and should be strongly constructed. The easiest method is to build over a stool or the seat of an old chair.

The larger thrones will have to be constructed with wood and board as illustrated on the next few pages.

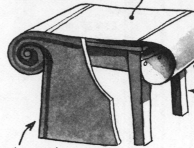

top of plywood or hardboard

curve of thick card, pinned to side of stool then glued and taped to top

stool or old chair with back removed

plywood cutout

Pilate's throne

A simple structure suitable for a primary school Passion play (see pages 240–242 for other Passion play items).

plywood or block board top

softwood frame

hardboard sides and front

hardboard edging to simulate thickness plywood backing and sides

shallow rostrum →

100 x 25 mm softwood framework in thin plywood or hardboard front and sides

side elevation

2 shallow rostra for steps

Simple thrones

Basic box shapes with a plinth underneath or a step in front to give importance to the seat.

The Snow Queen's throne

Shapes such as this are related to the fantastic and fairy tale. The throne shown above was designed for a primary school production of 'The Snow Queen' based on Hans Andersen's tale.

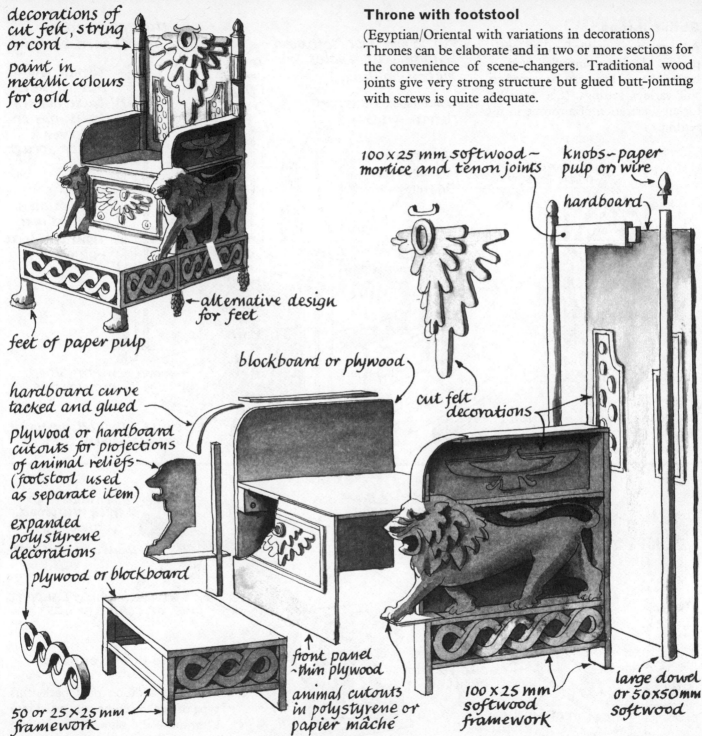

decorations of cut felt, string or cord

paint in metallic colours for gold

feet of paper pulp

←alternative design for feet

Throne with footstool

(Egyptian/Oriental with variations in decorations)
Thrones can be elaborate and in two or more sections for the convenience of scene-changers. Traditional wood joints give very strong structure but glued butt-jointing with screws is quite adequate.

100 x 25 mm softwood~ mortice and tenon joints

knobs~paper pulp on wire

hardboard

cut felt decorations

hardboard curve tacked and glued

plywood or hardboard cutouts for projections of animal reliefs (footstool used as separate item)

blockboard or plywood

expanded polystyrene decorations

plywood or blockboard

50 or 25 x 25 mm framework

front panel ~thin plywood

animals cutouts in polystyrene or papier mâché

100 x 25 mm softwood framework

large dowel or 50 x 50 mm softwood

151

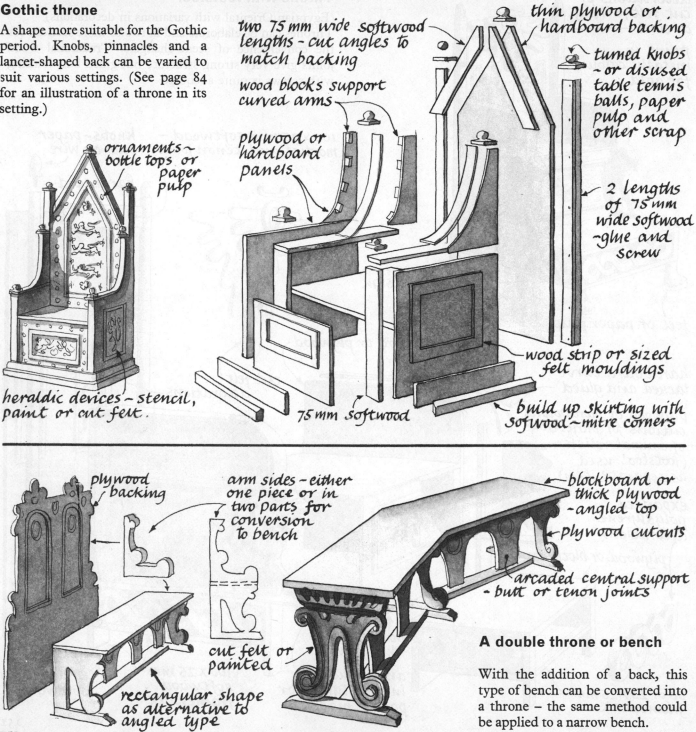

Gothic throne

A shape more suitable for the Gothic period. Knobs, pinnacles and a lancet-shaped back can be varied to suit various settings. (See page 84 for an illustration of a throne in its setting.)

ornaments ~ bottle tops or paper pulp

heraldic devices ~ stencil, paint or cut felt.

two 75 mm wide softwood lengths - cut angles to match backing

wood blocks support curved arms

plywood or hardboard panels

75 mm softwood

thin plywood or hardboard backing

turned knobs ~ or disused table tennis balls, paper pulp and other scrap

2 lengths of 75 mm wide softwood ~ glue and screw

wood strip or sized felt mouldings

build up skirting with softwood ~ mitre corners

plywood backing

arm sides - either one piece or in two parts for conversion to bench

cut felt or painted

rectangular shape as alternative to angled type

blockboard or thick plywood - angled top

plywood cutouts

arcaded central support - butt or tenon joints

A double throne or bench

With the addition of a back, this type of bench can be converted into a throne – the same method could be applied to a narrow bench.

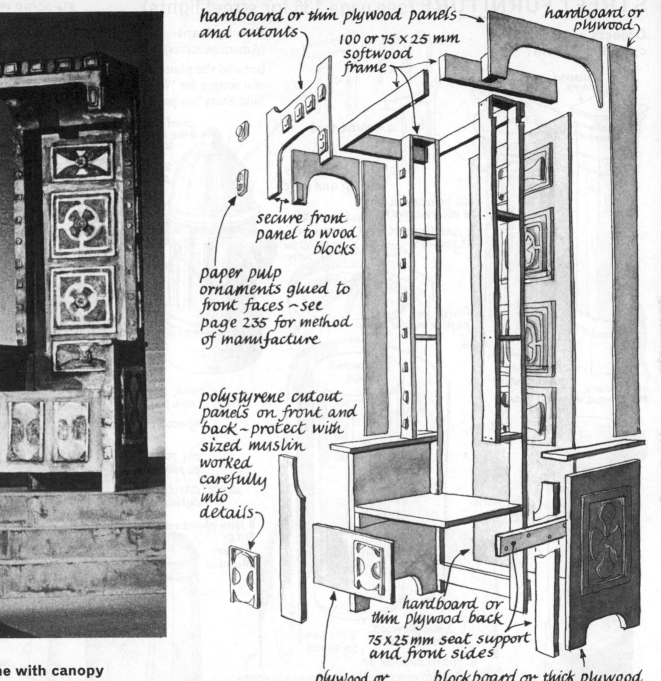

hardboard or thin plywood panels and cutouts

hardboard or plywood

100 or 75 x 25 mm softwood frame

secure front panel to wood blocks

paper pulp ornaments glued to front faces ~ see page 235 for method of manufacture

polystyrene cutout panels on front and back ~ protect with sized muslin worked carefully into details

hardboard or thin plywood back

75 x 25 mm seat support and front sides

plywood or hardboard front panel

blockboard or thick plywood seat and sides ~ butt joints and screws throughout ~ or mortice & tenon if preferred

Throne with canopy

A design giving more prominence to the throne; in this example for the court scene from 'The Merchant of Venice' (page 93). Also suitable for the Renaissance period. Built by 14 year old boys.

STREET FURNITURE (see page 136 for street lights)

Objects of basically cylindrical form:

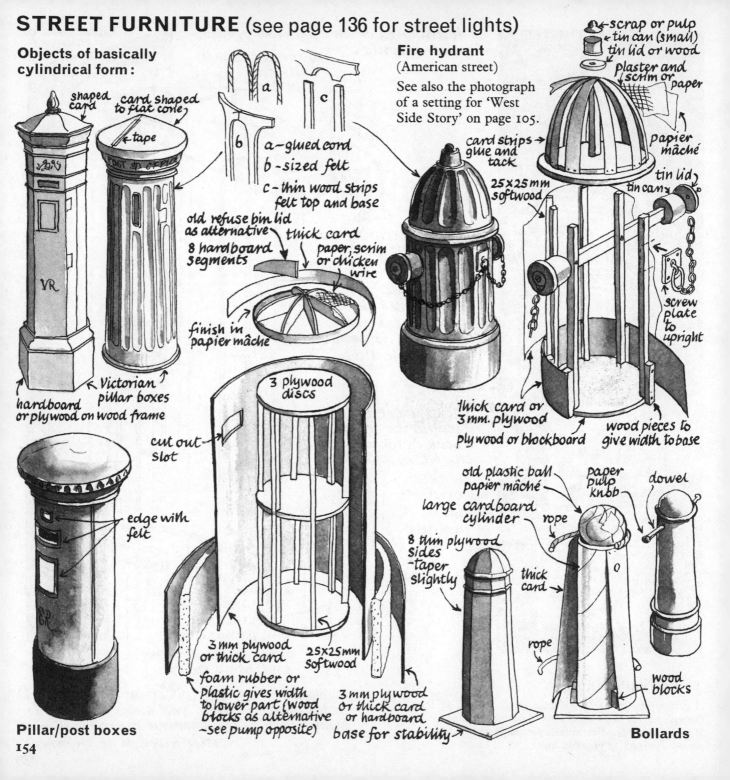

shaped card

card shaped to flat cone

tape

POST OFFICE

VR

hardboard or plywood on wood frame

Victorian pillar boxes

a
b
c

a – glued cord
b – sized felt
c – thin wood strips felt top and base

old refuse bin lid as alternative

8 hardboard segments

thick card

paper, scrim or chicken wire

finish in papier mâché

Fire hydrant
(American street)

See also the photograph of a setting for 'West Side Story' on page 105.

scrap or pulp
tin can (small)
tin lid or wood
plaster and scrim or paper

papier mâché

card strips glue and tack

25 × 25 mm softwood

tin lid

tin can

screw plate to upright

thick card or 3 mm. plywood

plywood or blockboard

wood pieces to give width to base

cut out slot

3 plywood discs

edge with felt

CR

3 mm plywood or thick card

25 × 25 mm softwood

foam rubber or plastic gives width to lower part (wood blocks as alternative ~ see pump opposite)

3 mm plywood or thick card or hardboard

base for stability

old plastic ball papier mâché

large cardboard cylinder

rope

8 thin plywood sides ~ taper slightly

thick card

rope

paper pulp knob

dowel

wood blocks

Pillar/post boxes

Bollards

154

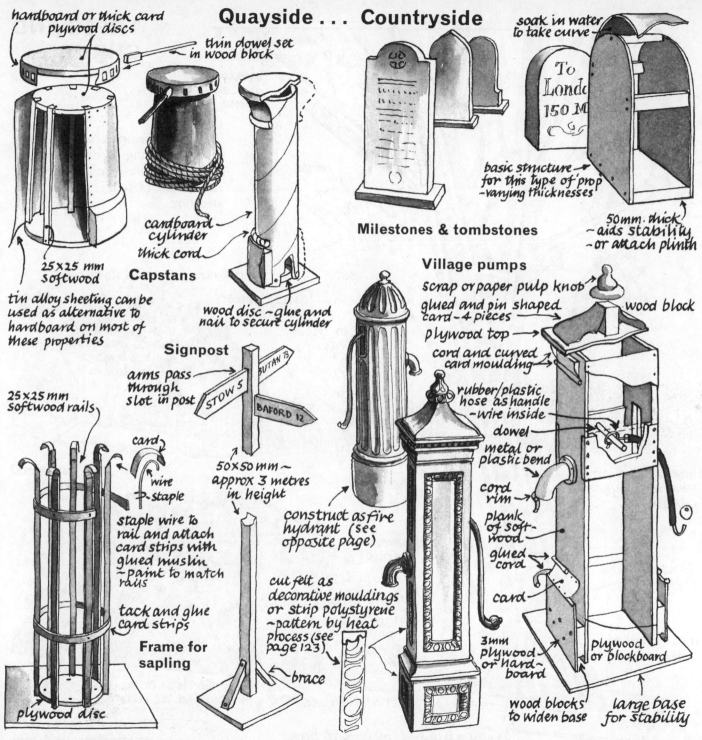

Quayside . . . Countryside

hardboard or thick card plywood discs

thin dowel set in wood block

soak in water to take curve

To London 150 M

cardboard cylinder

thick cord

basic structure for this type of prop ~ varying thicknesses

Milestones & tombstones

50 mm thick ~ aids stability ~ or attach plinth

25 × 25 mm softwood

tin alloy sheeting can be used as alternative to hardboard on most of these properties

wood disc ~ glue and nail to secure cylinder

Capstans

Village pumps

scrap or paper pulp knob

glued and pin shaped card ~ 4 pieces

wood block

plywood top

cord and curved card moulding

Signpost

BUTAN B

STOW 5

BAFORD 12

arms pass through slot in post

rubber/plastic hose as handle ~ wire inside

dowel

metal or plastic bend

25 × 25 mm softwood rails

card

wire staple

50 × 50 mm ~ approx 3 metres in height

construct as fire hydrant (see opposite page)

cord rim

plank of softwood

staple wire to rail and attach card strips with glued muslin ~ paint to match rails

glued cord

tack and glue card strips

cut felt as decorative mouldings or strip polystyrene ~ pattern by heat process (see page 123)

card

Frame for sapling

brace

3mm plywood or hardboard

plywood or blockboard

plywood disc

wood blocks to widen base

large base for stability

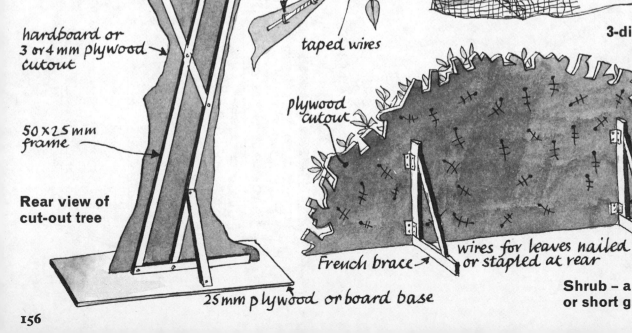

TREES AND SHRUBS

top edge concealed behind border

The two examples on this page properly belong to the section on flats, but are illustrated here to show the fixture of foliage to the main structure.

joints

wire mesh stapled to cutout

leaves/flowers wired on

braces inside shrub

felt or paper leaves

paint background to match leaves

staples

hardboard or 3 or 4 mm plywood cutout

taped wires

3-dimensional shrub

plywood cutout

50 × 25 mm frame

Rear view of cut-out tree

French brace

wires for leaves nailed or stapled at rear

25 mm plywood or board base

Shrub – a 'set piece' or short ground-row

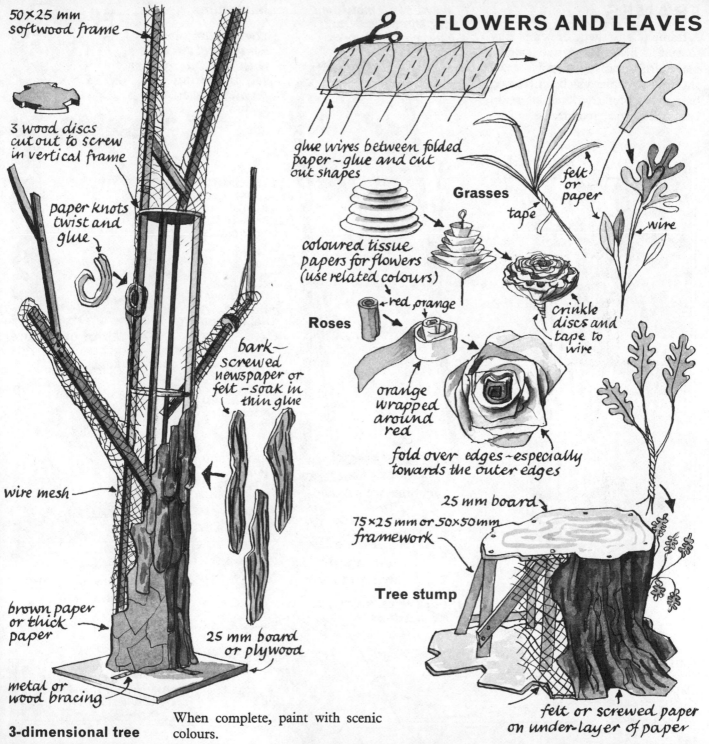

50×25 mm softwood frame

3 wood discs cut out to screw in vertical frame

paper knots twist and glue

glue wires between folded paper – glue and cut out shapes

Grasses

felt or paper

tape

coloured tissue papers for flowers (use related colours)

wire

bark– screwed newspaper or felt – soak in thin glue

Roses

red, orange

crinkle discs and tape to wire

orange wrapped around red

wire mesh

fold over edges – especially towards the outer edges

25 mm board

75×25 mm or 50×50 mm framework

brown paper or thick paper

25 mm board or plywood

Tree stump

metal or wood bracing

3-dimensional tree

When complete, paint with scenic colours.

felt or screwed paper on under-layer of paper

157

FRAMES

A frame of any shape or complexity to suit a historical period can be made from expanded polystyrene sheeting or papier mâché on a wood base or, if preferred, various scrap items glued to a wood frame.

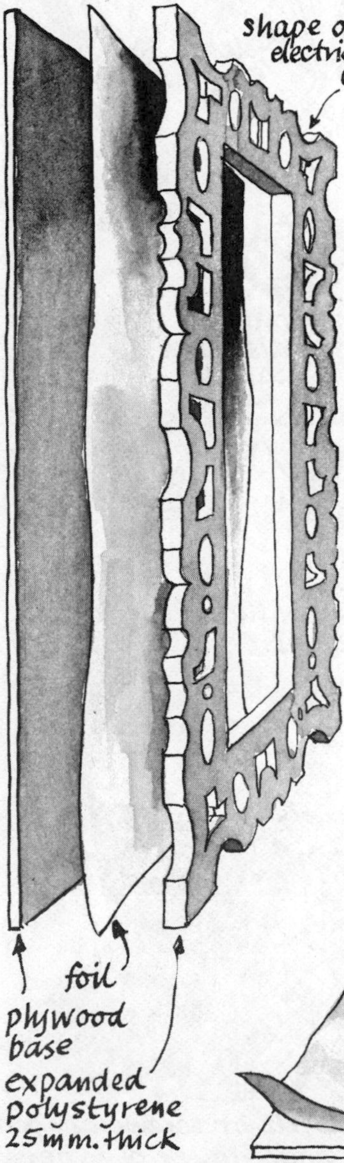

shape out with electric wire cutter

foil
plywood base
expanded polystyrene 25 mm. thick

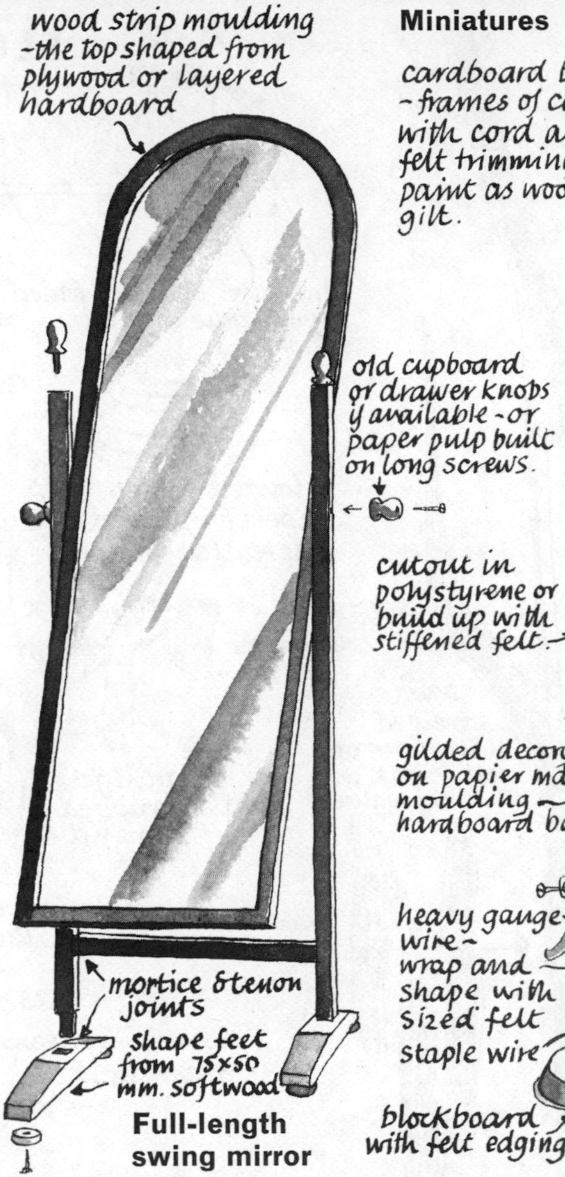

wood strip moulding - the top shaped from plywood or layered hardboard

Miniatures

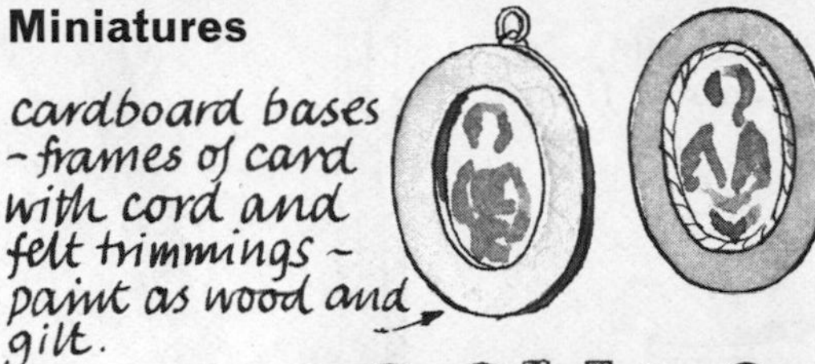

cardboard bases - frames of card with cord and felt trimmings - paint as wood and gilt.

old cupboard or drawer knobs if available - or paper pulp built on long screws.

cutout in polystyrene or build up with stiffened felt

Mirror or picture

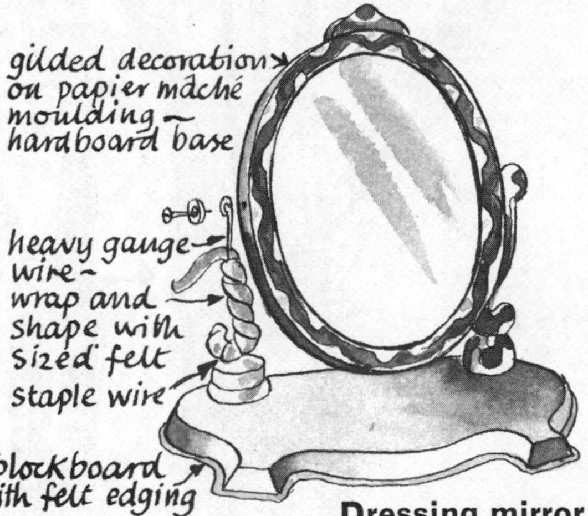

gilded decoration on papier mâché moulding - hardboard base

heavy gauge wire - wrap and shape with sized felt staple wire

blockboard with felt edging

mortice & tenon joints
shape feet from 75×50 mm. softwood

Full-length swing mirror

Dressing mirror on stand

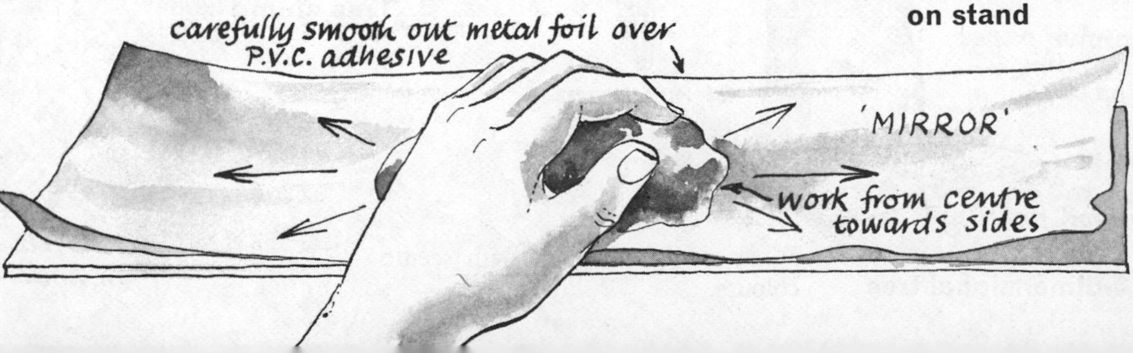

carefully smooth out metal foil over P.V.C. adhesive

'MIRROR'

work from centre towards sides

CLOCKS

Adapting modern timepieces to an antique body:

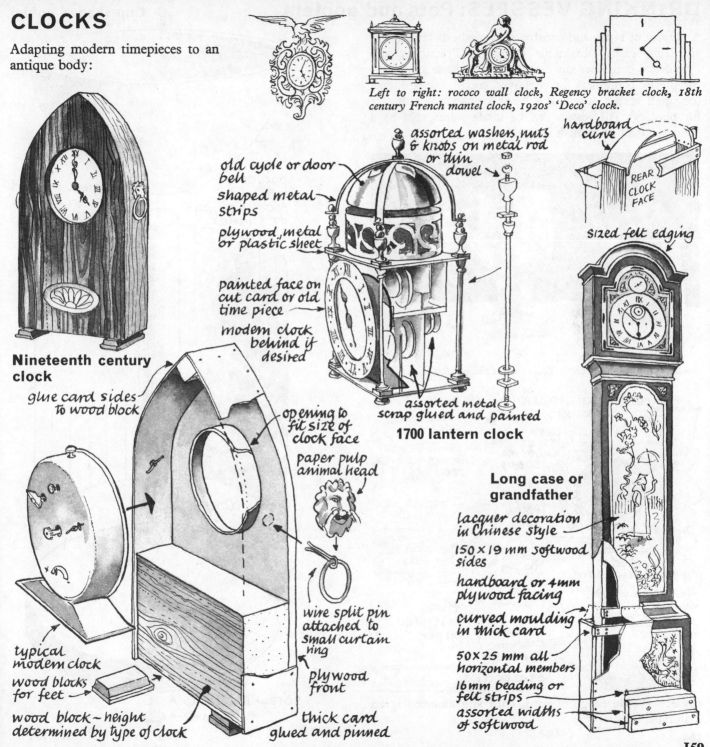

Left to right: rococo wall clock, Regency bracket clock, 18th century French mantel clock, 1920s' 'Deco' clock.

Nineteenth century clock

old cycle or door bell

shaped metal strips

plywood, metal or plastic sheet

painted face on cut card or old time piece

modern clock behind if desired

assorted washers, nuts & knobs on metal rod or thin dowel

hardboard curve

REAR CLOCK FACE

sized felt edging

assorted metal scrap glued and painted

1700 lantern clock

glue card sides to wood block

opening to fit size of clock face

paper pulp animal head

wire split pin attached to small curtain ring

plywood front

thick card glued and pinned

typical modern clock

wood blocks for feet

wood block – height determined by type of clock

Long case or grandfather

lacquer decoration in Chinese style

150 × 19 mm softwood sides

hardboard or 4mm plywood facing

curved moulding in thick card

50 × 25 mm all horizontal members

16mm beading or felt strips

assorted widths of softwood

159

DRINKING VESSELS: Pots and goblets

A variety of types and construction methods are shown, all using easily obtainable materials. Practically any cylindrical container can be adapted to make a goblet – the plastic containers for yoghourt, cream, etc. are ideal for small vessels (use a P.V.A. or polystyrene adhesive for plastics). All vessels can be made waterproof by a generous coat of varnish inside.

Some of the drinking vessels illustrated in this section.

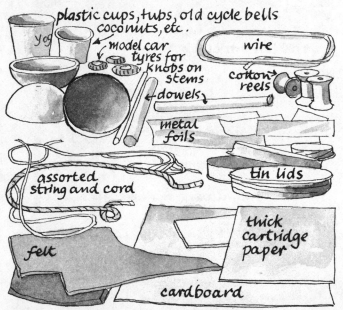

plastic cups, tubs, old cycle bells coconuts, etc.

yog

model car tyres for knobs on stems

wire

cotton reels

dowels

metal foils

tin lids

assorted string and cord

thick cartridge paper

felt

cardboard

Collect a wide range of card, cord and assorted scrap materials.

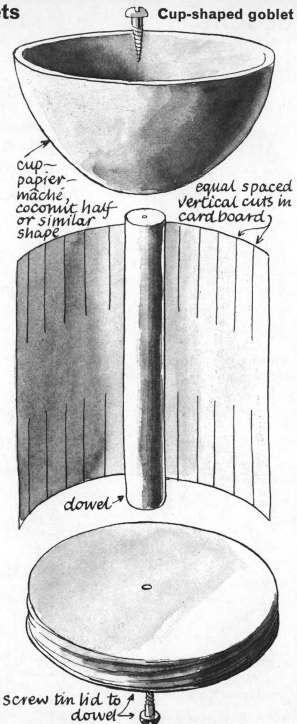

cup – papier-maché, coconut half or similar shape

equal spaced vertical cuts in cardboard

dowel

screw tin lid to dowel

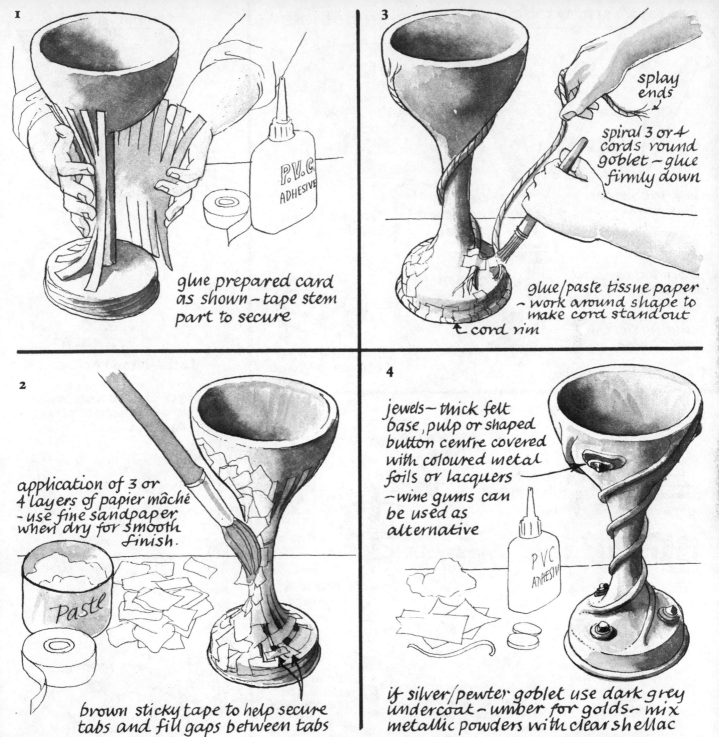

1 glue prepared card as shown – tape stem part to secure

P.V.C. ADHESIVE

2 application of 3 or 4 layers of papier mâché – use fine sandpaper when dry for smooth finish.

Paste

brown sticky tape to help secure tabs and fill gaps between tabs

3 splay ends

spiral 3 or 4 cords round goblet – glue firmly down

glue/paste tissue paper – work around shape to make cord stand out

← cord rim

4 jewels – thick felt base, pulp or shaped button centre covered with coloured metal foils or lacquers – wine gums can be used as alternative

P V C ADHESIVE

if silver/pewter goblet use dark grey undercoat – umber for golds – mix metallic powders with clear shellac

161

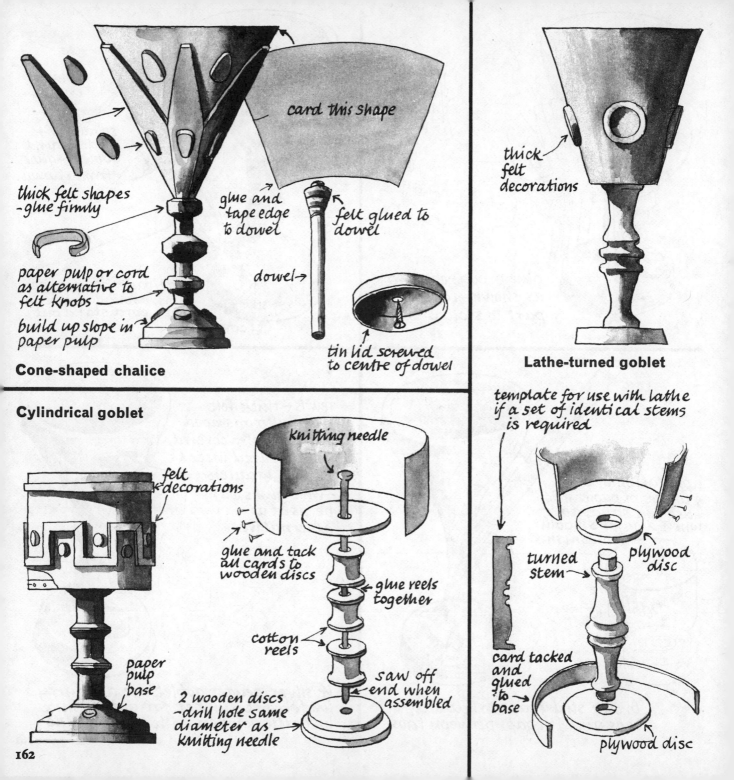

Cone-shaped chalice

thick felt shapes
- glue firmly

paper pulp or cord
as alternative to
felt knobs

build up slope in
paper pulp

card this shape

glue and
tape edge
to dowel

felt glued to
dowel

dowel →

tin lid screwed
to centre of dowel

Lathe-turned goblet

thick
felt
decorations

Cylindrical goblet

felt
decorations

knitting needle

glue and tack
all cards to
wooden discs

glue reels
together

cotton
reels

saw off
end when
assembled

paper
pulp
base

2 wooden discs
- drill hole same
diameter as
knitting needle

template for use with lathe
if a set of identical stems
is required

turned
stem

plywood
disc

card tacked
and
glued
to
base

plywood disc

162

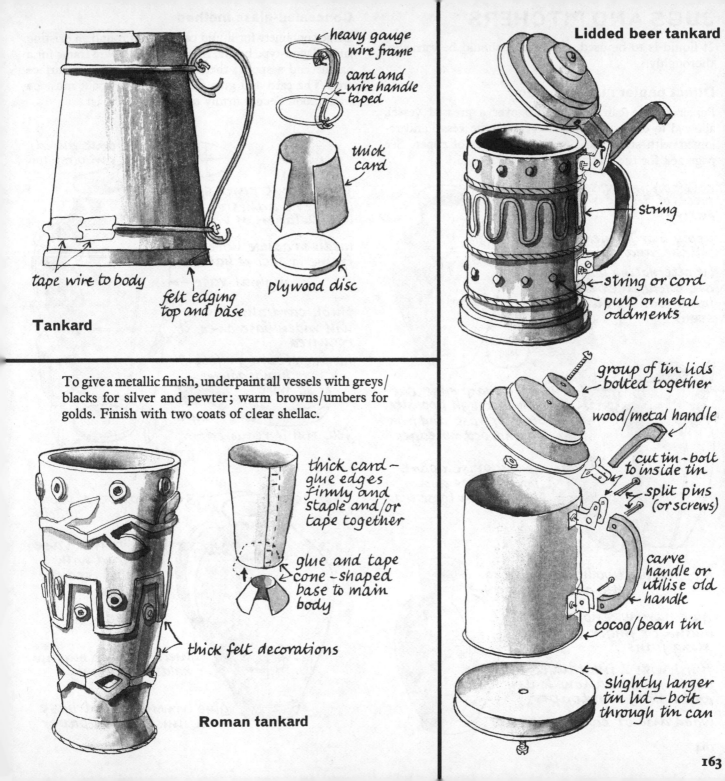

Tankard

heavy gauge wire frame

card and wire handle taped

thick card

tape wire to body

felt edging top and base

plywood disc

Lidded beer tankard

string

string or cord

pulp or metal oddments

To give a metallic finish, underpaint all vessels with greys/blacks for silver and pewter; warm browns/umbers for golds. Finish with two coats of clear shellac.

thick card — glue edges firmly and staple and/or tape together

glue and tape cone-shaped base to main body

thick felt decorations

Roman tankard

group of tin lids bolted together

wood/metal handle

cut tin-bolt to inside tin

split pins (or screws)

carve handle or utilise old handle

cocoa/bean tin

slightly larger tin lid — bolt through tin can

163

JUGS AND PITCHERS

If liquid is to be used, all surfaces should be varnished thoroughly.

Direct papier mâché method

Papier mâché can be built up over a greased vessel, allowed to dry, cut in half to remove the vessel and rejoined with sticky tape and a final layer of paper. See page 264 for the technique of papier mâché.

Concealed-glass method

Large containers for liquid can be built round an existing jar or flagon-type bottle. Simply attach a wire frame for a handle and a spout; then paste paper over the surface area. The card and glue for making the spout must be waterproof. Secure firmly to the top of the jar.

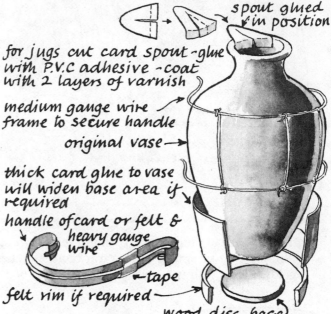

spout glued in position

for jugs cut card spout - glue with P.V.C adhesive - coat with 2 layers of varnish

medium gauge wire frame to secure handle

original vase →

thick card glue to vase will widen base area if required

handle of card or felt & heavy gauge wire

felt rim if required

tape

wood disc base

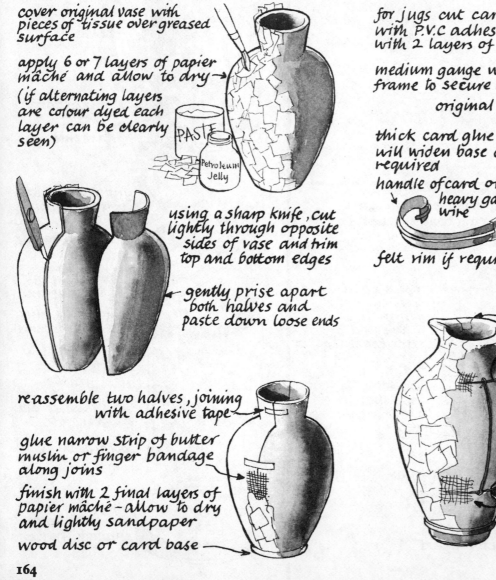

cover original vase with pieces of tissue over greased surface

apply 6 or 7 layers of papier mâché and allow to dry

(if alternating layers are colour dyed each layer can be clearly seen)

using a sharp knife, cut lightly through opposite sides of vase and trim top and bottom edges

gently prise apart both halves and paste down loose ends

reassemble two halves, joining with adhesive tape

glue narrow strip of butter muslin or finger bandage along joins

finish with 2 final layers of papier mâché - allow to dry and lightly sandpaper

wood disc or card base

3 or 4 layers of papier mâché

wires round vase tightened with pliers to secure handle

glued scrim or muslin holds wire firmly

glue trimmings and base with muslin and paper

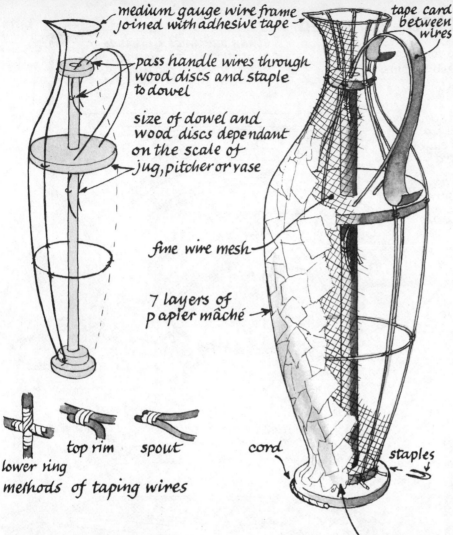

medium gauge wire frame joined with adhesive tape

tape card between wires

pass handle wires through wood discs and staple to dowel

size of dowel and wood discs dependant on the scale of jug, pitcher or vase

fine wire mesh

7 layers of papier mâché

cord

staples

shellac all parts before and after painting

lower ring
top rim
spout

methods of taping wires

Greek   Roman

Italian Renaissance

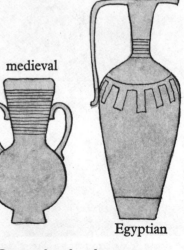

medieval

Egyptian

Some basic shapes

Wire mesh method

A further method is to make up a wire frame to your own design, based perhaps on a historical shape (see the outlines on the opposite page) and build up the surface with papier mâché. This is not practical if liquid is to be used – only for decorative purposes.

Another useful idea for creating an impression of pottery or porcelain: find a flagon-type cider bottle or some similar large glass bottle, pour paint into it, shake well and pour out the surplus. The effect from a distance will be of glistening porcelain. Mixtures of paint will produce marbling.

165

MUSICAL INSTRUMENTS – Stringed

Medieval instruments can be constructed for decorative purposes. Strings can be fitted and plucked to mime an actual (hidden) instrument or recording.

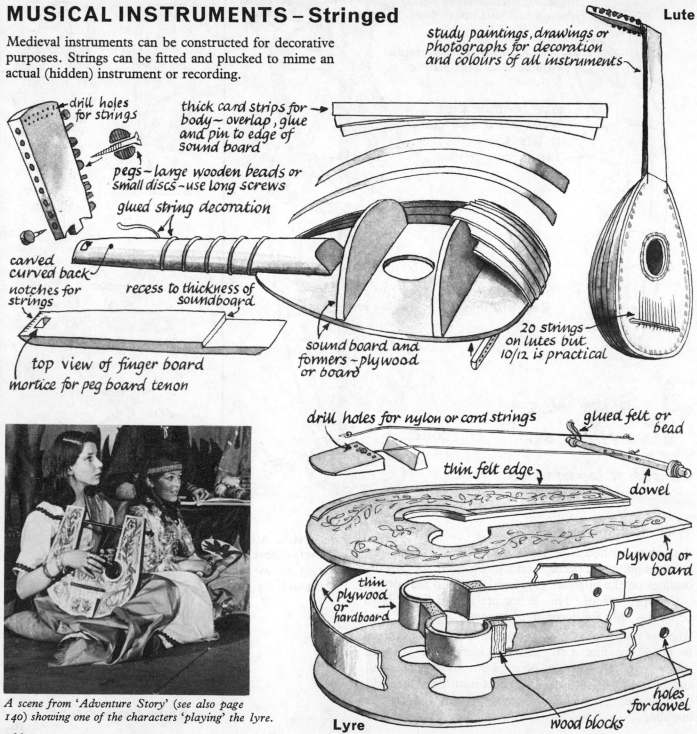

Lute

study paintings, drawings or photographs for decoration and colours of all instruments

drill holes for strings

thick card strips for body – overlap, glue and pin to edge of sound board

pegs – large wooden beads or small discs – use long screws

glued string decoration

carved curved back

notches for strings

recess to thickness of soundboard

sound board and formers – plywood or board

top view of finger board

mortice for peg board tenon

20 strings on lutes but 10/12 is practical

drill holes for nylon or cord strings

glued felt or bead

thin felt edge

dowel

plywood or board

thin plywood or hardboard

wood blocks

holes for dowel

A scene from 'Adventure Story' (see also page 140) showing one of the characters 'playing' the lyre.

Lyre

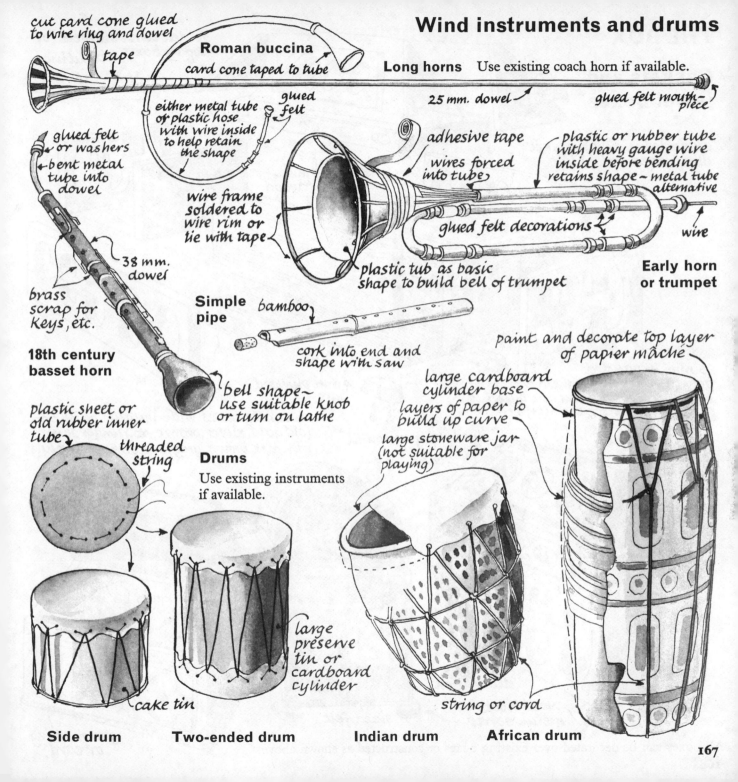

Wind instruments and drums

cut card cone glued to wire ring and dowel

tape

Roman buccina

card cone taped to tube

Long horns Use existing coach horn if available.

either metal tube or plastic hose with wire inside to help retain the shape

glued felt

25 mm. dowel

glued felt mouthpiece

glued felt or washers

bent metal tube into dowel

adhesive tape

wires forced into tube

plastic or rubber tube with heavy gauge wire inside before bending retains shape ~ metal tube alternative

wire frame soldered to wire rim or tie with tape

glued felt decorations

wire

38 mm. dowel

plastic tub as basic shape to build bell of trumpet

Early horn or trumpet

brass scrap for keys, etc.

Simple pipe

bamboo

18th century basset horn

cork into end and shape with saw

bell shape~ use suitable knob or turn on lathe

paint and decorate top layer of papier mâché

plastic sheet or old rubber inner tube

threaded string

large cardboard cylinder base

layers of paper to build up curve

large stoneware jar (not suitable for playing)

Drums

Use existing instruments if available.

large preserve tin or cardboard cylinder

cake tin

string or cord

Side drum   **Two-ended drum**   **Indian drum**   **African drum**

167

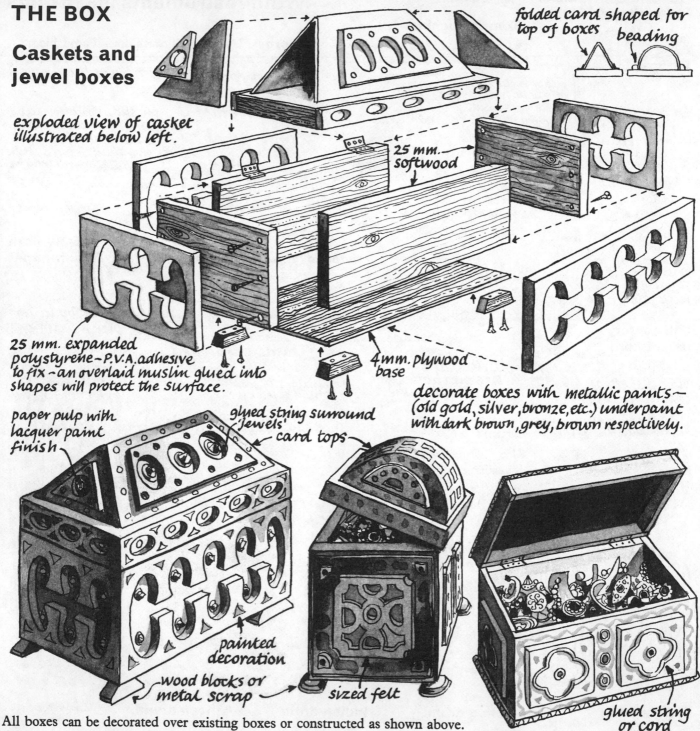

THE BOX

Caskets and jewel boxes

exploded view of casket illustrated below left.

folded card shaped for top of boxes

beading

25 mm. softwood

25 mm. expanded polystyrene – P.V.A. adhesive to fix – an overlaid muslin glued into shapes will protect the surface.

4 mm. plywood base

decorate boxes with metallic paints – (old gold, silver, bronze, etc.) underpaint with dark brown, grey, brown respectively.

paper pulp with lacquer paint finish

glued string surround 'jewels' card tops

painted decoration

wood blocks or metal scrap

sized felt

glued string or cord

All boxes can be decorated over existing boxes or constructed as shown above.

The chest

Large decorative boxes can be created out of existing old trunks or chests.

Medieval chest

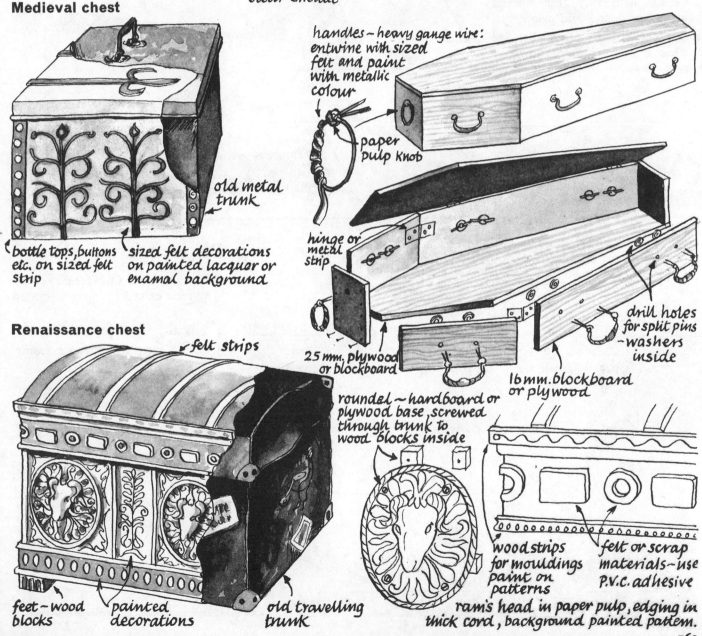

finish all felt decorations with a coat or two of clear shellac

bottle tops, buttons etc. on sized felt strip

sized felt decorations on painted lacquer or enamel background

old metal trunk

Renaissance chest

felt strips

feet ~ wood blocks

painted decorations

old travelling trunk

A coffin

A simple, plain shape, as used in a production of 'Oliver'. More ornate designs should be built over a simple shape with wood mouldings, and gilded as required.

handles ~ heavy gauge wire: entwine with sized felt and paint with metallic colour

paper pulp knob

hinge or metal strip

25 mm. plywood or blockboard

drill holes for split pins ~ washers inside

16 mm. blockboard or plywood

roundel ~ hardboard or plywood base, screwed through trunk to wood blocks inside

wood strips for mouldings paint on patterns

felt or scrap materials ~ use P.V.C. adhesive

ram's head in paper pulp, edging in thick cord, background painted pattern.

169

PAPER PROPS

Scrolls

1 Soften the edges or make ragged by tearing.

2 Colour with very thin uneven washes of ochres and pale greys.

3 Pull paper under a straight-edge when it is dry in order to effect curl.

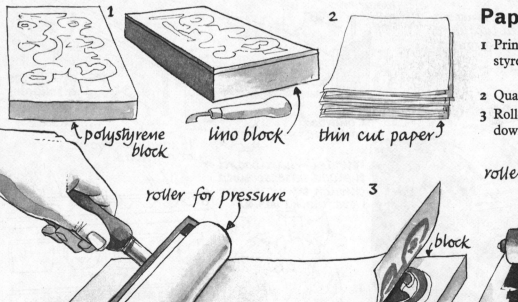

polystyrene block

lino block

thin cut paper

Paper money

1 Printing block of expanded polystyrene carved by electric cutter.

2 Quantity of thin paper cut to size.

3 Rollers for printing and pressing down.

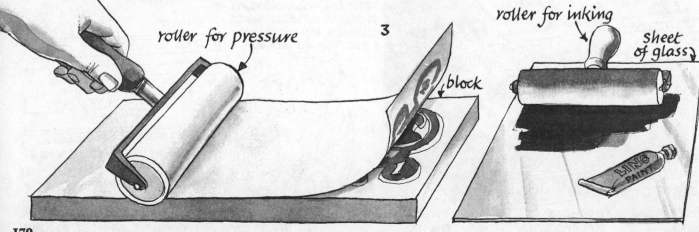

roller for pressure

block

roller for inking

sheet of glass

LINO PAINT

Books

If books are to be very large and dominant on stage, it will be preferable to seek out old dilapidated ones at jumble sales and secondhand shops. They can be repaired and decorated with felt, cord, beads, etc. and then painted and shellac varnished if required.

cut felt glued to cover

Letters and documents

They can be made in the same way as scrolls (without curling) and then ribboned together for bundles.

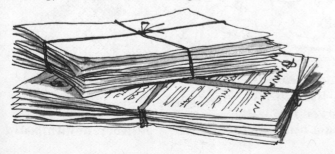

QUILLS AND INKWELLS

Select some goose quills and any small pot. It may be possible to obtain an old style of inkwell but an easy method of construction is shown below.

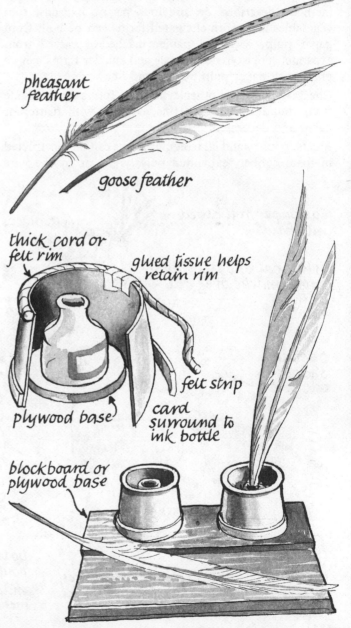

pheasant feather

goose feather

thick cord or felt rim

glued tissue helps retain rim

plywood base

felt strip

card surround to ink bottle

blockboard or plywood base

FOOD AND KITCHEN WARE

If a feast is to be held on stage, many of the items can be made in the workshop. Grapefruit, oranges, pumpkins, melons and other large fruits of a more or less spherical shape can be modelled over old plastic balls using papier mâché, or can be constructed in the wire and paper methods described on previous pages. Bananas, root vegetables and more elongated forms can be built from paper pulp, wire and papier mâché, or carved from expanded polystyrene. Grapes and smaller forms can be made with paper pulp built round fine wire.

Cheeses, cakes and other cylindrical forms can be made from round cake/biscuit tins, covered with plaster or paper and decorated.

Meats, poultry and all irregular forms can be constructed in foam rubber, expanded polystyrene or by the wire frame and papier mâché method. Plaster-of-Paris is useful for icing and creams.

Brush all surfaces with shellac for a bright, fresh appearance and to fix all colours.

Bread can be used after painting over with a coat of clear shellac.

Edible foods can be arranged among the 'prop' foods if eating is required. Care should be taken when choosing food from the table!

Cooking utensils, crockery, etc. can usually be obtained and used as found. A slight change of tone and colour may be necessary. If changes of style are necessary to suggest an earlier period, handles, spouts and other fittings can be attached to metal with P.V.A. adhesives. Such additions can be fashioned from wire and paper pulp as previously described and should be painted to match the basic article.

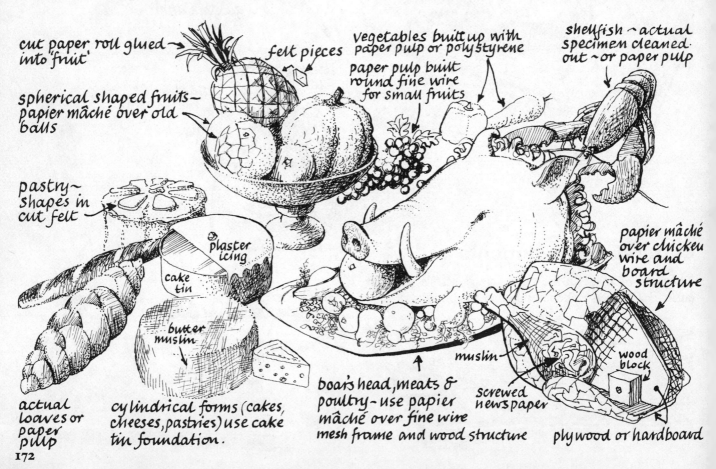

cut paper roll glued into 'fruit'

felt pieces

vegetables built up with paper pulp or polystyrene

paper pulp built round fine wire for small fruits

shellfish ~ actual specimen cleaned out ~ or paper pulp

spherical shaped fruits ~ papier mâché over old balls

pastry ~ shapes in cut felt

plaster icing

cake tin

butter muslin

papier mâché over chicken wire and board structure

muslin

wood block

actual loaves or paper pulp

cylindrical forms (cakes, cheeses, pastries) use cake tin foundation.

boar's head, meats & poultry ~ use papier mâché over fine wire mesh frame and wood structure

screwed newspaper

plywood or hardboard

Lighting

LAMPS AND EQUIPMENT · COLOUR · POSITIONING

Electrical supply and lamp types 174
Lanterns 175
Lighting control equipment 178
Positioning for proscenium and apron stages . . 180
Lighting circuits 182
Positioning for arena stages 183
Colour theory and practice 184
Designing the lighting layout 187
Cyclorama and back lighting 187
The lighting rehearsal 191

When equipping a stage, ensure that you get expert advice from local electricity boards and fire inspectors who are familiar with stage lighting and practice.

STAGE LIGHTING EQUIPMENT

The light source

Before you can plan a layout for your lighting it is necessary to know the limits of your electrical supply. Once you know the amount of your supply in amp(ere)s (x amps per socket) it is simply a matter of using the formula 'watts divided by volts equals amps'. For example, if your voltage is 240 and you wish to use lamps with a total wattage of 9600, you will need at least 40 amps in reserve. If the lighting operator already knows these facts, dangers of overloading can be avoided.

Lamp types

Three main groups are in use in the theatre: the General Lighting Service (G.L.S.) which is Tungsten, the Projection Lamp which is Tungsten, and the Tungsten Halogen Lamp. The G.L.S. is used in borderlights and flood lanterns, the Projection and Tungsten Halogen in spot lanterns. Illustrations on the right show the most commonly used lamps, their dimensions and type of base fitting.

Fittings are as follows:

1 Edison or Giant Edison screw (E.S. or G.E.S.) on most G.L.S. lamps in floods and compartment battens.
2 Pre-focus caps (P28 or P40) on Projection lamps in spot lanterns.
3 Twin pins for Tungsten Halogen lamps in spot lanterns.
4 Bayonet Cap (B.C.) on 60/100 watt lamps in some junior-size borderlights.

The lantern or lighting instrument

To give direction and control to all naked lights, the lamps are fitted within a variety of casings, called lanterns. The lamp is backed by a reflector which directs the light in a wide or narrow angled beam.

The lanterns fall into two main groups, known as *floods* and *spots*. The floods cast light over a wide area, whereas the spots concentrate light on a controlled small area of the stage.

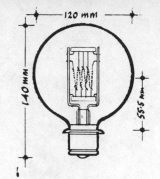

Above: medium pre-focus cap Projection lamp – 500 watt class T/20

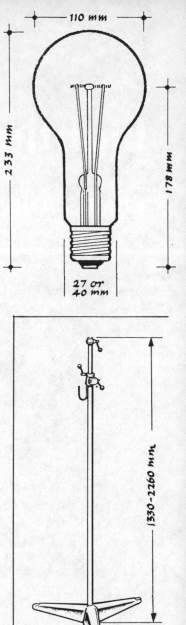

Right: G.L.S. lamp Edison screw 500 watt 40 mm diam. 200 watt 27 mm diam.

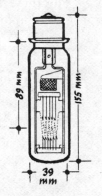

Above: 1000 watt class T/12 lamp – burns with base up as shown.

Below: 1000 watt Tungsten Halogen lamp (2 pins at 9.5 mm centres)

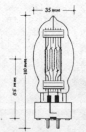

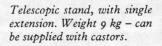

Telescopic stand, with single extension. Weight 9 kg – can be supplied with castors.

Floods

Floodlights are the large reflector units with a fixed wide angle beam that illuminate large areas of the stage or cyclorama. These beams of light can be intercepted and controlled by 'barn doors' (four doors fixed to the front edges of the lantern, rotatable for angling).

They are most useful as a form of general lighting for the backing, whether a backcloth, cyclorama or backing flat behind the door or window of an inner set.

The units are frequently attached to a mobile, telescopic stand. They can thus be swivelled and tilted to create modulations of colour and brightness.

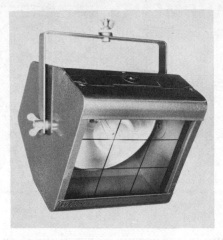

150/200 watt floodlight, or 500 watt floodlight (identical in shape, but larger) (Lamps 150/200 w, or 500 w General Lighting Service, G.L.S.).

The batten or borderlight

The other type of general lighting is supplied by the batten. This consists of 8 to 12 lamps in joined compartments and gives a diffused light over a long area. Several battens used in combination give an ideal light for skies on the cyclorama. They are usually suspended on bars above and at the base of the cyclorama, at a distance of 1 m – in the latter position on stage they are termed 'ground-row', not to be confused with scenic ground-rows (see glossary page 270). Each batten is wired in three or four circuits so that different colour filters can be used with each circuit.

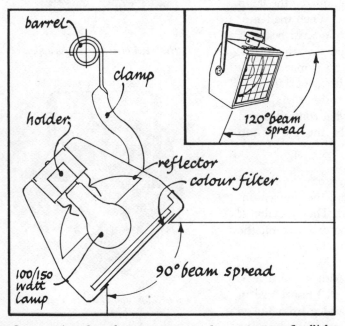

Cross-section through a compartment batten or any floodlight. Inset shows the 1000 watt floodlight giving a 120° beam spread.

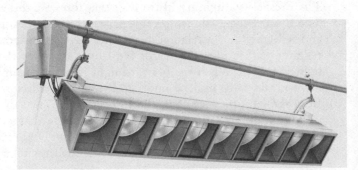

Borderlight – 3 circuit/3 colour with 100/150 watt lamps.

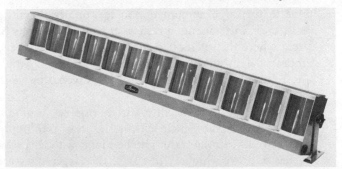

'Cylo' Trough used as a groundrow (circular colour filters give wide beam spread) – 3 circuit/3 colour with 60/100 w lamps.

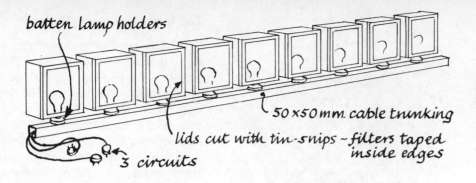

batten lamp holders

50 × 50 mm. cable trunking

lids cut with tin-snips ~ filters taped
inside edges

3 circuits

A home-made compartment batten, using biscuit/cake tins as reflectors and the lids with pieces cut out to accommodate colour filters. This batten, and another similar, lit the cyclorama for "Fiddler on the Roof" —see pages 26 and 70.

SPOTS

The spotlights are the second group of instruments—a type that can be focused, unlike the floods which belong to the 'fixed' group. The advantage of spreading the light to meet particular requirements is gained by altering the relationship between the lamp and the lens. Spots themselves fall into two groups: Fresnels and ellipsoidals.

Fresnels

The Fresnel is a lighting instrument that throws a soft-edged beam of light. The Fresnel spots (shown on this page) vary the beam by moving the lamp and reflector (A) in relation to the lens (B)—see diagram. When the lamp-reflector unit is moved towards the lens, the size of the projected beam of light increases. When the beam of light is at its maximum size, the instrument is said to be in flood position. If the lamp-reflector unit is moved away from the lens, the size of the beam decreases. When the beam of light is at its minimum size, the instrument is said to be in spot position. As is the case with the floodlights, the beams of light can be somewhat controlled and shaped with 'barn doors,' or made into smaller circles by the use of 'top hats.'

Due to the large amount of spillage, or peripheral light, from the Fresnel lens, these instruments are most useful in positions behind the proscenium arch, where the set itself can control the spill of the light. They are almost impractical in any house position, for the spill would be excessive on the proscenium arch, and using barn doors would prove inefficient.

Fresnel spotlights come in a variety of sizes, beginning with a 3-inch lens. The next size, the 6-inch lens, is the most commonly used Fresnel size in theatre today. Fresnels can also be found with lens sizes varying from 8 to 20 inches and even higher; however, the larger sizes are rarely found on the conventional stage, being mostly used in television lighting.

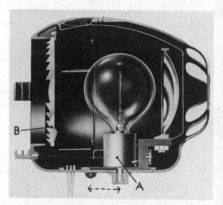

Half-section 500 w Fresnel spot.

1000 w Tungsten Halogen Fresnel spot.

176

Half-section 500 w ellipsoidal spot. A second lens, nearest beam-shaping shutters, is added when wider beam spread is required.

The Ellipsoidal Spotlight

The ellipsoidal spotlight, unlike the Fresnel, uses a lens (1) to focus a variable shaped gate (2) through which the light is directed by a mirror system—see diagram.

While the Fresnel throws a very soft-edged beam, the ellipsoidal throws a sharp-edged beam. This beam may be softened somewhat by moving the lens barrel in or out, but it can never reach the softness of the Fresnel. Another major difference between the two instruments is the method of shaping the beam. In the Fresnel, this is accomplished by the use of barndoors, while in the ellipsoidal, it is done by moving shutters located at the gate, which provides far better control of the shape of the beam. The ellipsoidal therefore proves invaluable in front-of-house positions where it is important to prevent the light from illuminating the proscenium arch, or even worse, the audience.

Another feature of the ellipsoidal that is not found in the Fresnel is the ability to use gobos. These are templates made from any heat-resistant material and cut with a desired pattern such as leaves or a window frame. When the instrument is properly focused, it will project this image onto the stage.

Like the Fresnel, the ellipsoidal comes in a variety of sizes, starting with a 4½ inch lens (very useful for covering a large area with a short throw) and going as high as 12 inches (excellent for extremely long throws). The exact ratio of length-of-throw to the diameter of the circle of light for each size ellipsoidal (or Fresnel) can be found in any complete catalogue from the various lighting manufacturers.

500 w narrow angle ellipsoidal spot.

Lighting control equipment

To control the various lamps it is preferable that each should be on a separate circuit for independent control. In the case of the batten floods, three circuits will control three sets of primary colours (page 184 for colour); in larger battens, four circuits will control the primaries and white.

A gradual transition from full brightness to a black-out requires a dimmer connected to the switch controlling the circuit.

Ideally each circuit should be controlled by a dimmer but it is seldom economically possible to give one dimmer to each circuit so it is usual to connect two circuits to one.

It is, however, rare that all the circuits require dimming at the same time and it is therefore possible to connect one dimmer to one circuit up to the number of dimmers fitted, while the rest of the circuits are controlled by switches only. Switches and dimmers can be interchanged by plug/socket changes during performance to give greater flexibility, provided that this has been well thought out and noted during the lighting rehearsal (see pages 191 and 192).

EDRC control system showing an 18 channel board arrangement with '2 pre-set' desk.

STM Thyristor Dimmer Rack.

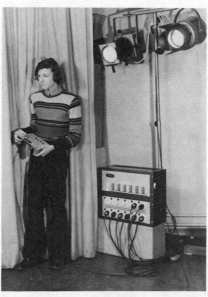

EDRC six-way system in operation. Note plug/sockets on rack with two per channel.

Electronic switchboards

EDRC (Electronic Dimmer Remote Control) systems have now generally replaced the resistance-style dimmer. The latter, widely used by many schools and the amateur stage, have been phased out by stage lighting suppliers as uneconomical to manufacture.

The EDRC systems (above and centre) comprise a remote control desk and a separate dimmer rack. The panel will allow master control with two pre-sets. The dimmers are 2 kw with two 5 amp socket outlets, giving combinations of up to 24 circuits.

The STM Thyristor Dimmer Rack (left) is for permanent installation. Multiples of these 20-dimmer racks are used for large stage controls.

Portable lighting systems

Improvised drama in schools and colleges, small one-act plays and groups of travelling players will find the portable control unit more convenient than permanent control units. In its simplest form a control can be from a single 1 kw Box Dimmer (see illustration right) running from a 13 amp wall socket and clipped to a telescopic stand supplying two 500 w or one 1000 w lamps. Two, three or more of these units in a hall (up to the number of sockets available) could provide sufficient lighting for any combination required. (A complete unit of Dimmer, Stand and lamps is available commercially under the name 'Drama Pack'.)

A home-made control unit

A portable control unit can be tailor-made by a lighting/electrical technician to suit any local need. In the example shown here, four 600 w dimmers (commercial 'Dimma switches') and four 5 amp socket outlets and switch are built into an old tape recorder case.

Right: circuit diagram of home-made portable dimmer board.

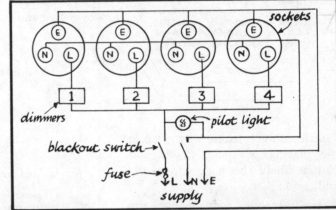

The complete unit has a total loading of 2400 watts and can be run from one 13 amp or 15 amp socket without overload. Any of the following lanterns may be used:

One Patt. 23 Profile spot ⎫
One Patt. 123 Fresnel spot ⎬ 500 w
One Patt. 60 flood ⎟ lamps
One Patt. 45 Fresnel spot ⎭
Two Patt. 137 floods – 200 w lamps.

Right: the tape recorder case with four dimmers, master switch and fuse built inside.
Far right: rear view of case showing the four 5 amp socket outlets.

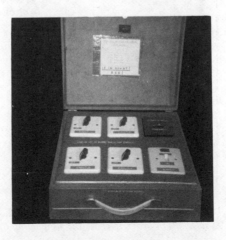

POSITIONING
for proscenium and apron stages

The tubular 'barrels' suspended between the borders (when in position, called 'bars') provide support for all lamps above the stage. On very small stages only a No. 1 bar position is needed, whereas large stages will need two or three positions.

The most used position is always No. 1 bar immediately behind the proscenium arch, as this carries the lamps for the centre stage area as well as for downstage left and right. The lanterns normally clamped here will be a variety of soft and hard edge spots.

Perches or *booms* (originally a platform for lamps) are barrels fixed in a vertical position – usually between front tabs and the proscenium arch. The spots can swivel on brackets clamped to these vertical bars. Booms are necessary on the larger stage – a small stage can achieve light downstage by using two telescopic stage stands.

Sometimes a 'ladder' is suspended from No. 2 or No. 3 bar to carry lamps between the wings when additional light is required on centre stage left or right.

Wall brackets are used to carry front-of-house (F.O.H.) lighting for illumining downstage and the apron.

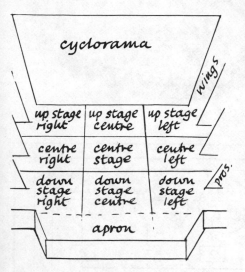

Consideration must now be given to the placing of spots, floods and battens about the stage and in the auditorium.

The illustration above shows the main areas of a proscenium stage that require lighting (the proscenium arch is not marked).

The areas are conveniently grouped as follows:

a the centre stage
b downstage and apron
c upstage
d the cyclorama
e backings

Most lighting is directed diagonally across the stage to avoid 'flattening' the setting and actors.

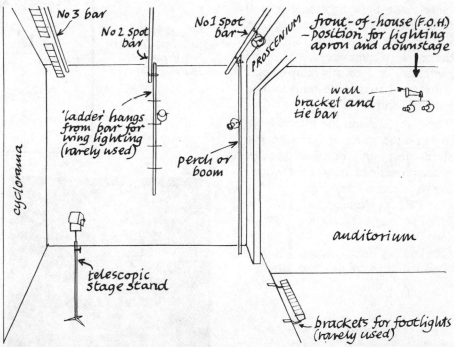

Side view of the stage and part of the auditorium stripped of all scenery, curtains, borders and wings in order to show the supporting apparatus for stage lighting.

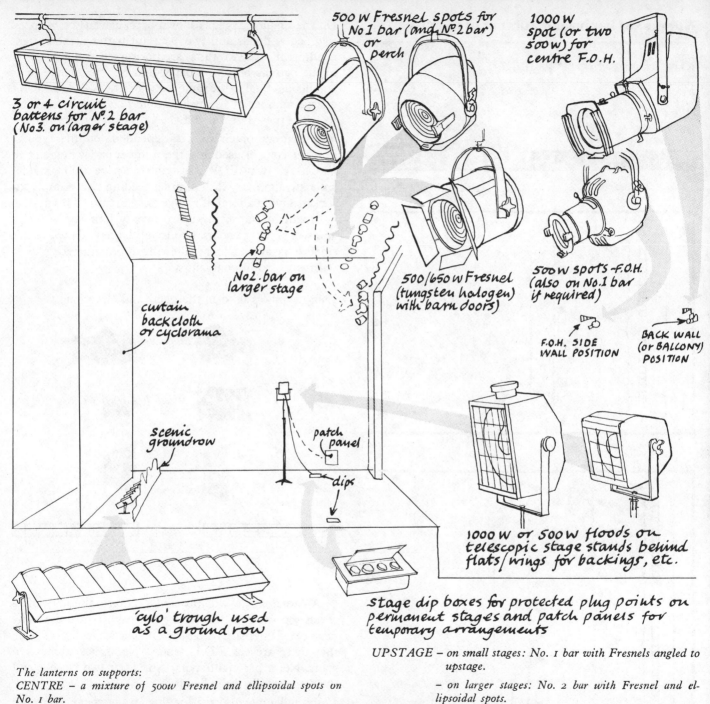

3 or 4 circuit battens for No 2 bar (No 3. on larger stage)

500 W Fresnel spots for No 1 bar (and No 2 bar) or perch

1000 W spot (or two 500 w) for centre F.O.H.

No 2. bar on larger stage

curtain back cloth or cyclorama

500/650 W Fresnel (tungsten halogen) with barn doors)

500 W spots - F.O.H. (also on No 1 bar if required)

F.O.H. SIDE WALL POSITION

BACK WALL (or BALCONY) POSITION

scenic groundrow

patch panel

dips

1000 W or 500 W floods on telescopic stage stands behind flats/wings for backings, etc.

'cyclo' trough used as a ground row

Stage dip boxes for protected plug points on permanent stages and patch panels for temporary arrangements

The lanterns on supports:
CENTRE – a mixture of 500w Fresnel and ellipsoidal spots on No. 1 bar.
DOWNSTAGE and APRON – front-of-house lighting using ellipsoidal 500w spots, one centred in hall for a larger apron.

UPSTAGE – on small stages: No. 1 bar with Fresnels angled to upstage.

– on larger stages: No. 2 bar with Fresnel and ellipsoidal spots.
CYCLORAMA and BACKINGS – two or more compartment battens and/or small floods.

181

Number of lamps and number of circuits

Above: elevation   Below: plan

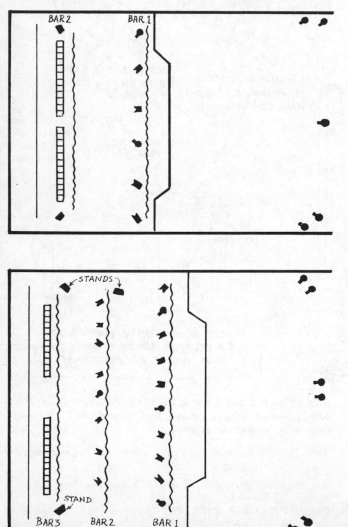

On the smaller stage, as shown here, eleven 500 w spots, two 500 w floods and two 3-circuit battens (the battens needing up to 2400 watts) are positioned. An alternative to the battens on No. 2 bar would be four or five spots and floods equal to the same wattage. If you have available a large number of Fresnels and no floods or battens, try to utilise these lights and make your own arrangement.

The number of circuits is dependent on the type of dimmer control used and the number and wattage of the lamps. A 6-way EDRC system (see page 178) provides six 2 kw dimmers, each dimmer feeding two 5 amp 1 kw sockets giving a total of twelve 1kw circuits. This system is capable of supplying up to twenty-four 500 w lamps and will serve the spots, floods and battens shown in this small stage arrangement, allowing approximately 3 kw in reserve for additional lamps.

Lamp symbols used in the plans and elevation:

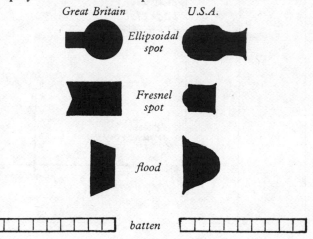

A larger stage will probably require about twenty-seven 500 w lamps (excluding battens) to give the same balance of intensity as on the smaller stage above. Note that there are six F.O.H. spots, No. 1 bar carries ten spots, No. 2 bar eight spots, No. 3 bar two battens and the stage stands three floods.

If 500 w lamps are used for this arrangement, then two 6-way EDRC systems will be needed. These will allow approximately 8 kw in reserve for any additional lamps.

POSITIONING

for arena stages

In arena productions, it is important to avoid light beams that cause discomfort to the audience. Lanterns have to be focused with great care to cover the stage without any spillage beyond. Barn doors are invaluable for this purpose.

Another problem arises over suspension. If the production is to be staged in a hall regularly used for such events, wall brackets can be fitted; if in a temporary place (possibly at a local youth club for one night only), then some means of portable telescopic stands will be more suitable.

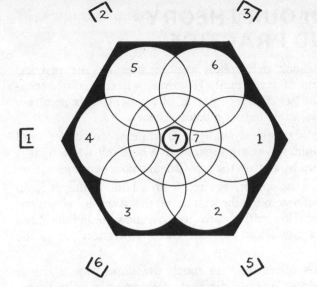

Plan view showing lantern positions.

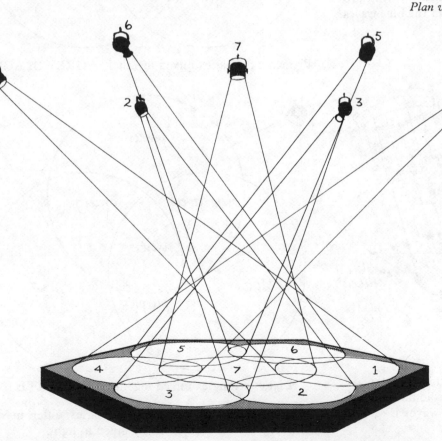

It is preferable to direct the beam of each lantern diagonally across, as shown on the plan above and in the general view on the left. This avoids the heavy shadows on actors' faces from a light source directly above them. Ellipsoidal are the most practical lanterns for the purpose as their beams can be focused accurately to the edge of the stage. Some Fresnels can be used. Floods should be avoided, except in the centre position where spillage is negligible, or when used with hoods.

183

COLOUR THEORY AND PRACTICE

This book deliberately concentrates on the practical aspects of stage craft. However, where colour is concerned (whether of light or of pigment) it is necessary to give a few notes on colour theory.

Light (daylight or sunlight) is white or 'colourless' until the light waves are separated. When any white light is split up by a prism the constituent colours emerge.

To get the colour required from a lamp a filter is fitted that allows only the colour of the filter to penetrate: a blue filter will absorb green, yellow, orange and red waves and allow the blue waves to 'reflect' on to the stage.

Colour filters work in much the same way as colour pigments. A blue pigment, for example, will absorb yellow, orange, red and green, and reflect the blue waves back to our retinas.

These two diagrams may help:

The two diagrams below show the difference in colour mixing between pigment and light.

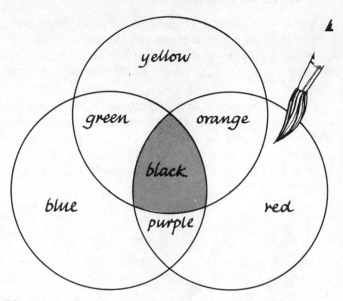

Pigment: primaries mixed together = GREY/BLACK

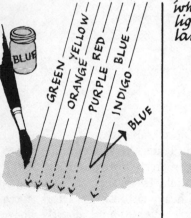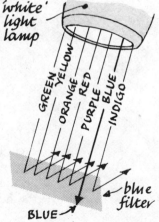

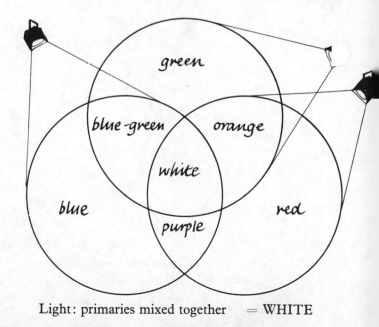

Light: primaries mixed together = WHITE

So an object seen as BLUE absorbs all other colours and a light seen as BLUE has had all other colours removed. An object or light reflecting all colour waves is seen as WHITE.

Note that light and pigment primaries differ in one respect – yellow is replaced by green in light.

Coloured light on coloured surfaces

The effect of a coloured light on coloured settings and costumes can be best explained by a further diagram:

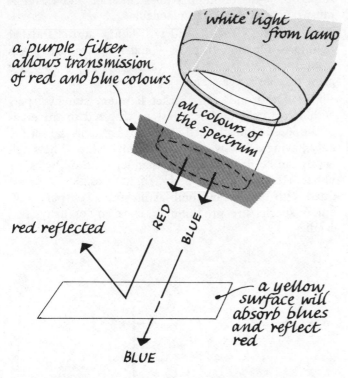

In the illustration above, a purple light is seen as red on reflection. A yellow pigment reflects yellow, orange and red and absorbs blue – a purple light falling on such a surface will appear as RED, since the blue will be absorbed and the red reflected.

The general principles can be applied to any colour of light falling on any other colour of pigment. Here is a chart showing only primary colours of light falling on primary colours of pigment:

PIGMENT	LIGHT		
	red	green	blue
red	red	dark brown	dark purple
yellow	red	green	black
blue	black	green/blue	blue

Note: these colours are approximate only, depending entirely on the purity of light and pigment.

Colour mixing

The practical application of the colour mixing of primaries is best seen with cyclorama batten lighting where red, green and blue compartments are mixed in varying proportions by dimmers to produce any hue or tint in the spectrum.

If lights are hired from suppliers, the colours usually fitted to battens are No. 6 red, 39 green and 20 blue. These will produce a satisfactory white light from a 3-circuit batten but it will be noted that the blue will be of lesser intensity. This is because of the weakness of blue light waves in tungsten filament lamps. (These lamps are in general use for battens. The tungsten halogen lamp eliminates the blue light wave problem.) To compensate for this loss, it is advisable to increase the wattage of lamps in the 'blue' circuit. The colours just mentioned are suitable for use on the cyclorama for sky or for symbolic background effects. But these filters, because of their depth of colour, are not really adequate for lighting the general acting area which demands a greater intensity of light. Other filters will be found preferable.

To avoid waste of light, use either of the following groups in battens for lighting acting areas:

1 No. 36 pale lavender, 3 straw, 17 steel blue
2 No. 7 pink, 51 gold, 32 medium blue

All the primary light waves are included in these two groups and much better illumination will result.

Apart from cyclorama lighting, primary colours are also effective for revues, pantomime, musical plays and symbolic lighting.

Colour selection

Colour filters, which are sheets of gelatine or acetate, are sold under the trade name Cinemoid in two sizes. (The large sheet will make 12 batten filters the small sheet 6 filters.) Over sixty colours are available from the suppliers (see page 276) and the problem is to select a limited number to meet the requirements of a particular production.

Successful choice will come with experience but a guide to essential filters will be helpful to those who have not experimented with lighting. Very few tints and primaries are needed, provided that a balance is achieved between warm and cool tints. The most useful for a small production or curtain set are:

No.

3 straw (warm)	52 pale gold
17 steel blue (cool)	53 pale salmon
31 light frost	54 pale rose
50 pale yellow	

31 light frost is useful for softening the edges of spotlights, either with or without the colour filter. (Frost does not affect the colour of the light.)

Below is a useful selection of filters for a more ambitious production, being about a third of the colours from the available list:

3 straw	36 pale lavender
5 orange	39 primary green
6 primary red	40 pale blue
7 light rose	50 pale yellow
10 middle rose	51 gold tint
15 peacock blue	52 pale gold
16 blue green	53 pale salmon
17 steel blue	54 pale rose
19 dark blue (as alternative to primary)	55 chocolate
	62 turquoise
31 light frost	63 sky blue

Amber is better avoided as it tends to spoil all cool colours in costumes and settings.

Sources of visible light

General lighting creates mood and atmosphere but the source of light for night scenes (interior and exterior) must be particularly well planned.

The fireplace, standard and wall lights, and chandelier lighting – for modern plays – and fireplace, torch, gas mantle and oil lamps – for earlier periods – can give great emphasis to a scene.

For standard and wall-bracket lighting, suitable spots with warm colour filters must be directed to the areas of supposed light, the actual light or lights in the setting only having a low-wattage or 'pygmy' lamp. The small lamps can be fitted into a gas mantle, as an oil 'wick' or under a lampshade on a wall light. Candles are best fitted with battery and bulb as illustrated on page 139, unless special fire precautions are taken for using real candles.

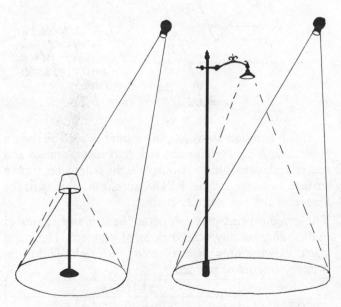

Supposed light areas from spotlights.

Special optical effects are beyond the scope of this book. If methods of projecting light on to cyclorama, showing slides, etc. are required, see the book list on page 277 – or contact one of the stage lighting suppliers listed on page 276.

DESIGNING THE LIGHTING LAYOUT

The approaches to lighting a play will be as many and as varied as there are designers and directors. Some directors will depend entirely on the visual concept from the designer whilst others may submit rough sketches or a plan of their own for the designer to develop.

A Shakespearean play with its many scenes will obviously require more thought to be given to variety of lighting than, say, a revue sketch. But even a short revue or one-act play will demand equal care in the placing of the lights.

Priorities in placing the lights

The priorities are:

1 to light the actors, especially their faces. The actors must *show* what they are thinking, feeling and saying;

2 to enhance the grouping of actors on the stage, so that certain of the characters dominate by virtue of suitable lighting as well as costume;

3 to illuminate the set;

4 to indicate time and season;

5 to set a mood or atmosphere.

Plan the lighting carefully to suit the movement of actors around the stage, avoiding 'black spots' where an actor cannot be properly seen.

There must be sufficient light to make the settings convincing in atmosphere and contrast. Remember that contrast is of prime importance, that variety of light in different areas of the stage is most essential for dramatic impact.

Lighting the cyclorama

An important role in dramatic lighting is played by the placing of cyclorama lights.

If used without front lighting, a silhouette is achieved.

The scene on the right (from a production of 'The Tempest') illustrates the use of the cyclorama at the beginning of a scene or play – the cyclorama is lit by a top batten and two side floods.

Back lighting

Other dramatic effects are achieved by combining cyclorama lights with spots directed *forward* towards the downstage. In a scene requiring strong sunlight a 1000w flood, together with a Fresnel, was directed downstage on to the temple wall to the right of the head of Apollo. Battens lit the cyclorama (in this case, the wall of the hall). Always ensure that such lighting does not spill into the audience.

Left and bottom left: the scene shows the temple at Delphi from 'Adventure Story'. As Alexander climbs over a sculptured sill by the statue of Apollo, the sun strikes his back, casting his shadow on the temple wall. The priestess downstage is softly illuminated by ellipsoidal and Fresnel spots.

Below right: a scene from 'West Side Story' shows the use of back and front lighting with a dark centre stage area – a use of localised lighting for a dramatic purpose.

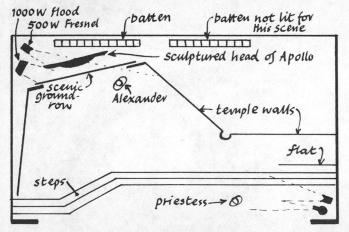

Lighting plan for Act I Scene 2 of 'Adventure Story'.

Positioning lights in a limited stage space

On very small stages and where no space is available for 'flies' (galleries above the stage area of the same height as the stage area itself) or for hanging lights from above, lanterns must be carefully placed behind flats and in the auditorium.

In the illustrations on this page, note the nearness of ceiling to stage level. In the scene from 'Julius Caesar' the lanterns are grouped immediately behind the narrow temporary proscenium arch (which does not appear in the picture) and in F.O.H. positions. The main light source is on stage left – note the shadows.

Scene before battle in Shakespeare's 'Julius Caesar' (a school production with arms and armour made in the school workshop. See pages 202–203.)

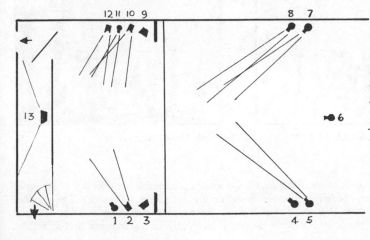

Left: diagrammatic plan of lighting for the scene above, with switched-on lighting indicated by beam lines in the diagram. Most lights, because of the lack of space, are situated behind the proscenium arch (built up from flats – see page 14). The battens are fixed vertically (3 and 9) on booms. The scene is lit mainly from stage left with 7 and 8 F.O.H., 10, 11 and 12; 2 is lit on stage right and 5 F.O.H.; 13 is a large 1000w flood placed behind the large wall-flat to illuminate the back wall. If the colour of an existing wall is pale in tint, it is often possible, as in this case, to light direct without a curtain or backcloth.

Light positioning for 'Oliver' in a small hall

Below is a plan view of light positions for a particular production.

All available lights were placed in the most advantageous positions to ensure that all essential acting areas were covered. A variety of gels (colour filters) were fitted to enable the changing moods to be created effectively.

Act I Scene 1: workhouse.

Act I Scene 6: Thieves' kitchen.

Act I Scene 2: workhouse parlour.

Act II Scene 1: Inn.

Act I Scenes 3 and 4: street and undertaker's.

Act II Scene 2: Brownlow's house.

Act I Scene 5: Paddington Green.

Final scene: riverside.

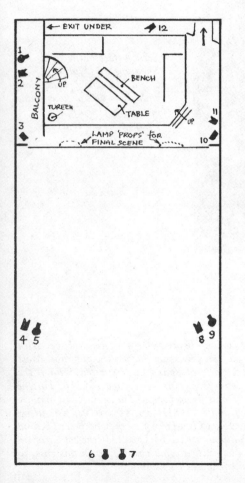

Plan for the workhouse setting in Act I Scene 1 of 'Oliver' by Lionel Bart.

The eight small sketches above illustrate the variations obtainable with the lights arranged as in the diagram on the left (variations in colour are not shown, of course). The sketches show eight scenes from 'Oliver'. (See also pages 74–75 on sketch methods.) On the next page the placing of the lights is explained in relation to certain requirements and priorities.

This illustration explains the lighting for the scene below. F.O.H. lights **4** and **5** illuminate the group of workhouse boys, whilst Oliver is emphasised by an additional Fresnel spot (**2**) from above stage right. An ellipsoidal 500 w spot (**1**) lights part of the background wall.

Left: a scene from the musical 'Oliver'. Note how Oliver, the main character, is made the focal point of the lighting in this scene.

THE LIGHTING REHEARSAL

Before the lighting rehearsal the director should give the chief electrician some idea of the quantity of light that he would like for each scene, the moods he wants to create, the time of day, the place and any particular effects (e.g. a fire, a thunderstorm). The electricians will also need to know the placing of windows, doors, furniture and the main acting areas.

When the relevant facts are established, the electricians can check the equipment available and hire additional lamps, dimmers and 'gels'.

All lights will be placed before the rehearsal, focused on the most useful area. Appropriate gels can be fitted. Each light should be given a number and the number marked on a sketch plan for reference and easy plotting during the rehearsal. (*continued on the next page*)

The lighting rehearsal (continued)

When such arrangements have all been made, the producer and designer should each be informed of the number and colour positions of each light on a sketch plan.

Finally before the rehearsal, make sure that the electricians have a comprehensive list of all the effects needed, including sound effects; also a text with sound cues, exits and entrances marked – indeed anything that may affect the work of the electricians.

The director and designer should be present at the rehearsal, together with some members of the cast dressed in costume. The latter can move, sit or stand in appropriate positions to ensure that the lights cover them and create around them the desired mood.

It is essential to mark clearly in the margins of the text script every light, sound and other effect. If there is to be a slow dimming of the light over two and a half pages, indicate in the margin with a long arrow from the start of the appropriate cue.

Two important points: unless a sudden change of light is relevant, always fade lights in and out slowly – if lights 'jump in' the effect is spoilt and the audience is distracted; when a blackout is required, ensure that it is a blackout – no working lights left on!

Working at the lighting plot

Start with a blackout and gradually bring up the lights to the required setting for the play to open – this is usually called the pre-setting and is visible to the audience on arrival. Mark this on the script as Cue 1, noting on the plot the exact number of lights and their exact dimmer calibrations. You then move on to the next cue – and so on throughout the play. Always note exactly which lights are added and which removed, also which lights are changed to a higher or lower dimmer calibration.

During the lighting rehearsal give yourself time to experiment in order to achieve the best effect. If the number of lights is small, be prepared to change positions and gels.

A typical lighting plot will look rather like this:

Cue No.	CUE	Bank A Master	Dimmers: 'A' bank						Bank B Master	Dimmers: 'B' bank					
			1	2	3	4	5	6		1	2	3	4	5	6
1	presetting	full	o	o	o	o	4	o	off	o	o	o	o	o	o
*2	houselights fade as music builds up	full	o	o	o	o	3	o	off	o	o	o	o	o	o
*3	curtain up slow fade in	full	3	7	F	F	F	7	full	3	o	o	7	4	o
4	Mr Brown enters	full	3	F	F	F	F	F	full	3	o	o	7	4	o
5	Elizabeth exits, begin sunset	full	3	F	F	6	F	7	full	o	o	o	4	4	o
5a	sunset complete (3 pages text)	full	3	F	F	6	F	7	off	o	o	o	o	o	o
6	blackout	off	o	F	F	6	F	7	off	o	o	o	o	o	o

* if there is no curtain, cues 2 and 3 crossfade, i.e. 2 goes down as 3 comes up.

F = full on.

Arms and armour 8

ARMATURES AND DUMMIES · ARMOUR THROUGH
THE AGES · WEAPONS AND GUNS

Dummies for breast, arm and leg armour . . . 194
Dummy for helmets 196
Ancient civilisations 198
Gauls, Saxons and Vikings 199
Armour: Greek 200
　　　　 Roman 202
　　　　 Romanesque and early gothic (Norman) . 204
　　　　 Late gothic 206
　　　　 Late Renaissance (Elizabethan) . . . 208
　　　　 17th, 18th, 19th and 20th century . . . 210
Arms: 　 Greek (including a device for a spear sticking
　　　　 in a body) 212
　　　　 Roman 213
　　　　 11th and 12th century 214
　　　　 13th to 14th century 216
　　　　 15th and 16th century (including a device for
　　　　 making a bloody cut) 218
　　　　 17th, 18th and 19th century . . . 220
Guns of all periods 222

COSTUME ARMOUR

A comprehensive range of excellent illustrated books is available to any-one seeking methods of making stage costumes – the variety is such that no additional material is necessary in this book – see the book list on page 277.

However, there is a definite lack of information about techniques for making armour, whether the basic leather jacket or the elaborate plate armour of the sixteenth century. Most costume books make some textual reference but there is little in the way of illustrations from which to work.

This section on arms and armour is, therefore, an attempt to rectify the situation, showing the development of arms and armour by grouping them into historical periods, and showing methods of construction and decoration. Most of the examples can be made by school-children but care must be exercised in measurements and in securing the fixing points. Where a very high standard of finish is desirable, or time and labour demands a quick solution, costume armour can be hired – see the list of suppliers on page 276.

On the next few pages a group of dummies is shown. They serve as supports for building up the various pieces of armour subsequently shown.

DUMMIES FOR BREAST ARMOUR

Ideally an old adjustable shop dummy or tailor's dummy is most suitable but a strong well-shaped dummy can be built as shown. It may be necessary to make three sizes: large, medium and small if a large cast of military is demanded. Measure the actors involved.

When the final covering of scrim in plaster has been applied, the dimensions can be made more accurate, or adjusted, by applying papier mâché pulp and paper.

The whole surface should be painted with enamel paint when it has dried out. Waxing or varnishing afterwards will produce a surface ideal for repeated use and resistant to glues.

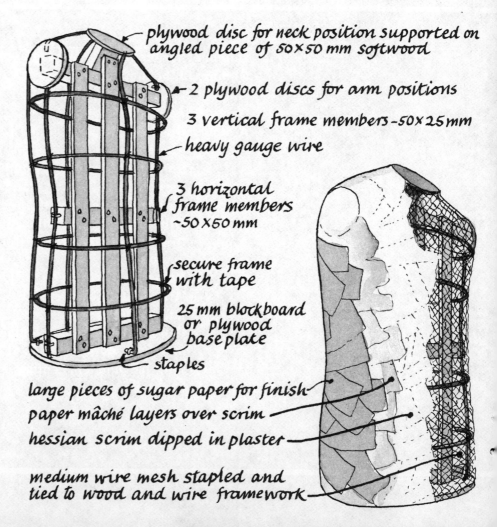

plywood disc for neck position supported on angled piece of 50×50 mm softwood

2 plywood discs for arm positions

3 vertical frame members - 50×25 mm

heavy gauge wire

3 horizontal frame members ~50×50 mm

secure frame with tape

25 mm blockboard or plywood base plate

staples

large pieces of sugar paper for finish

paper mâché layers over scrim

hessian scrim dipped in plaster

medium wire mesh stapled and tied to wood and wire framework

Basic breast garment over the dummy

The basic garment for all breast armour: an old blanket (or similar material) is cut as above, in one piece to the required length for back and front. The neck opening can be cut square or circular as required. Shoulder pieces may be used to widen and/or strengthen the armour.

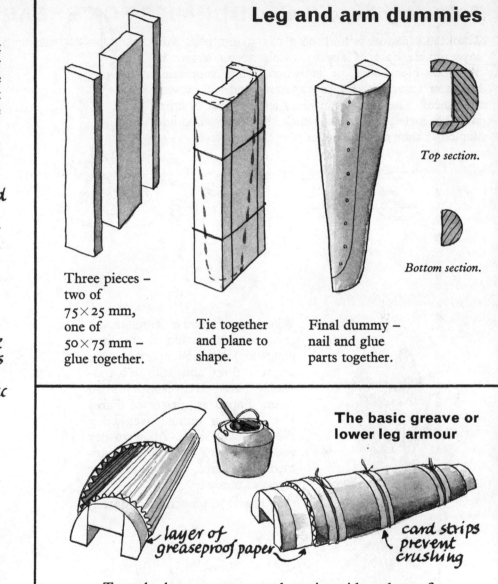

surface sanded down and painted with lacquer or enamel

three coats of shellac

neck opening

2 shoulder pieces

Leg and arm dummies

Three pieces – two of 75 × 25 mm, one of 50 × 75 mm – glue together.

Tie together and plane to shape.

Final dummy – nail and glue parts together.

Top section.

Bottom section.

The basic greave or lower leg armour

layer of greaseproof paper

card strips prevent crushing

To make leg armour, cover dummies with a sheet of greaseproof paper, to prevent armour from sticking to dummies.

For the armour, use corrugated cardboard, the first layer with the corrugations uppermost – glue the surface.

The second layer with corrugations down – glue the surface. Work the two layers into each other.

Finally tie dummy and cardboard together lightly. Leave for two or three days to dry thoroughly.

A dummy head (helmets)

The head armature is built on a 50 × 50 mm post, with any suitable base of approximately 30 cm square in plywood, blockboard or softwood. Four supporting braces of approximately 50 × 25 mm wood will prevent movement. The piping can be of lead, copper or other available metal or plastics, which should be wired and stapled as shown to the upper part of the post.

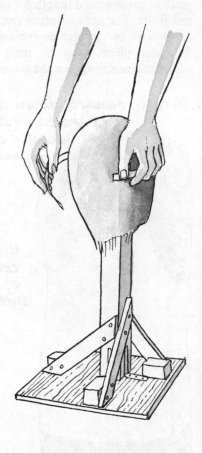

When the armature is complete, use galvanised wire, thin or medium gauge, and wire mesh over the whole surface. Snip and trim all protruding parts and cover with hessian scrim dipped in plaster of Paris. Use one layer without over-laying the pieces of scrim. Allow to dry and make quick check of measurements required. Apply further layers as necessary.

(See page 276 for scrim suppliers.)

When complete the head surface should be smoothed out with plaster and/or cotton scrim. *At all stages the measurements should not exceed those of the actor.*

So make sure that the armature is much smaller at the beginning. At the final stage the dummy head can be 1 cm larger in circumference to allow for shrinkage of helmet materials.

Steam felts over a can of boiling water, then press down firmly over a dummy. Repeat the process until the right shape is achieved.

Add nasals and cheek pieces with a hand-stapler. Pieces can be added or removed as required. Glue before stapling.

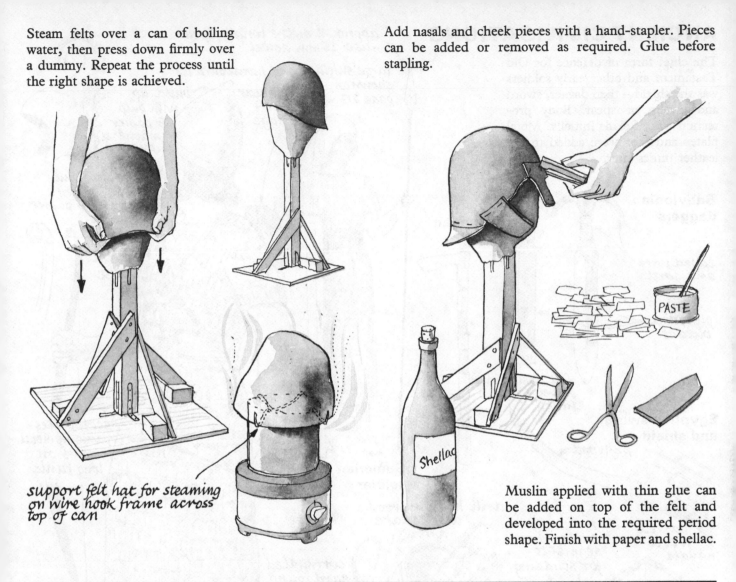

support felt hat for steaming on wire hook frame across top of can

Muslin applied with thin glue can be added on top of the felt and developed into the required period shape. Finish with paper and shellac.

Before using the dummy head, ensure that all measurements have been taken from the actor concerned. Helmet materials should be cut or fitted to the actor – this will not be possible with an old felt hat which has first to be steamed out (see above).

A large production, involving ten or more armour costumes, will require more than one dummy. If two or three are built, ensure that you make three sizes – large, medium and small – using the smaller with paper or felt padding to build up the in-between sizes of head measurement.

Also available from some hairdressers, haberdashers and local stores are cheap expanded polystyrene wig stands. They are adequate for small head sizes. Some means of securing to a base will be essential.

ANCIENT CIVILISATIONS

The chief form of defence for Old Testament and other early soldiers was the shield – then dagger, sword and javelin or spear. Body protection was of skins initially. Metal plates and tabs were added to the leather tunics later.

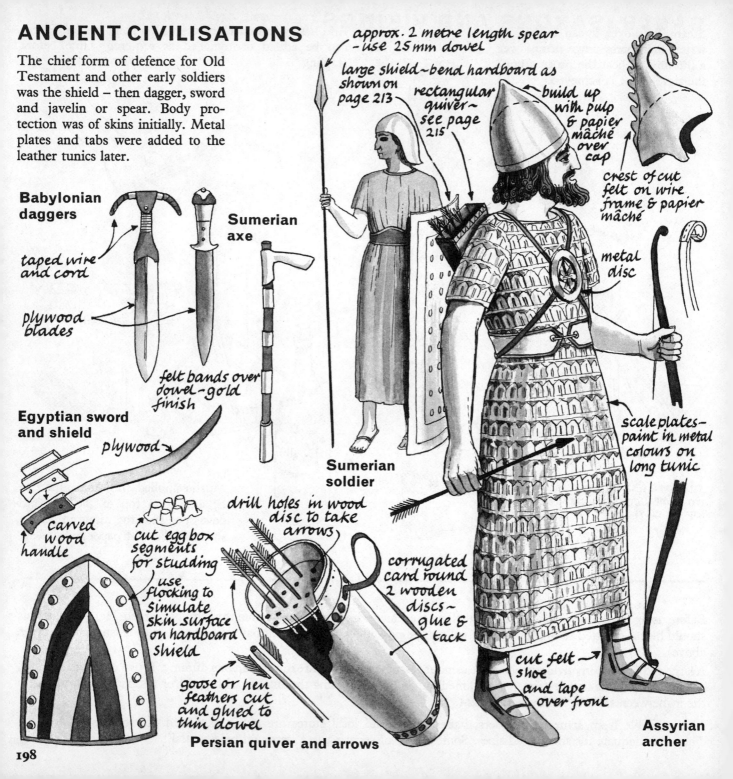

approx. 2 metre length spear – use 25 mm dowel

large shield ~ bend hardboard as shown on page 213

rectangular quiver ~ see page 215

build up with pulp & papier mâché over cap

crest of cut felt on wire frame & papier mâché

metal disc

Babylonian daggers

taped wire and cord

plywood blades

Sumerian axe

felt bands over dowel – gold finish

Egyptian sword and shield

plywood

carved wood handle

cut egg box segments for studding

use flocking to simulate skin surface on hardboard shield

drill holes in wood disc to take arrows

corrugated card round 2 wooden discs ~ glue & tack

scale plates – paint in metal colours on long tunic

cut felt shoe and tape over front

goose or hen feathers cut and glued to thin dowel

Persian quiver and arrows

Sumerian soldier

Assyrian archer

198

GAULS, SAXONS AND VIKINGS

Defensive equipment was basically similar to that of earlier peoples – the shield, often with a large boss was the main item. The helmet was probably worn only by leaders in battle. Metal strips and tabs were added to tunics to give added protection.

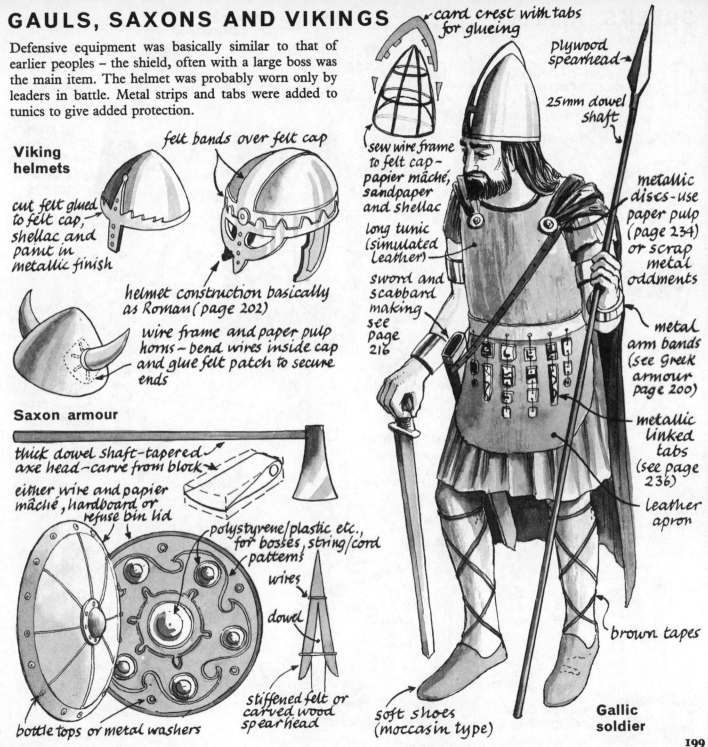

Viking helmets

felt bands over felt cap

cut felt glued to felt cap, shellac and paint in metallic finish

helmet construction basically as Roman (page 202)

wire frame and paper pulp horns – bend wires inside cap and glue felt patch to secure ends

Saxon armour

thick dowel shaft – tapered axe head – carve from block

either wire and papier mâché, hardboard or refuse bin lid

polystyrene/plastic etc., for bosses, string/cord patterns

wires

dowel

bottle tops or metal washers

stiffened felt or carved wood spearhead

card crest with tabs for glueing

plywood spearhead

25mm dowel shaft

sew wire frame to felt cap – papier mâché, sandpaper and shellac

long tunic (simulated leather)

sword and scabbard making see page 216

metallic discs – use paper pulp (page 234) or scrap metal oddments

metal arm bands (see Greek armour page 200)

metallic linked tabs (see page 236)

leather apron

brown tapes

soft shoes (moccasin type)

Gallic soldier

199

GREEKS - Armour

See page 212 for weapons.

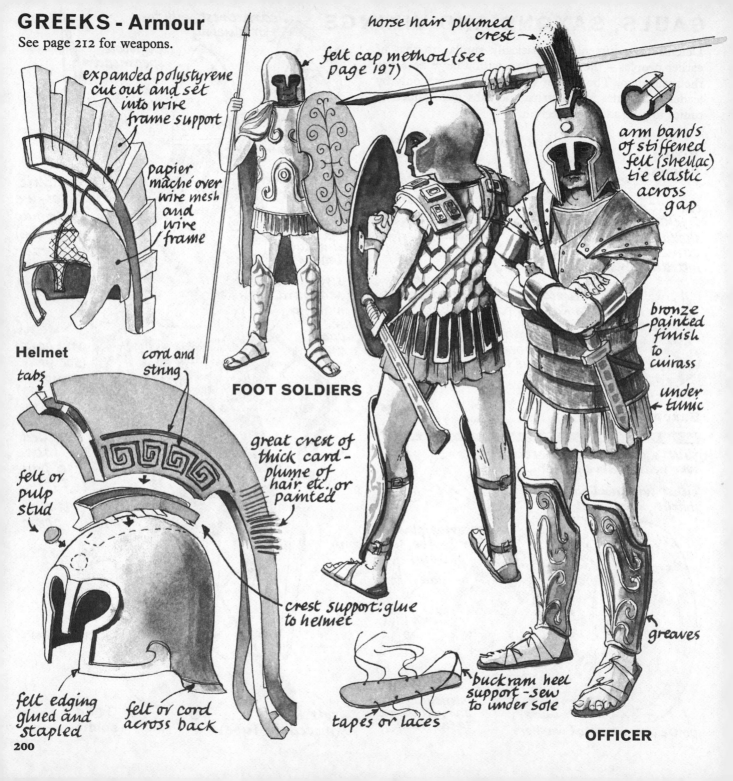

horse hair plumed crest

felt cap method (see page 197)

expanded polystyrene cut out and set into wire frame support

papier mâché over wire mesh and wire frame

arm bands of stiffened felt (shellac) tie elastic across gap

Helmet

tabs

cord and string

great crest of thick card - plume of hair etc., or painted

felt or pulp stud

crest support: glue to helmet

bronze painted finish to cuirass

under tunic

FOOT SOLDIERS

felt edging glued and stapled

felt or cord across back

tapes or laces

buckram heel support - sew to under sole

greaves

OFFICER

200

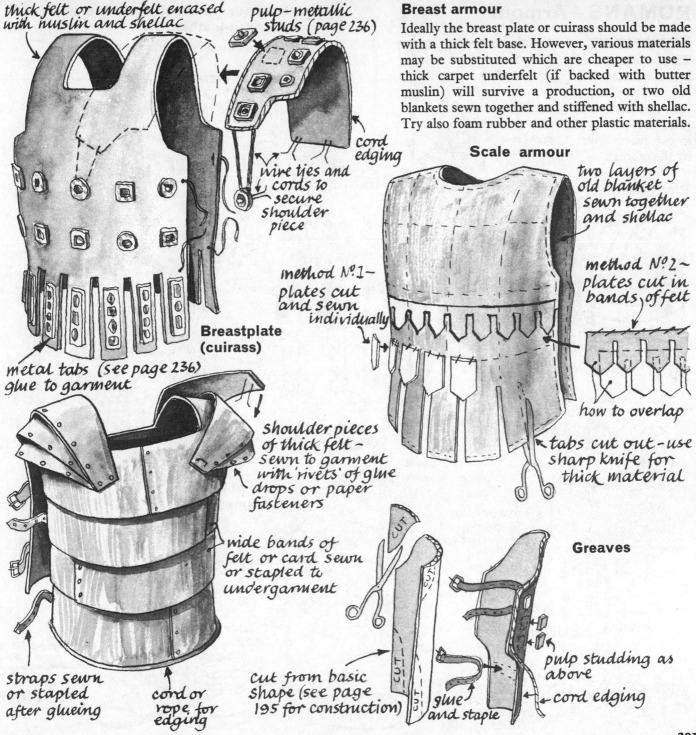

thick felt or underfelt encased with muslin and shellac

pulp-metallic studs (page 236)

cord edging

wire ties and cords to secure shoulder piece

metal tabs (see page 236) glue to garment

Breastplate (cuirass)

shoulder pieces of thick felt - sewn to garment with 'rivets' of glue drops or paper fasteners

wide bands of felt or card sewn or stapled to undergarment

straps sewn or stapled after glueing

cord or rope for edging

cut from basic shape (see page 195 for construction)

glue and staple

Breast armour

Ideally the breast plate or cuirass should be made with a thick felt base. However, various materials may be substituted which are cheaper to use – thick carpet underfelt (if backed with butter muslin) will survive a production, or two old blankets sewn together and stiffened with shellac. Try also foam rubber and other plastic materials.

Scale armour

two layers of old blanket sewn together and shellac

method Nº 1- plates cut and sewn individually

method Nº 2- plates cut in bands of felt

how to overlap

tabs cut out - use sharp knife for thick material

Greaves

pulp studding as above

cord edging

ROMANS – Armour

Breast armour

Three types of breast armour are shown: plate, scale and cast plate (the last in two pieces worn by the officer).

Standards, spears and other arms on page 213.

All armour: finish either in bronze, leather or bronzed-leather

(use metal powders described on page III)

Plate armour

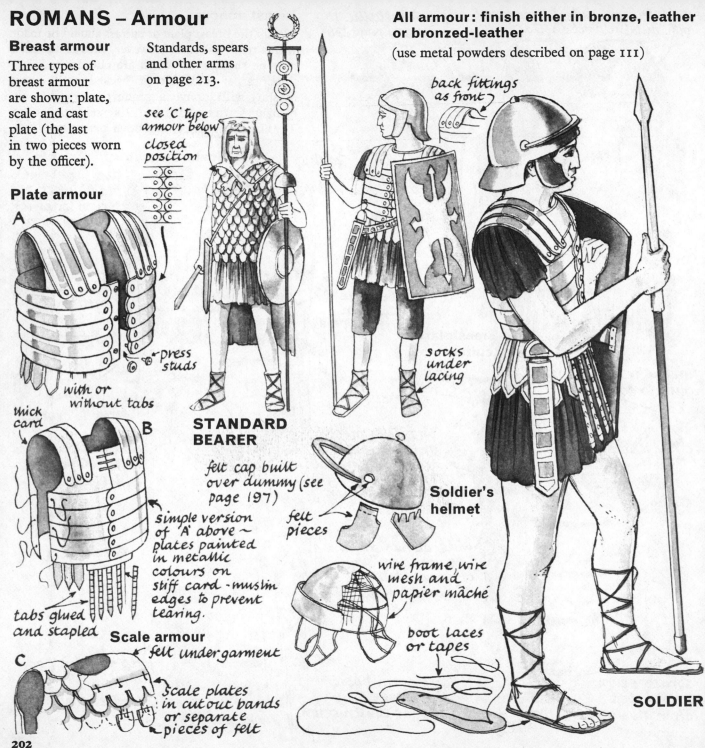

A

○ press studs

with or without tabs

see 'C' type armour below

closed position

thick card

B

simple version of 'A' above ~ plates painted in metallic colours on stiff card - muslin edges to prevent tearing.

tabs glued and stapled

Scale armour

C

felt undergarment

Scale plates in cutout bands or separate pieces of felt

STANDARD BEARER

felt cap built over dummy (see page 197)

felt pieces

wire frame, wire mesh and papier mâché

back fittings as front

socks under lacing

Soldier's helmet

boot laces or tapes

SOLDIER

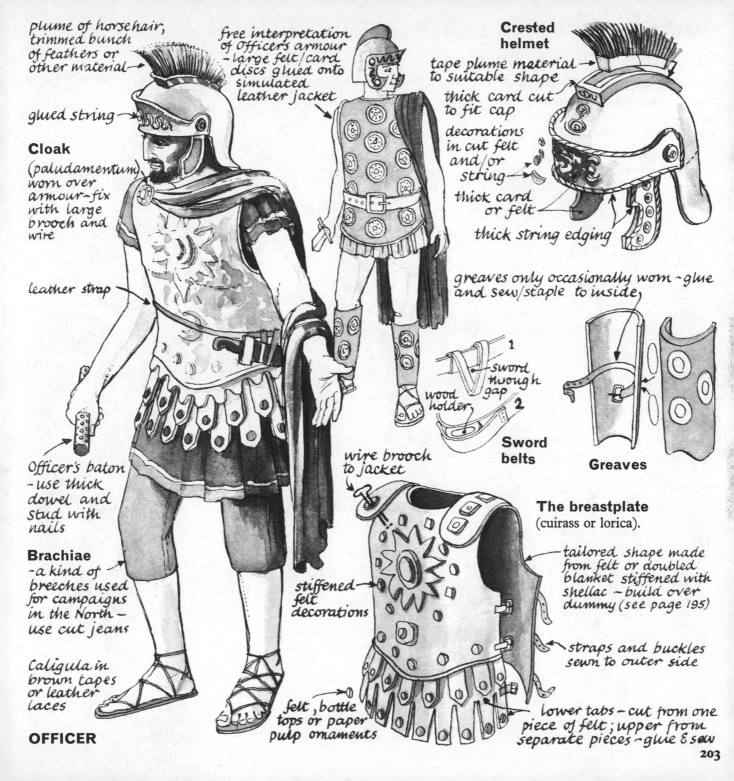

plume of horsehair, trimmed bunch of feathers or other material

glued string

Cloak
(paludamentum) worn over armour ~ fix with large brooch and wire

leather strap

Officer's baton ~ use thick dowel and stud with nails

Brachiae ~ a kind of breeches used for campaigns in the North ~ use cut jeans

Caligula in brown tapes or leather laces

OFFICER

free interpretation of Officer's armour ~ large felt/card discs glued onto simulated leather jacket

Crested helmet

tape plume material to suitable shape

thick card cut to fit cap

decorations in cut felt and/or string

thick card or felt

thick string edging

greaves only occasionally worn ~ glue and sew/staple to inside

1
sword through gap
wood holder
2

Sword belts

Greaves

wire brooch to jacket

stiffened felt decorations

felt, bottle tops or paper pulp ornaments

The breastplate
(cuirass or lorica).

tailored shape made from felt or doubled blanket stiffened with shellac ~ build over dummy (see page 195)

straps and buckles sewn to outer side

lower tabs ~ cut from one piece of felt; upper from separate pieces ~ glue & sew

203

ROMANESQUE AND EARLY GOTHIC ARMOUR

10–13th centuries: Normans

Basic garment of hood and tunic was made of chain mail. Various helmets and scaled tunics were worn by knights over this mail.

Swords and other weapons on pages 214 and 215.

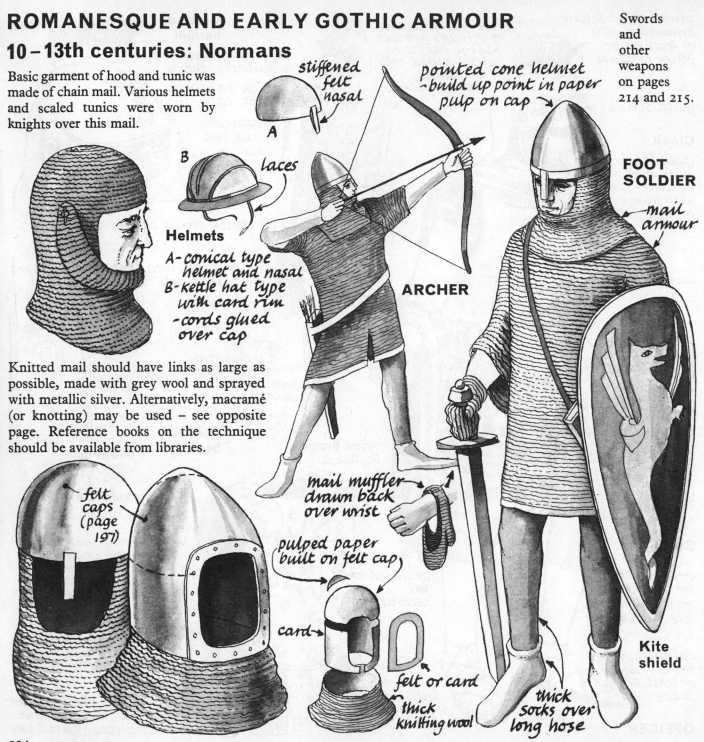

stiffened felt nasal

A

pointed cone helmet – build up point in paper pulp on cap

B

laces

Helmets

A – conical type helmet and nasal
B – kettle hat type with card rim – cords glued over cap

ARCHER

Knitted mail should have links as large as possible, made with grey wool and sprayed with metallic silver. Alternatively, macramé (or knotting) may be used – see opposite page. Reference books on the technique should be available from libraries.

FOOT SOLDIER

mail armour

felt caps (page 197)

mail muffler drawn back over wrist

pulped paper built on felt cap

card →

felt or card

thick knitting wool

thick socks over long hose

Kite shield

204

flat topped helmet

mail as shown opposite

Scale armour

mail hood drawn back

An old jersey or jumper can be used as an undergarment. Scales may be enlarged to reduce working time.

either individual card scales or cutout bands of felt sewn to undergarment

flat topped tubular helms of thick card with felt strips glued over

surcoat over mail

thick card shape

felt

card

felt

Knight's helms

KNIGHT

Chain mail

Macramé, or knotting with yarns/cords

metal washers

long laces or tape washers sewn to undergarment

front of leg mail with enclosed toe cap

If a large quantity of washers is available, they will be very suitable but must each be stitched to the undergarment.

205

LATE GOTHIC ARMOUR:
14th and 15th centuries

Chain mail, although still in use as a basic garment, was more and more often covered by various paddings and plates. Knights were guarded by protective plate from head to foot. Helmets developed to include visors. Knees and elbows had special armour pieces and feet and hands were covered by overlapping plates.

Weapons shown on pages 216 and 217.

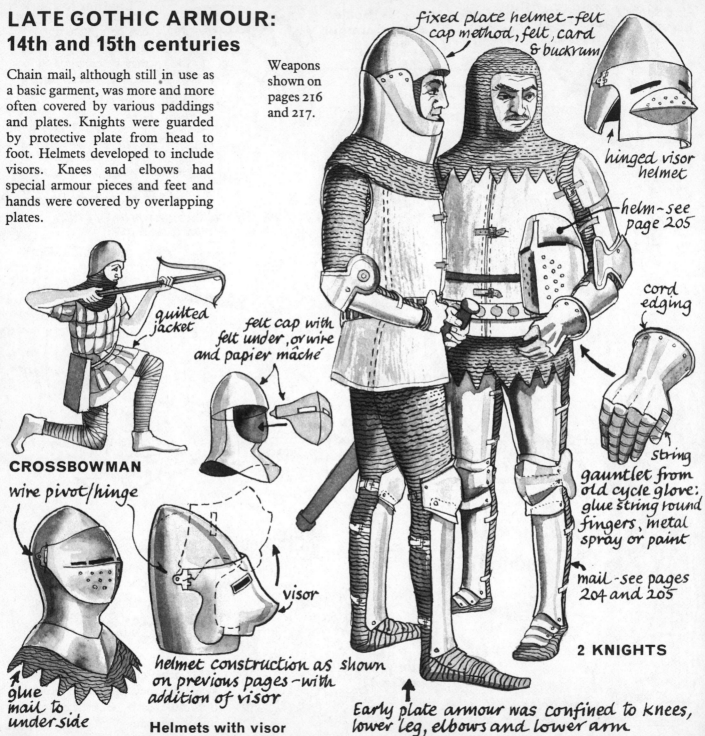

fixed plate helmet-felt cap method, felt, card & buckrum

hinged visor helmet

helm-see page 205

cord edging

quilted jacket

felt cap with felt under, or wire and papier mâché

CROSSBOWMAN

wire pivot/hinge

visor

string gauntlet from old cycle glove: glue string round fingers, metal spray or paint

mail-see pages 204 and 205

glue mail to underside

helmet construction as shown on previous pages-with addition of visor

Helmets with visor

2 KNIGHTS

Early plate armour was confined to knees, lower leg, elbows and lower arm

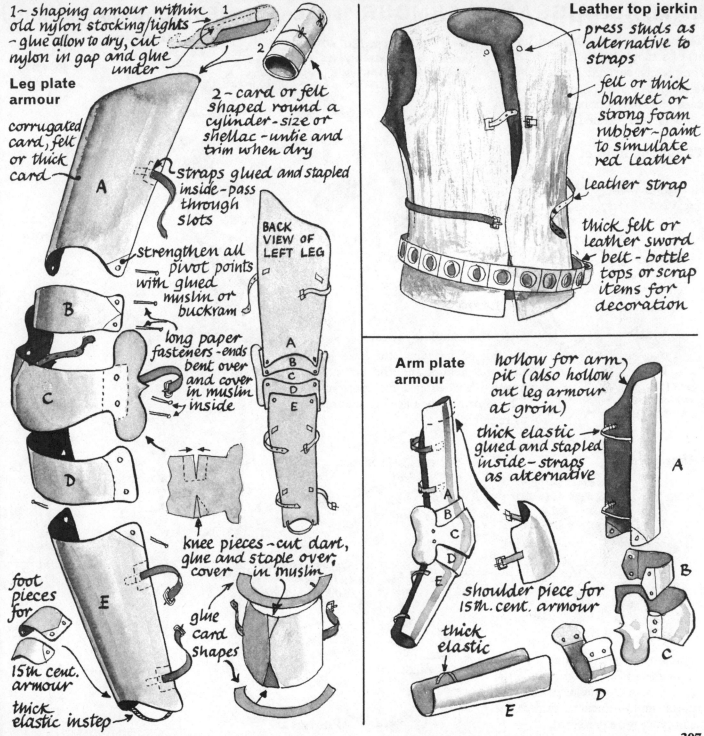

1~ shaping armour within old nylon stocking/tights ~ glue allow to dry, cut nylon in gap and glue under

2 ~ card or felt shaped round a cylinder ~ size or shellac ~ untie and trim when dry

Leg plate armour

corrugated card, felt or thick card

straps glued and stapled inside ~ pass through slots

strengthen all pivot points with glued muslin or buckram

long paper fasteners ~ ends bent over and cover in muslin inside

BACK VIEW OF LEFT LEG

A
B
C
D
E

knee pieces ~ cut dart, glue and staple over; cover in muslin

glue card shapes

foot pieces for

15th cent. armour

thick elastic instep

Leather top jerkin

press studs as alternative to straps

felt or thick blanket or strong foam rubber ~ paint to simulate red leather

leather strap

thick felt or leather sword belt ~ bottle tops or scrap items for decoration

Arm plate armour

hollow for arm pit (also hollow out leg armour at groin)

thick elastic glued and stapled inside ~ straps as alternative

A

shoulder piece for 15th. cent. armour

thick elastic

A
B
C
D
E

B

C

D

E

207

LATE RENAISSANCE ARMOUR: 16th century (Elizabethan England)

This period shows the peak in the art of armour design. The body was completely covered by plate, with overlapping ribs over all mobile parts. Swords were large and heavy, helmets often crested.

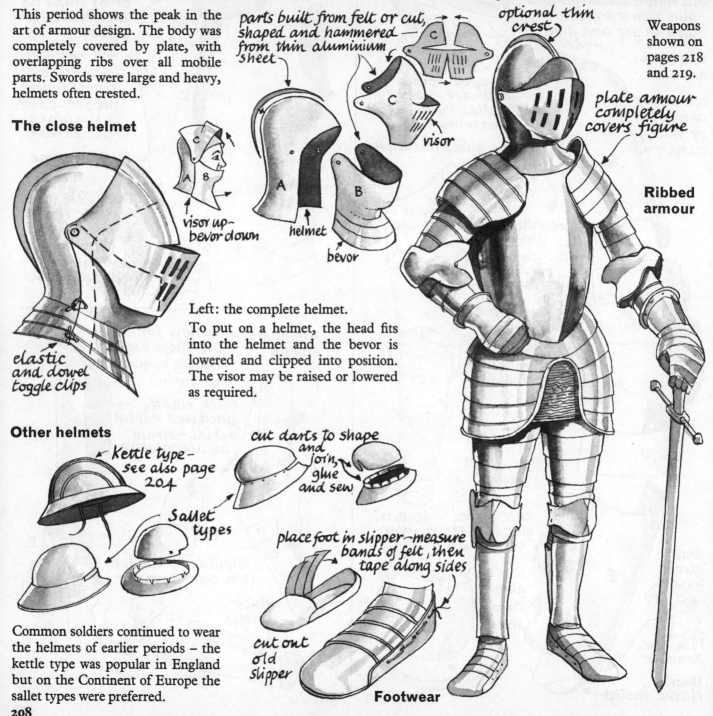

parts built from felt or cut, shaped and hammered from thin aluminium sheet

optional thin crest

Weapons shown on pages 218 and 219.

visor

C

C

plate armour completely covers figure

The close helmet

C

A B

visor up – bevor down

helmet

A

B

bevor

elastic and dowel toggle clips

Left: the complete helmet.

To put on a helmet, the head fits into the helmet and the bevor is lowered and clipped into position. The visor may be raised or lowered as required.

Ribbed armour

Other helmets

Kettle type – see also page 204

Sallet types

cut darts to shape and join, glue and sew

place foot in slipper – measure bands of felt, then tape along sides

cut out old slipper

Footwear

Common soldiers continued to wear the helmets of earlier periods – the kettle type was popular in England but on the Continent of Europe the sallet types were preferred.

208

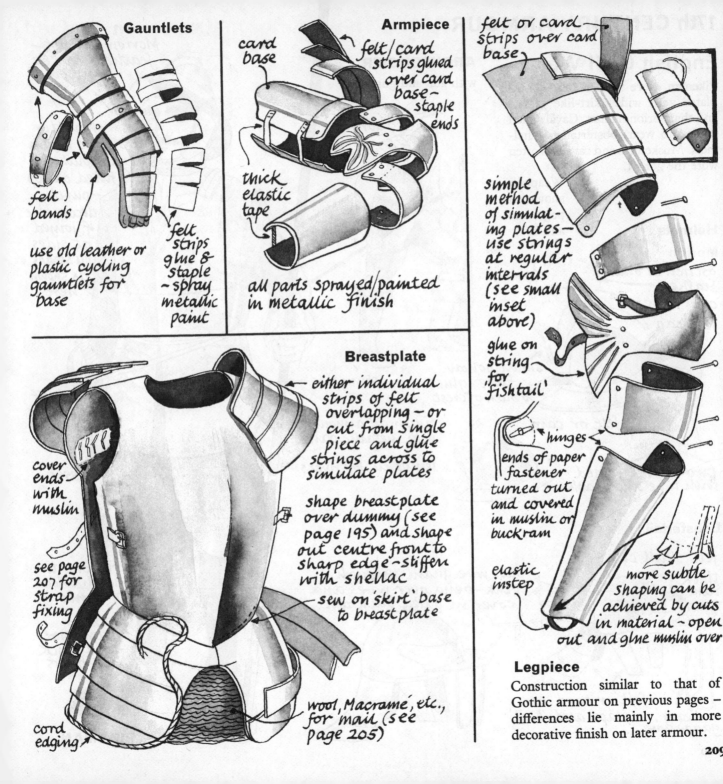

Gauntlets

use old leather or plastic cycling gauntlets for base

felt bands

felt strips glue & staple ~ spray metallic paint

Armpiece

card base

felt/card strips glued over card base ~ staple ends

thick elastic tape

all parts sprayed/painted in metallic finish

felt or card strips over card base

simple method of simulating plates ~ use strings at regular intervals (see small inset above)

glue on string for 'fishtail'

hinges

ends of paper fastener turned out and covered in muslin or buckram

elastic instep

more subtle shaping can be achieved by cuts in material ~ open out and glue muslin over

Breastplate

either individual strips of felt overlapping ~ or cut from single piece and glue strings across to simulate plates

shape breastplate over dummy (see page 195) and shape out centre front to sharp edge ~ stiffen with shellac

sew on 'skirt' base to breastplate

cover ends with muslin

see page 207 for strap fixing

cord edging

wool, Macramé, etc., for mail (see page 205)

Legpiece

Construction similar to that of Gothic armour on previous pages ~ differences lie mainly in more decorative finish on later armour.

209

17th CENTURY ARMOUR

English Civil War

Pikemen wore breast- and back-plates with wide skirt-like tassets and the morion helmet. Cavalrymen tended to wear lobstertail pot helmets. Musketeers and cavaliers often wore the gorget.

Weapons shown on pages 220 and 221.

ARQUEBUSIER
with gun and gun-rest

gorget

Helmets
Morion

ostrich or other feathers

card crest

felt cap

small hollow tube - glue to back of crest

felt or card

Two halves joined with tape and staples

finish all armour with metallic paint

lentils, etc. for rivets

Lobstertail

felt skull cap

thick card

pass wire guard through peak - bend over wires and cover in glued buckram

heavy gauge wire

felt or card ear-flaps and 'tail'

Morion helmet— feathers can be omitted

shoulder straps to join breastplate if fitted at top — purely decorative if joined at sides by straps as shown here

string ribs

buff leather gloves

tasset

ribbons to match colour of tunic

common brown shoes - add thick bows

PIKEMAN

210

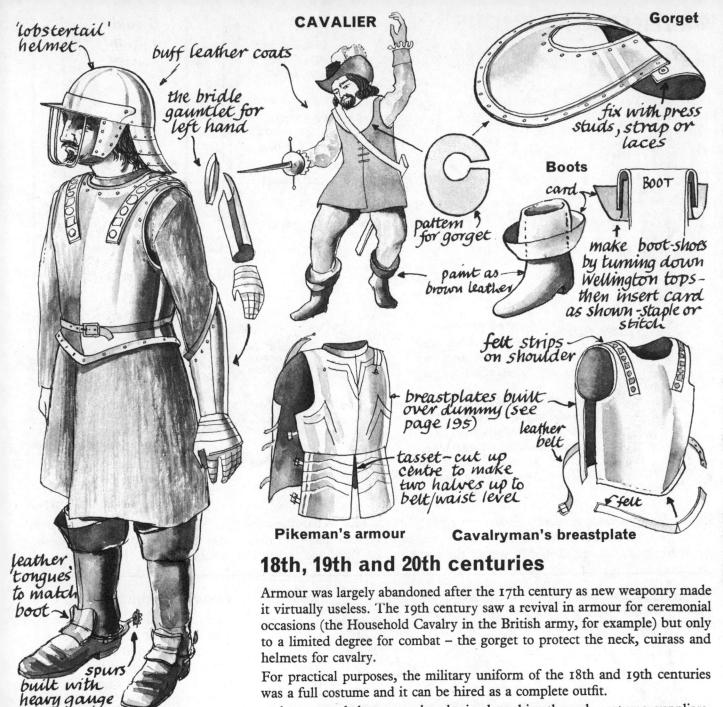

'lobstertail' helmet

buff leather coats

the bridle gauntlet for left hand

CAVALIER

Gorget

fix with press studs, strap or laces

pattern for gorget

paint as brown leather

Boots

card

BOOT

make boot-shoes by turning down Wellington tops— then insert card as shown —staple or stitch

felt strips on shoulder

breastplates built over dummy (see page 195)

tasset—cut up centre to make two halves up to belt/waist level

leather belt

felt

Pikeman's armour

Cavalryman's breastplate

leather tongues to match boot

spurs built with heavy gauge wire

CAVALRYMAN

18th, 19th and 20th centuries

Armour was largely abandoned after the 17th century as new weaponry made it virtually useless. The 19th century saw a revival in armour for ceremonial occasions (the Household Cavalry in the British army, for example) but only to a limited degree for combat – the gorget to protect the neck, cuirass and helmets for cavalry.

For practical purposes, the military uniform of the 18th and 19th centuries was a full costume and it can be hired as a complete outfit.

20th century helmets can be obtained on hire through costume suppliers, local antique dealers or the enthusiastic collector of military paraphernalia.

GREEKS – Arms

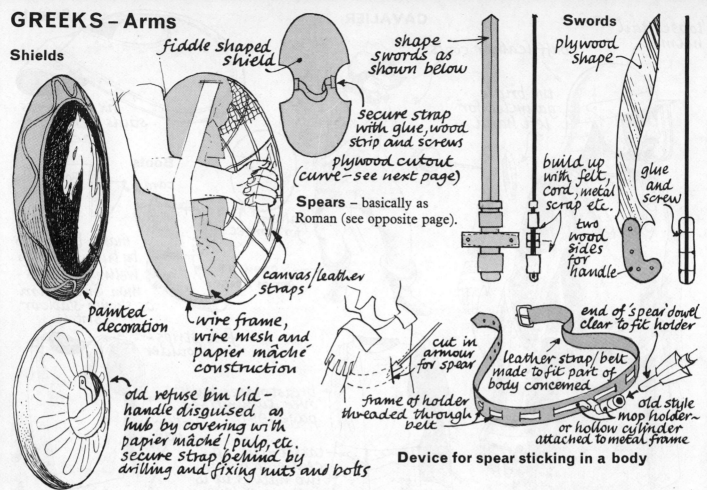

Shields

fiddle shaped shield

shape swords as shown below

Swords

plywood shape

secure strap with glue, wood strip and screws

plywood cutout (curve – see next page)

Spears – basically as Roman (see opposite page).

build up with felt, cord, metal scrap etc.

two wood sides for handle

glue and screw

painted decoration

wire frame, wire mesh and papier mâché construction

canvas/leather straps

old refuse bin lid – handle disguised as hub by covering with papier mâché/pulp, etc. secure strap behind by drilling and fixing nuts and bolts

cut in armour for spear

frame of holder threaded through belt

end of 'spear' dowel clear to fit holder

leather strap/belt made to fit part of body concerned

old style mop holder – or hollow cylinder attached to metal frame

Device for spear sticking in a body

Shield construction

Shields for all periods are easily made from a pliable board such as hardboard or thin (skin) plywood. If a deep curve is required, steam the board and allow to dry between two fixed points to mould into shape (see diagram opposite). Wood formers or straps should fit within the curve and be glued and tacked into position.

softwood shape – dimensions dependent on type and period

screw together

cut back handle

1

plane sides approx. 15° from centre line

2

thin sheet aluminium – fold to shape & tack at centre

glued cord or string

3

Sword construction

The basic shape for Greek and Roman swords is made from softwood. Plane to the correct angle and build hilt across shaft as shown in (2). Cover with thin sheet alloy; glue on metal foil; or paint with metallic colours if realism is required.

212

ROMANS – Arms

Shields

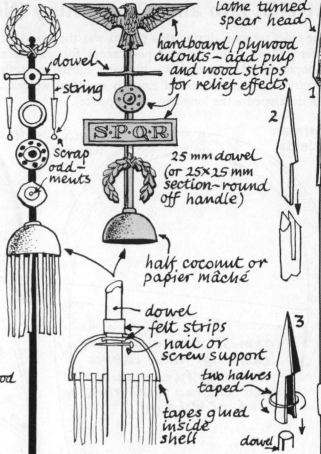

felt cutout decoration scrap metal

basic shape after setting curve (see below)

shield arm support – cut to fit curve

thick felt edging – studs/rivets of seeds, cereals etc.,

battens screwed to board (or old wood floor)

hardboard/plywood, soaked and shaped between two fixed battens

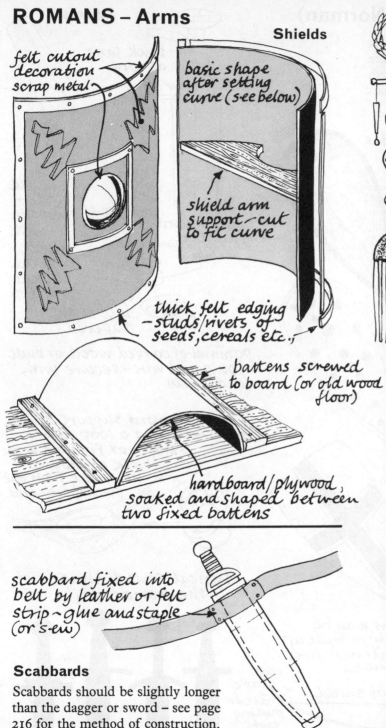

dowel

string

Scrap odd-ments

lathe turned spear head

hardboard/plywood cutouts – add pulp and wood strips for relief effects

S·P·Q·R

25 mm dowel (or 25×25 mm section – round off handle)

half coconut or papier mâché

dowel
felt strips
nail or screw support

two halves taped

tapes glued inside shell

dowel

1

2

3

scabbard fixed into belt by leather or felt strip – glue and staple (or sew)

Scabbards

Scabbards should be slightly longer than the dagger or sword – see page 216 for the method of construction.

Standards and spears

All pole-like weapons and standards are constructed on a suitable length of dowel rod or broom handle (25 mm to 35 mm diameter). Spear heads are formed of carved wood pieces drilled to take the shaft – or the dowel can be spliced and the blade fitted inside. Larger heads are built of two or more pieces of thin plywood, bound with wire and shaped to a point. Decorative pieces on standards can be of wood and board with paper pulp modelling. Gild with metallic colours (see page 111).

ARMS: 11th and 12th century (Norman)

The chief weapon during this period was the sword. It differed little from earlier types except for the more elaborate hilt. However, it was probably during the 12th century that the greatest of English medieval weapons was developed – the longbow (see opposite).

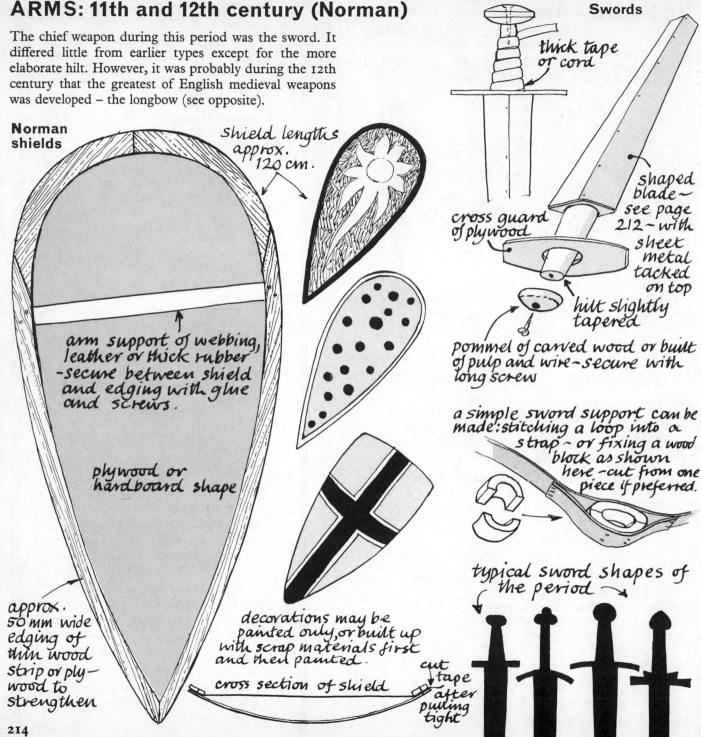

Swords

thick tape or cord

shaped blade ~ see page 212 ~ with sheet metal tacked on top

cross guard of plywood

hilt slightly tapered

pommel of carved wood or built of pulp and wire ~ secure with long screw

a simple sword support can be made: stitching a loop into a strap ~ or fixing a wood block as shown here ~ cut from one piece if preferred.

typical sword shapes of the period

Norman shields

Shield lengths approx. 120 cm.

arm support of webbing, leather or thick rubber ~ secure between shield and edging with glue and screws.

plywood or hardboard shape

approx. 50 mm wide edging of thin wood strip or plywood to strengthen

decorations may be painted only, or built up with scrap materials first and then painted.

cross section of shield

cut tape after pulling tight

214

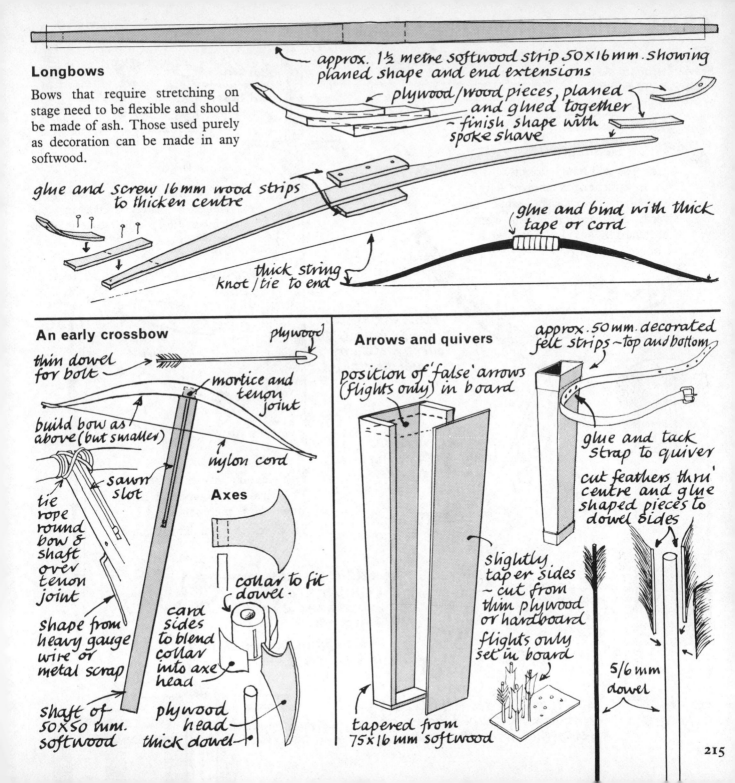

Longbows

Bows that require stretching on stage need to be flexible and should be made of ash. Those used purely as decoration can be made in any softwood.

approx. 1½ metre softwood strip 50×16 mm. showing planed shape and end extensions

plywood/wood pieces, planed and glued together
~ finish shape with spoke shave

glue and screw 16mm wood strips to thicken centre

glue and bind with thick tape or cord

thick string knot/tie to end

An early crossbow

plywood

thin dowel for bolt

build bow as above (but smaller)

mortice and tenon joint

nylon cord

sawn slot

tie rope round bow & shaft over tenon joint

shape from heavy gauge wire or metal scrap

shaft of 50×50 mm. softwood

Axes

collar to fit dowel.

card sides to blend collar into axe head

plywood head

thick dowel

Arrows and quivers

position of 'false' arrows (flights only) in board

approx. 50 mm. decorated felt strips ~ top and bottom

glue and tack strap to quiver

cut feathers thru' centre and glue shaped pieces to dowel sides

slightly taper sides ~ cut from thin plywood or hardboard

flights only set in board

tapered from 75×16 mm softwood

5/6 mm dowel

ARMS: Gothic period, 13th – 14th centuries

During this period the sword developed into a longer heavier weapon. Axes and maces (metal-headed clubs) became more popular.

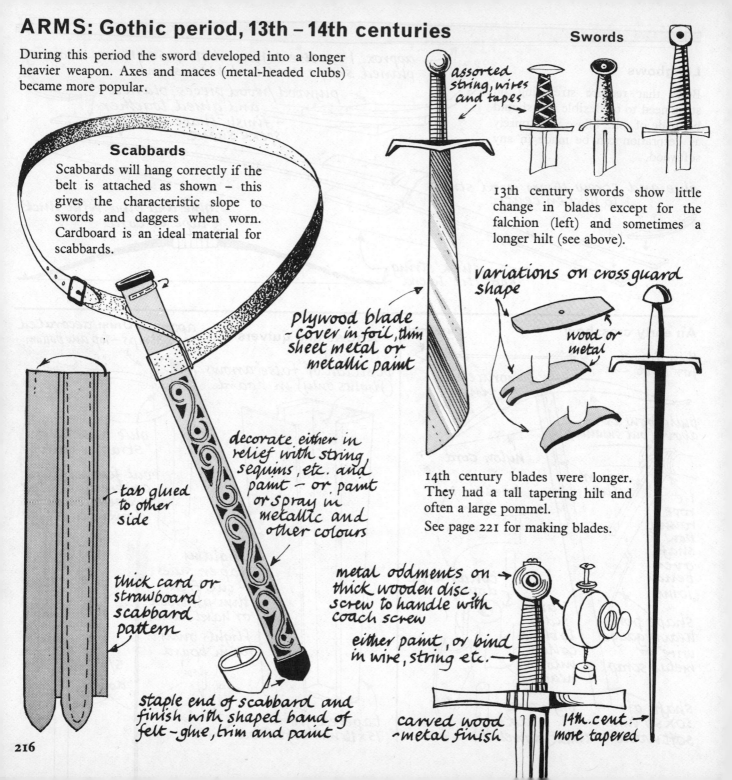

Swords

assorted string, wires and tapes

13th century swords show little change in blades except for the falchion (left) and sometimes a longer hilt (see above).

Variations on crossguard shape

wood or metal

14th century blades were longer. They had a tall tapering hilt and often a large pommel.

See page 221 for making blades.

Scabbards

Scabbards will hang correctly if the belt is attached as shown – this gives the characteristic slope to swords and daggers when worn. Cardboard is an ideal material for scabbards.

Plywood blade – cover in foil, thin sheet metal or metallic paint

tab glued to other side

decorate either in relief with string, sequins, etc. and paint – or paint or spray in metallic and other colours

thick card or strawboard scabbard pattern

metal oddments on thick wooden disc screw to handle with coach screw

either paint, or bind in wire, string etc.

staple end of scabbard and finish with shaped band of felt – glue, trim and paint

carved wood ~metal finish

14th. cent.→ more tapered

216

Other arms

Maces

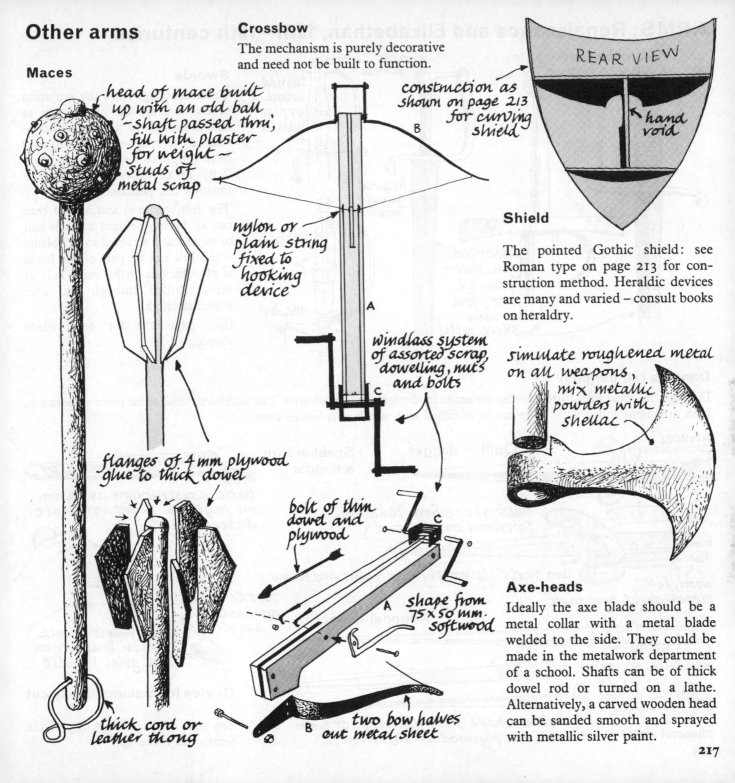

head of mace built up with an old ball – shaft passed thru; fill with plaster for weight – studs of metal scrap

flanges of 4 mm plywood glue to thick dowel

thick cord or leather thong

Crossbow

The mechanism is purely decorative and need not be built to function.

construction as shown on page 213 for curving shield

B

nylon or plain string fixed to hooking device

A

C

windlass system of assorted scrap, dowelling, nuts and bolts

bolt of thin dowel and plywood

C

A

shape from 75 × 50 mm softwood

B

two bow halves cut metal sheet

REAR VIEW

hand void

Shield

The pointed Gothic shield: see Roman type on page 213 for construction method. Heraldic devices are many and varied – consult books on heraldry.

simulate roughened metal on all weapons, mix metallic powders with shellac

Axe-heads

Ideally the axe blade should be a metal collar with a metal blade welded to the side. They could be made in the metalwork department of a school. Shafts can be of thick dowel rod or turned on a lathe. Alternatively, a carved wooden head can be sanded smooth and sprayed with metallic silver paint.

ARMS: Renaissance and Elizabethan, 15th – 16th centuries

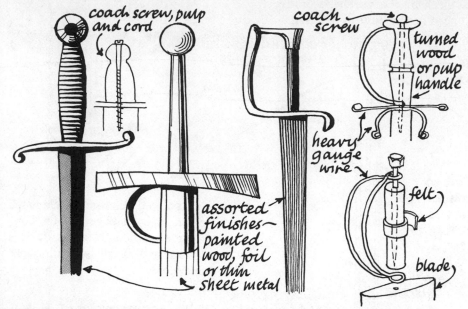

coach screw, pulp and cord

coach screw

turned wood or pulp handle

heavy gauge wire

felt

blade

assorted finishes – painted wood, foil or thin sheet metal

Swords

These drawings show the evolution of the knucklebow (which was to lead eventually to the enclosed cup-hilts of the 17th and 18th centuries) from simple curved and looped bars (left) to the curving of the hilt towards the pommel.

The hilt, pommel and looped bars can all be built round a coach bolt or large screw attached to the 'blade' – the hilt can be part of the blade if of sufficient girth, but a bolt or screw drilled through will give added strength.

(See page 221 for basic blade shaping.)

Daggers (all periods)

Daggers (in effect miniature swords) are made in the same way as swords. The scabbards tend to be more elaborate in both ornament and colour. Hilts can be enriched with nail heads, 'jewels', etc.

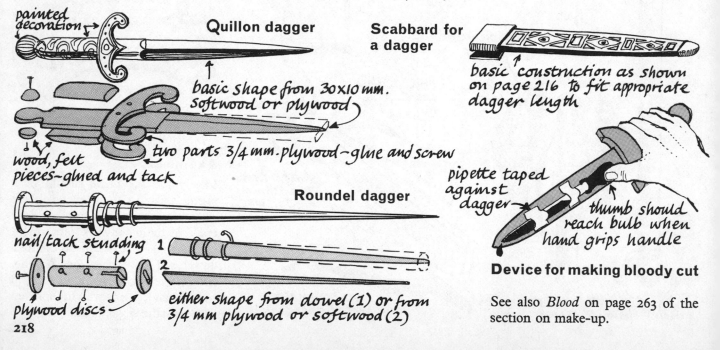

painted decoration

Quillon dagger

basic shape from 30 × 10 mm. softwood or plywood

Scabbard for a dagger

basic construction as shown on page 216 to fit appropriate dagger length

wood, felt pieces – glued and tack

two parts 3/4 mm. plywood – glue and screw

Roundel dagger

nail/tack studding

plywood discs

either shape from dowel (1) or from 3/4 mm plywood or softwood (2)

pipette taped against dagger

thumb should reach bulb when hand grips handle

Device for making bloody cut

See also *Blood* on page 263 of the section on make-up.

218

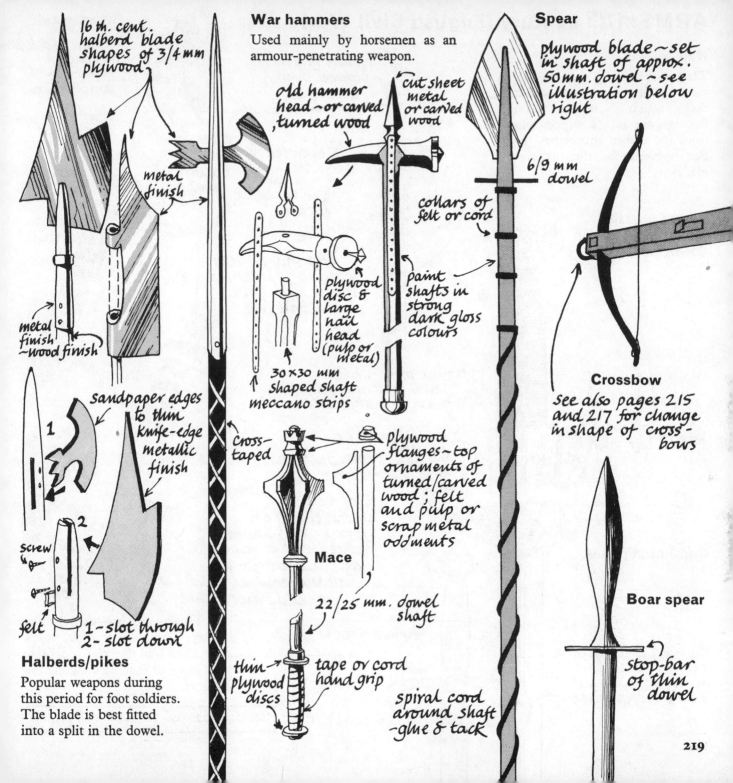

16th. cent. halberd blade shapes of 3/4 mm plywood

metal finish

metal finish ~wood finish

sandpaper edges to thin knife-edge metallic finish

1

2

screw

felt

1 – slot through
2 – slot down

Halberds/pikes

Popular weapons during this period for foot soldiers. The blade is best fitted into a split in the dowel.

War hammers

Used mainly by horsemen as an armour-penetrating weapon.

old hammer head ~ or carved, turned wood

cut sheet metal or carved wood

plywood disc & large nail head (pulp or metal)

30 × 30 mm shaped shaft meccano strips

collars of felt or cord

paint shafts in strong dark gloss colours

cross-taped

plywood flanges ~ top ornaments of turned/carved wood; felt and pulp or scrap metal oddments

Mace

22/25 mm. dowel shaft

thin plywood discs

tape or cord hand grip

spiral cord around shaft ~ glue & tack

Spear

plywood blade ~ set in shaft of approx. 50mm. dowel ~ see illustration below right

6/9 mm dowel

Crossbow

see also pages 215 and 217 for change in shape of cross-bows

Boar spear

stop-bar of thin dowel

219

ARMS: 17th century (English Civil War)

Rapier

The rapier is a long, thin two-edged blade sword for quick cut-and-thrust action. Note how the hilt has evolved into a cupped shape from the earlier knucklebow type. See opposite for the making of blades.

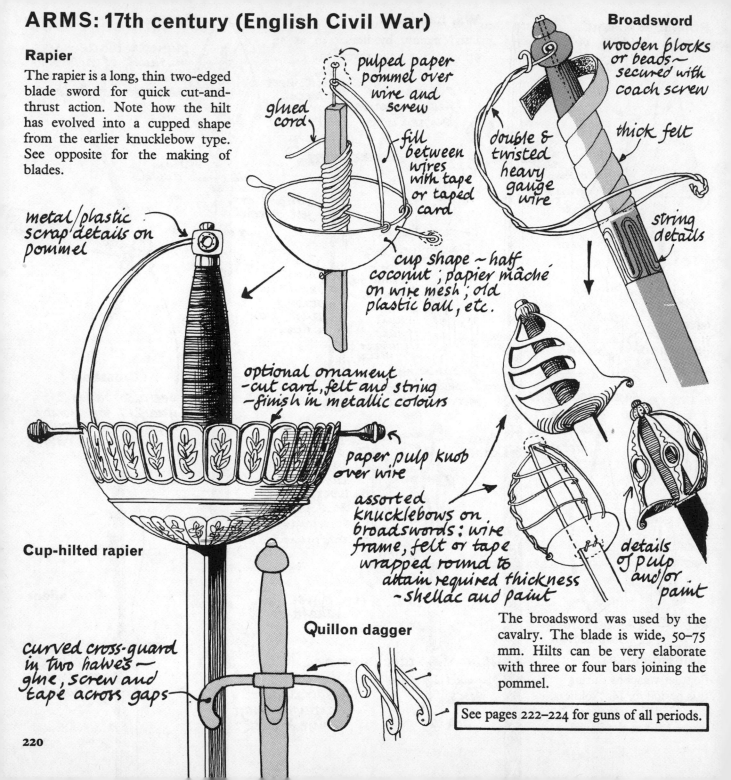

metal/plastic scrap details on pommel

glued cord

pulped paper pommel over wire and screw

fill between wires with tape or taped card

cup shape ~ half coconut; papier mâché on wire mesh; old plastic ball, etc.

Broadsword

wooden blocks or beads ~ secured with coach screw

double & twisted heavy gauge wire

thick felt

string details

optional ornament
- cut card, felt and string
- finish in metallic colours

paper pulp knob over wire

assorted knucklebows on broadswords: wire frame, felt or tape wrapped round to attain required thickness ~ shellac and paint

details of pulp and/or paint

Cup-hilted rapier

curved cross-guard in two halves ~ glue, screw and tape across gaps

Quillon dagger

The broadsword was used by the cavalry. The blade is wide, 50–75 mm. Hilts can be very elaborate with three or four bars joining the pommel.

See pages 222–224 for guns of all periods.

220

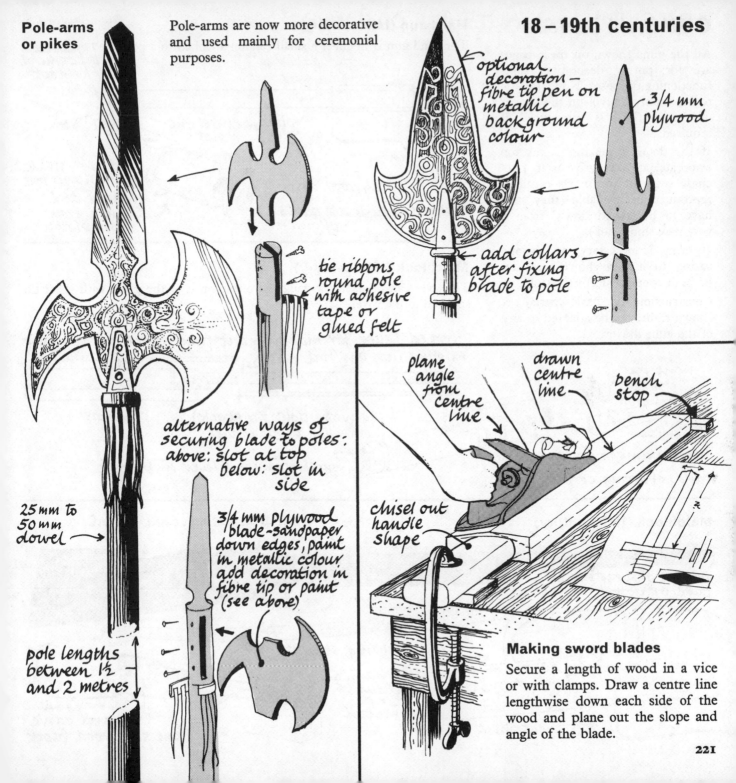

Pole-arms or pikes

Pole-arms are now more decorative and used mainly for ceremonial purposes.

optional decoration — fibre tip pen on metallic background colour

3/4 mm plywood

add collars after fixing blade to pole

tie ribbons round pole with adhesive tape or glued felt

25mm to 50mm dowel

pole lengths between 1½ and 2 metres

alternative ways of securing blade to poles:
above: slot at top
below: slot in side

3/4 mm plywood blade - sandpaper down edges, paint in metallic colour add decoration in fibre tip or paint (see above)

plane angle from centre line

drawn centre line

bench stop

chisel out handle shape

Making sword blades

Secure a length of wood in a vice or with clamps. Draw a centre line lengthwise down each side of the wood and plane out the slope and angle of the blade.

221

GUNS: all periods

All the guns shown on these pages are for purely decorative, non-functioning purposes. None is made to fire – only a pivot on the trigger of the flintlock is introduced if required.

If the detailed making seems too elaborate, an alternative is to purchase some of the many excellent reproductions available (they may have to be 'toned down' from a very new shiny look).

If firing is necessary, an antique casing (from those shown here) can be built round a starting pistol.

Construction of basic parts, as shown right, can be adapted to any of the guns illustrated.

Hand gun (14th century)

The hand gun is in effect a small cannon attached to a pole.

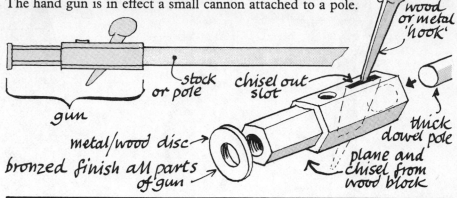

wood or metal 'hook'

stock or pole

chisel out slot

gun

metal/wood disc

bronzed finish all parts of gun

thick dowel pole

plane and chisel from wood block

Matchlock (15th century)

The lever can be of heavy-gauge wire thickened at the pivot with sheet tin soldered to the wire.

pivoted lever for match ~ cut from sheet metal or use existing iron bar/rod

'match'

cannon

long wood pole (the stock) ~ use thick dowel

finish cannon & lever in bronze

cut out slot

screw pivot

large bamboo for cannon

bands of string, cord or wire

Matchlock (16th century)

stock ~ simulate weathered wood

barrel of scrap metal tube or dowel

webbing strap

mechanical details of scrap metal

cut sheet tin

saw and carve from softwood block

222

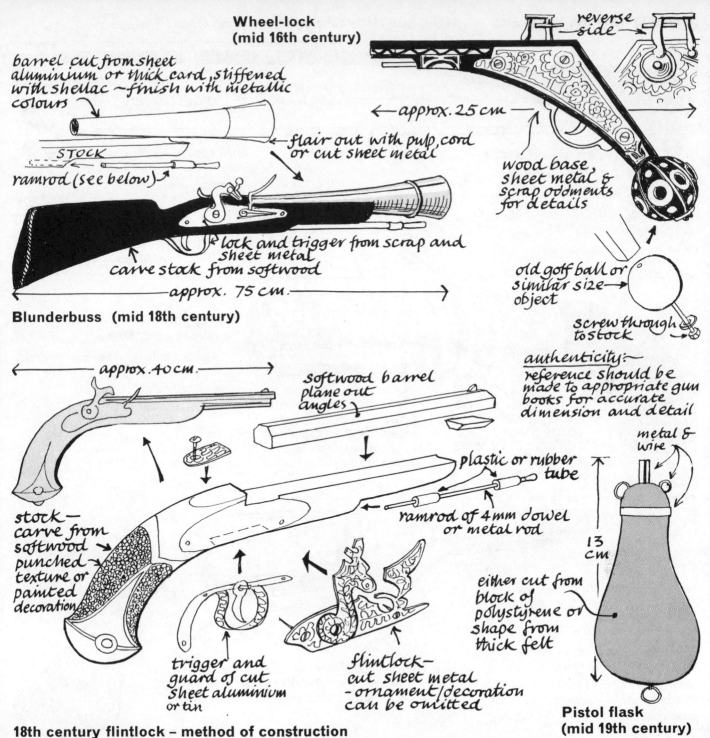

Wheel-lock (mid 16th century)

barrel cut from sheet aluminium or thick card, stiffened with shellac ~ finish with metallic colours

STOCK

ramrod (see below)

flair out with pulp, cord or cut sheet metal

reverse side

← approx. 25 cm →

wood base, sheet metal & scrap oddments for details

lock and trigger from scrap and sheet metal

carve stock from softwood

approx. 75 cm.

old golf ball or similar size object

screw through to stock

Blunderbuss (mid 18th century)

approx. 40 cm.

softwood barrel plane out angles

authenticity:~ reference should be made to appropriate gun books for accurate dimension and detail

plastic or rubber tube

ramrod of 4mm dowel or metal rod

metal & wire

stock — carve from softwood punched texture or painted decoration

trigger and guard of cut sheet aluminium or tin

flintlock ~ cut sheet metal - ornament/decoration can be omitted

13 cm

either cut from block of polystyrene or shape from thick felt

Pistol flask (mid 19th century)

18th century flintlock – method of construction

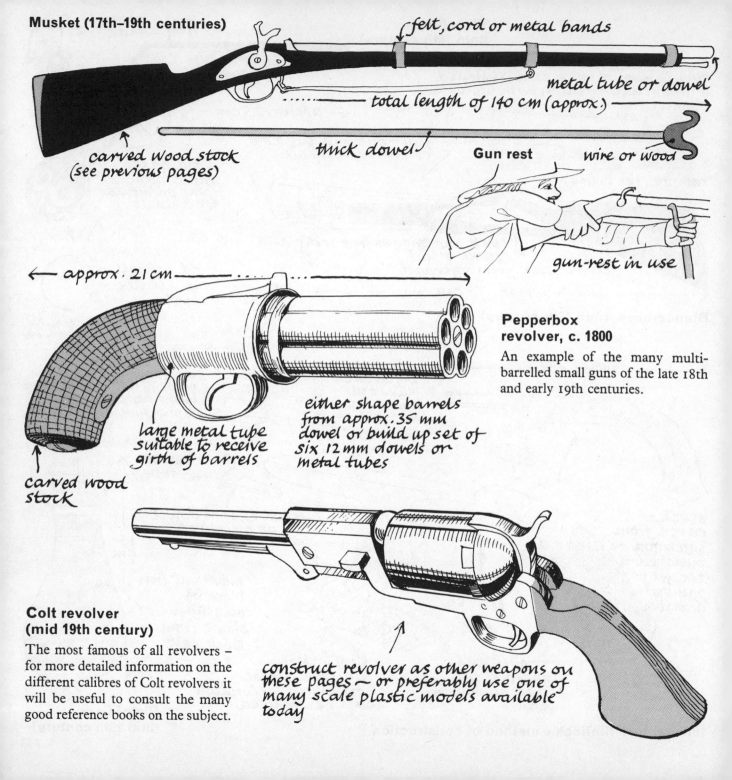

Musket (17th–19th centuries)

felt, cord or metal bands

metal tube or dowel

total length of 140 cm (approx.)

carved wood stock (see previous pages)

thick dowel

Gun rest

wire or wood

gun-rest in use

approx. 21 cm

large metal tube suitable to receive girth of barrels

carved wood stock

Pepperbox revolver, c. 1800

An example of the many multi-barrelled small guns of the late 18th and early 19th centuries.

either shape barrels from approx. 35 mm dowel or build up set of six 12 mm dowels or metal tubes

Colt revolver (mid 19th century)

The most famous of all revolvers – for more detailed information on the different calibres of Colt revolvers it will be useful to consult the many good reference books on the subject.

construct revolver as other weapons on these pages – or preferably use one of many scale plastic models available today

Costume accessories 9

CROWNS · OCCUPATIONAL ACCESSORIES · PAPER PULP AND MOULDS · JEWELLERY

Crowns 226

Footwear 229

Occupational costume accessories 230

Fans 232

Spectacles 233

Purses and pomanders 233

Jewellery and ornaments (including the use of paper pulp and moulds) . . . . . · . . . 234

Items for a school Nativity Play 240

Items for a school Passion Play 241

CROWNS – 1: a basic design and some construction methods

Materials

1 Cut shapes of stiff cartridge paper, stencil paper, felt or similar flexible material. **2** Scrap metals, buttons, beads, springs, etc. **3** Cord and string. **4** Muslin and scrim. **5** Pulp and paper. **6** Tissue paper and torn newsprint. **7** Stapler. **8** Adhesives, scissors, knife. **9** Light and medium gauge wire. **10** Felt pieces. **11** Paint.

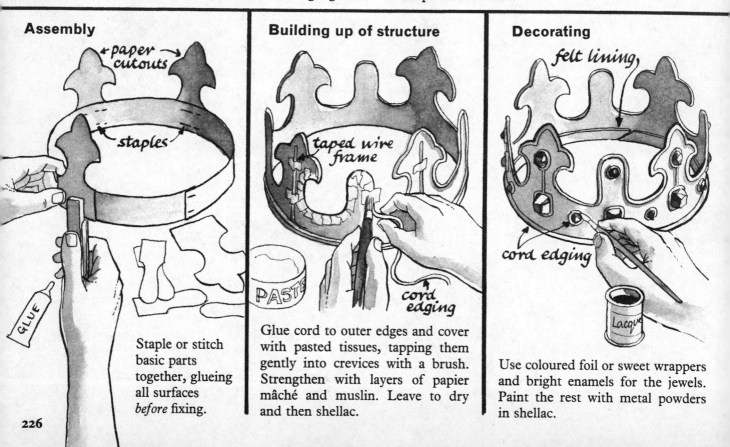

Assembly

paper cutouts

staples

Staple or stitch basic parts together, glueing all surfaces *before* fixing.

Building up of structure

taped wire frame

cord edging

Glue cord to outer edges and cover with pasted tissues, tapping them gently into crevices with a brush. Strengthen with layers of papier mâché and muslin. Leave to dry and then shellac.

Decorating

felt lining

cord edging

Use coloured foil or sweet wrappers and bright enamels for the jewels. Paint the rest with metal powders in shellac.

Felt method

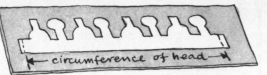

Cut out a paper pattern, the circumference determined by the actor's head + 2 cm flaps.

Lay out on felt or similar material stiffened with shellac. Chalk round the pattern and cut out. Use leftover pieces for decorations.

felt decorations

Stitch or staple the flaps together. Bend the crown to the required shape before the shellac hardens.

Jewels are small cut pieces of felt covered with foil or paint. Metal paints and powders can be applied to the whole crown with a brush or spraygun.

Felt cap method

Steam an old felt hat (see helmet-making on page 197) to the right size. Cut round with scissors to give a smooth edge.

Staple or stitch a 5 cm rim outside the cap. Shellac both parts.

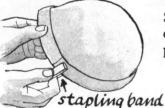

stapling band

Build up the crown over the cap, with strips across and a centre bob.

Try variations on string decorations.

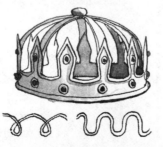

Wire method

A strip of card or paper is wrapped round the actor's head to get the right circumference.

staple

medium gauge wire frame

fine wire mesh

taped wire

A wire frame is built round the paper pattern ring – the paper is later removed. Tie wires as shown on page 233.

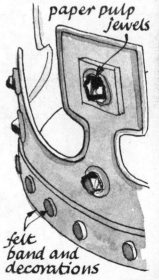

paper pulp jewels

Paper mâché is pasted over the wire mesh (approximately 4 layers). The decorative parts are added with more pulp or felt. Apply a coat of shellac, then a coat of paint, then another coat of shellac. Finish with metal powders, etc. See notes on page 111.

felt band and decorations

227

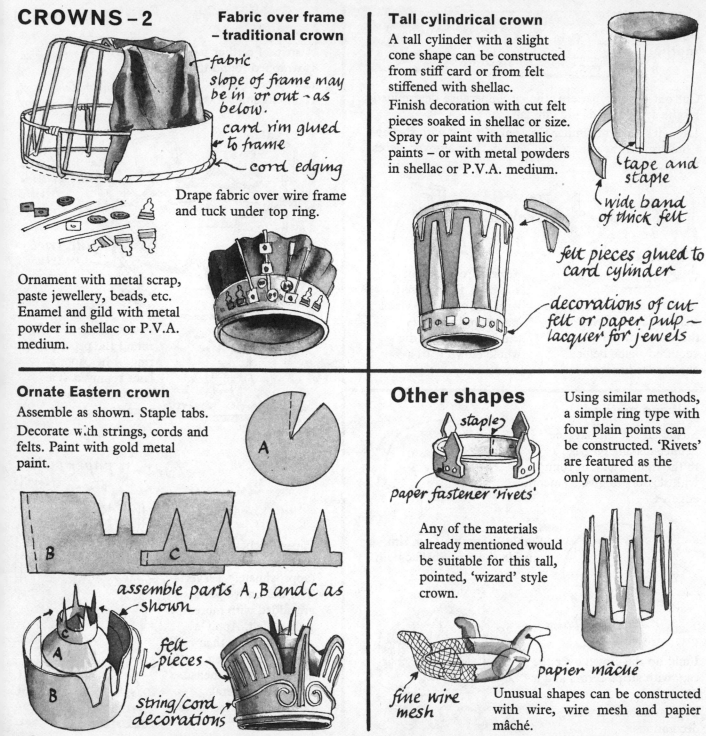

CROWNS – 2

Fabric over frame – traditional crown

- fabric
- slope of frame may be in or out – as below.
- card rim glued to frame
- cord edging

Drape fabric over wire frame and tuck under top ring.

Ornament with metal scrap, paste jewellery, beads, etc. Enamel and gild with metal powder in shellac or P.V.A. medium.

Tall cylindrical crown

A tall cylinder with a slight cone shape can be constructed from stiff card or from felt stiffened with shellac.

Finish decoration with cut felt pieces soaked in shellac or size. Spray or paint with metallic paints – or with metal powders in shellac or P.V.A. medium.

- tape and staple
- wide band of thick felt
- felt pieces glued to card cylinder
- decorations of cut felt or paper pulp – lacquer for jewels

Ornate Eastern crown

Assemble as shown. Staple tabs. Decorate with strings, cords and felts. Paint with gold metal paint.

assemble parts A, B and C as shown

- felt pieces
- string/cord decorations

Other shapes

- staple
- paper fastener 'rivets'

Using similar methods, a simple ring type with four plain points can be constructed. 'Rivets' are featured as the only ornament.

Any of the materials already mentioned would be suitable for this tall, pointed, 'wizard' style crown.

- fine wire mesh
- papier mâché

Unusual shapes can be constructed with wire, wire mesh and papier mâché.

Coronets

Coronets are more delicate than crowns and need fine detail on the top edge. Interesting spaces can be created by adding raised parts to the top edge.

Variety can be achieved by the use of various scrap items – feathers, beads, etc.

This illustration shows a ring of felt surmounted by feathers, combs, sticks, hat-pins and scrap metal, all secured by fine wire.

felt band

wire or shellac string

cut metal, beads, etc.

Tiered crowns

card disc glued inside top

string pattern

shorter version

bands of felt or card

Tall Biblical crowns can be made from simple cones of card, as shown above.

Bishop's mitre

sequins beads, etc for decoration

glue two halves inside band

The mitre requires two halves bound at the bottom by a band, with two 'tassels' attached.

Greek/Roman sandals

buckram or felt sewn to sock

cords or leather thongs threaded through boot socks

Footwear

Simple footwear can be constructed over canvas shoes, old shoes and rubber boots. Old shoe soles and shoe socks can have tapes and felt glued and stapled underneath.

high tongue of stiffened felt

shoe

17th cent. shoe

plimsoll with felt over ~ stitched to sole

plimsoll

14th cent. shoe

card and silver paper

18th cent. buckled shoe

shoes ~ elastic sided type

stitch thick white blanket/felt etc.

19th cent. riding boot

wellington top turned down and felt rim glued or stitched to low edge

17th cent. boot shoe

OCCUPATIONAL COSTUME ACCESSORIES

Certain plays and musicals demand accessories relating to particular occupations often of an early period. The musical 'Oliver', for example, requires various street traders: strawberry sellers, a knife grinder, a milkmaid, etc. Costumes for such trades are beyond the scope of this book (but see page 277 for book list) but a few items illustrated on these two pages can be useful and are not difficult to make.

Milkmaid's yoke and pail

heavy gauge wire frame
wire mesh
wood or metal strip under for strength
papier mâché
tin can - rivetted metal strip
ladle →
leather strap
pails built over bucket in thick card or plywood - or construct entirely in plywood and wire for handle
thick felt →

A yoke and early wooden pail (17th century). Pail can be fixed to yoke or carried on the head.

Chef's hat

white starched cotton - pleat and glue/sew to inside of card band

Chef's hat of the 19th century. The band gradually became deeper to reach the height seen today.

Postman's caps

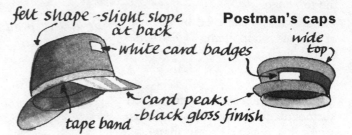

felt shape - slight slope at back
white card badges
wide top
card peaks
black gloss finish
tape band

The double-peaked postman's cap (1904) can be made from an existing cap with peaks added.

Sweep's brush and cap

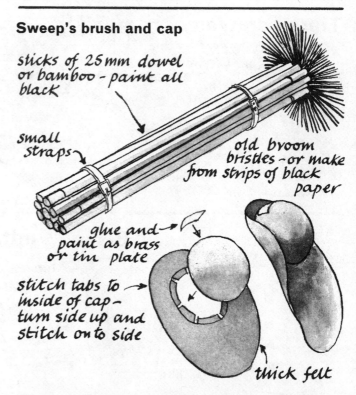

sticks of 25mm dowel or bamboo - paint all black

small straps

old broom bristles - or make from strips of black paper

glue and paint as brass or tin plate

stitch tabs to inside of cap - turn side up and stitch on to side

thick felt

The sweep's brush is shown in a closed position.

The sweeps' fantail hat was also used by dustmen in the 1800s.

230

Carpenter's tools and paper cap

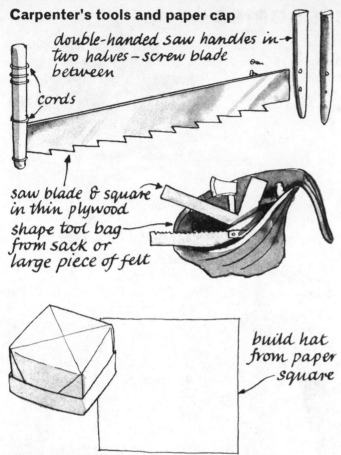

double-handed saw handles in two halves – screw blade between

cords

saw blade & square in thin plywood

shape tool bag from sack or large piece of felt

build hat from paper square

The paper cap was common to many trades in the 19th century but was associated chiefly with carpenters. The paper-folding method is complicated but can be found in most **origami** books.

Stove-pipe hat

tabs – glue top and brim – trim edge when dry – paint black

hat under if preferred

These tall hats are useful for Dickensian pageboys, Bow Street Runners and some tradesmen of 19th century.

Hawker's tray

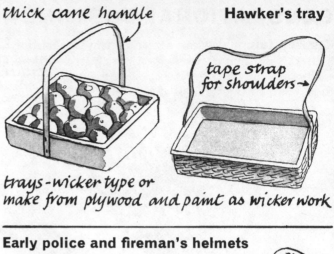

thick cane handle

tape strap for shoulders →

trays – wicker type or make from plywood and paint as wicker work

Early police and fireman's helmets

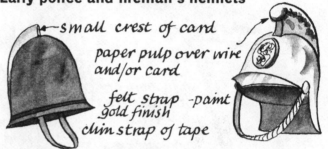

small crest of card

paper pulp over wire and/or card

felt strap – paint gold finish

chin strap of tape

These helmets can be constructed as Roman helmets – see page 202.

Water seller's tankard

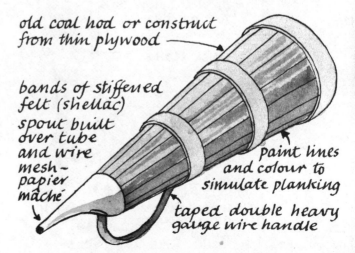

old coal hod or construct from thin plywood

bands of stiffened felt (shellac)

spout built over tube and wire mesh – papier mâché

paint lines and colour to simulate planking

taped double heavy gauge wire handle

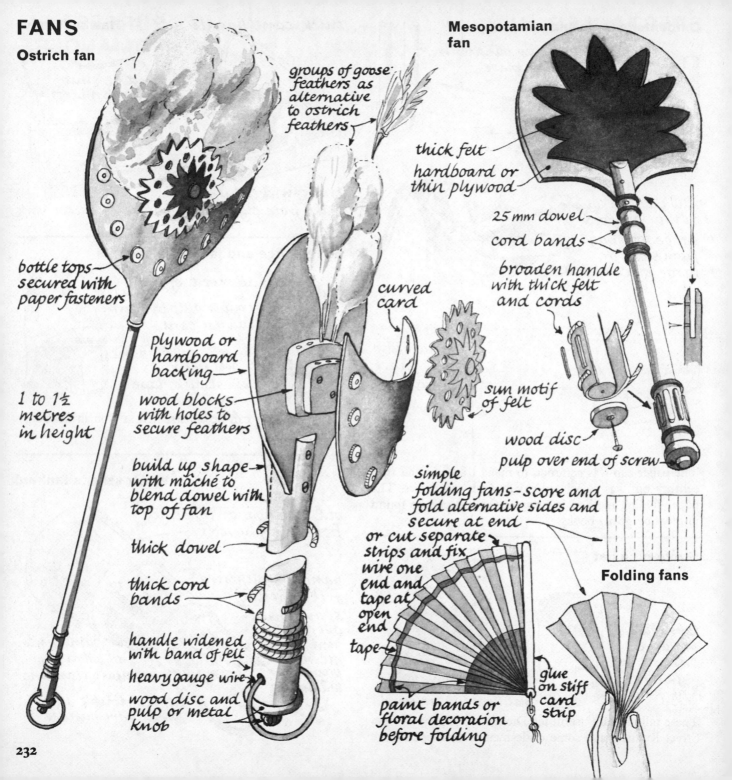

FANS

Ostrich fan

Mesopotamian fan

groups of goose feathers as alternative to ostrich feathers

thick felt

hardboard or thin plywood

25 mm dowel

cord bands

broaden handle with thick felt and cords

bottle tops secured with paper fasteners

1 to 1½ metres in height

curved card

plywood or hardboard backing

wood blocks with holes to secure feathers

sun motif of felt

wood disc

pulp over end of screw

build up shape with maché to blend dowel with top of fan

thick dowel

thick cord bands

handle widened with band of felt

heavy gauge wire

wood disc and pulp or metal knob

simple folding fans – score and fold alternative sides and secure at end

or cut separate strips and fix wire one end and tape at open end

tape

paint bands or floral decoration before folding

Folding fans

glue on stiff card strip

232

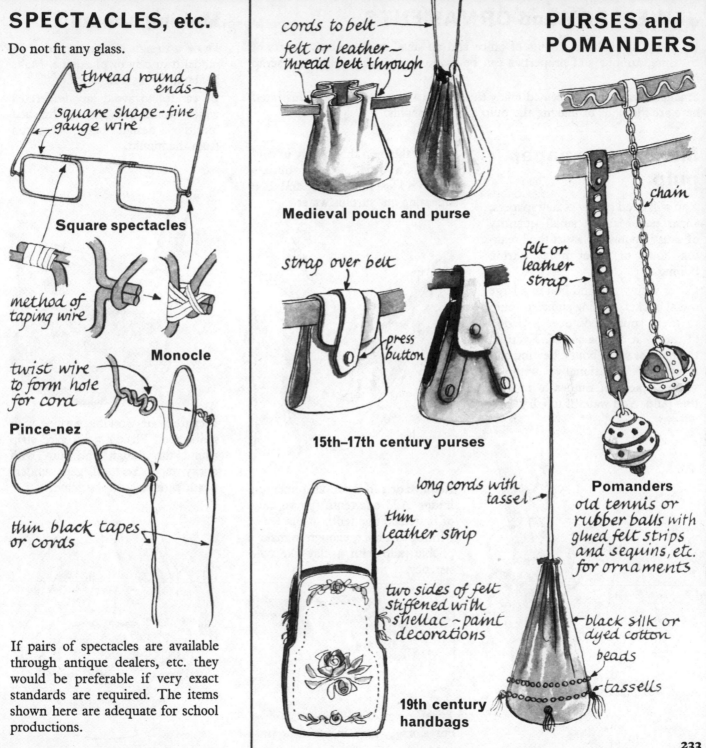

SPECTACLES, etc.

Do not fit any glass.

thread round ends

square shape-fine gauge wire

Square spectacles

method of taping wire

Monocle

twist wire to form hole for cord

Pince-nez

thin black tapes or cords

If pairs of spectacles are available through antique dealers, etc. they would be preferable if very exact standards are required. The items shown here are adequate for school productions.

cords to belt

felt or leather — thread belt through

Medieval pouch and purse

strap over belt

press button

15th–17th century purses

long cords with tassel

thin leather strip

two sides of felt stiffened with shellac ~ paint decorations

19th century handbags

PURSES and POMANDERS

chain

felt or leather strap

Pomanders

old tennis or rubber balls with glued felt strips and sequins, etc. for ornaments

black silk or dyed cotton beads

tassells

233

JEWELLERY and ORNAMENTS

Jewellery, medallions, chains of office and all small and decorative parts of costume, armour and properties can be made from plaster, pulp and scrap materials.

Smaller items can be repeated many times from a common mould. Illustrated here are methods of making the pulp and the moulds.

Making fine paper pulp

You will need plenty of newspapers, sugar paper and a small quantity of caustic potash to assist the breaking down of paper fibres during boiling.

Cover with water and boil in a large metal bucket, making sufficient pulp to meet your needs over a period of time – it can be stored. Keep on the boil for some hours, beating and thumping occasionally with a squared piece of timber to make a fine pulp. Add water if too dry.

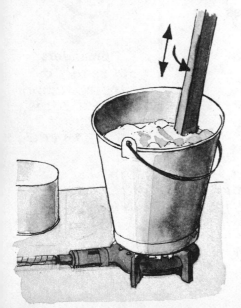

Cleanse the pulp thoroughly in cold water – a wide piece of butter-muslin is ideal for draining and then squeezing out surplus water.

Remove or rub down all remaining lumps. Add one tenth (by volume) of paste and one tenth of plaster or whiting as a filler, enough to make a pliable pulp with a clay-like consistency.

For storage, pack in air-tight tins.

Making a mould

Draw a design on paper and then model it in clay or plasticine. Make it about 10–15 mm thick.

Be careful to avoid any undercuts which would prevent the finished 'positive' design being removed from the mould.

Prepare your working surface with newspaper. Place a 3 cm card strip round the design and join with sticky tape. Seal off gaps underneath with clay or plasticine.

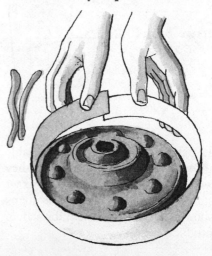

Sift plaster through the fingers into a cup or small bowl about a third full of water. Continue until the plaster appears just above the surface of the water. Stir gently with the fingers until all lumps and air bubbles have been removed.

When the plaster has set turn the mould over and carefully prise out the original model, taking care not to damage the plaster.

Using the prepared paper pulp, press a sufficient quantity into the greased mould. Flatten off with a straight-edge, pulled across at an angle.

Pour the prepared plaster inside the card circle until it reaches the top edge. Any leftover plaster should be used immediately on other prepared moulds.

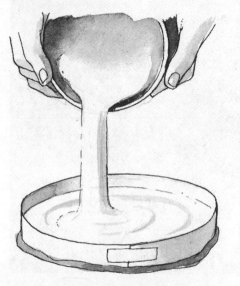

Thoroughly clean out all traces of clay or plasticine. Use a stiff brush (hog bristle will do) to work oil or Vaseline into all parts of the 'negative' mould. It is usual to leave the plaster for a few days to dry out, but it can be used immediately if time is pressing.

Leave for some hours before removing the 'positive' design from the mould. If it sticks, prise gently around the edges – check that no undercuts are preventing the pulp cast from coming clear.

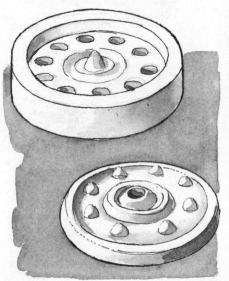

Using moulds

Should a large number of ornaments be needed, multiple moulds can be prepared. Sets of moulds of approximately the same size and design can be placed closely together inside the card frame before pouring in the plaster. The illustrations on this page show examples – and the photograph on the facing page shows a chain made up of the 'positive' shapes from these moulds.

Right: Two illustrations showing the ornaments used on armour and helmets. The small squares over the shoulder piece and the oblongs on the lower edge were pressed out of the moulds below.

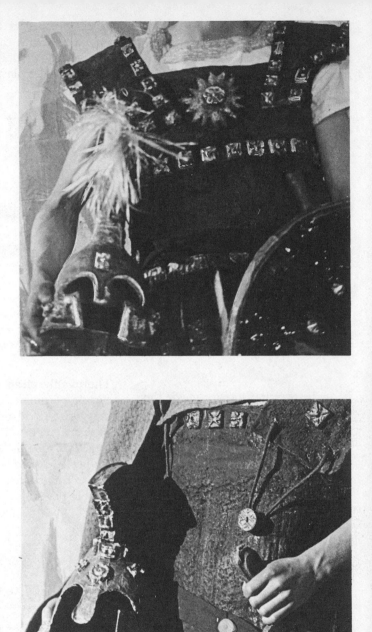

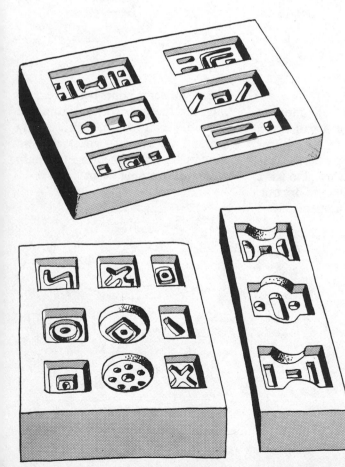

Bases and supports for jewellery

Large items of jewellery such as collars or heavy medallions are best built up on a plywood, hardboard or felt base. If in felt, stiffen first with shellac or P.V.A. medium.

Collars

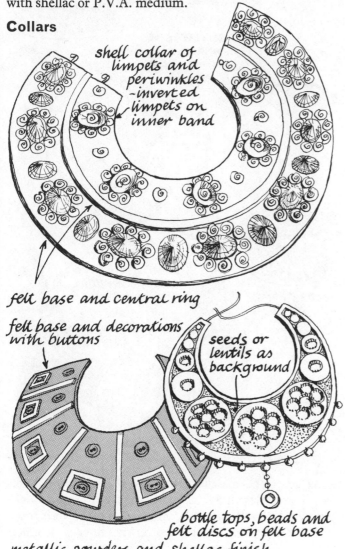

shell collar of limpets and periwinkles – inverted limpets on inner band

felt base and central ring

felt base and decorations with buttons

seeds or lentils as background

bottle tops, beads and felt discs on felt base

metallic powders and shellac finish

Collars require large bold designs. Experiment with all kinds of scrap materials: metal scrap, wire, felt, cord, pieces of plastic, etc. All can be securely fixed with P.V.A. adhesive .

Above: chain of office or chain with pendant. Each piece is firmly glued to a narrow finger bandage or, if preferred, to a thin, strong tape. A staple can be carefully driven into the back of each piece through the fabric.

Pendants on a golden or silver chain. The chain can be built around a medium-gauge wire with small beads, etc. threaded on to the wire and glued in position – spaced out as required.

alternative pendants for bead necklace →

card base string

card cutouts and beads

suspender clips and hair grips

beads →

237

Various kinds of jewellery

Necklaces

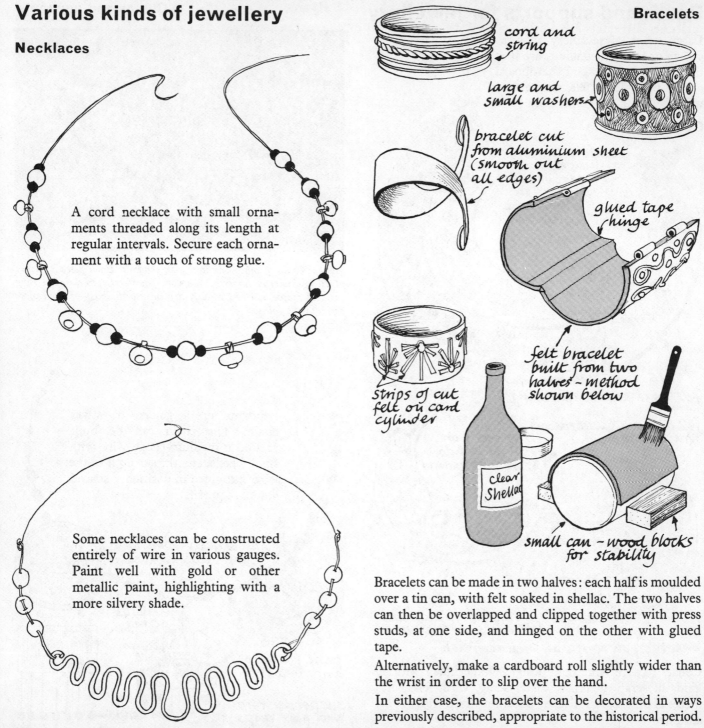

A cord necklace with small ornaments threaded along its length at regular intervals. Secure each ornament with a touch of strong glue.

Some necklaces can be constructed entirely of wire in various gauges. Paint well with gold or other metallic paint, highlighting with a more silvery shade.

cord and string

large and small washers

bracelet cut from aluminium sheet (smooth out all edges)

glued tape hinge

felt bracelet built from two halves - method shown below

strips of cut felt on card cylinder

Clear Shellac

small can - wood blocks for stability

Bracelets can be made in two halves: each half is moulded over a tin can, with felt soaked in shellac. The two halves can then be overlapped and clipped together with press studs, at one side, and hinged on the other with glued tape.

Alternatively, make a cardboard roll slightly wider than the wrist in order to slip over the hand.

In either case, the bracelets can be decorated in ways previously described, appropriate to the historical period.

238

Brooches

Brooches can either be pressed out of moulds or built up from wire (soldered or tied), seeds or cereals.

Another method: use a small base and glue to it small beads, etc. surrounded by metal strips in a sun-ray effect.

seeds and cereals

Girdles, with buckles, clasp, etc.

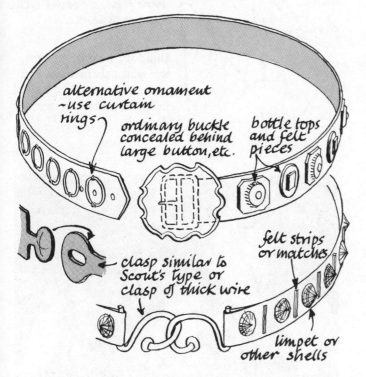

alternative ornament ~ use curtain rings

ordinary buckle concealed behind large button, etc.

bottle tops and felt pieces

clasp similar to Scout's type or clasp of thick wire

felt strips or matches

limpet or other shells

Use an existing belt and mount various ornaments along the entire length, leaving gaps if desired. Secure with P.V.A. medium – leave to dry thoroughly.

Buttons

These can be made as brooches, but with holes for threading. Or they can be existing large buttons decorated with added scraps.

macaroni glued to card base

washers

thick cards

card bases

string patterns

Rings and earrings

Make rings by twisting strands of medium-gauge wire round the finger – tie into knot and build up with pulp. Cheap paste jewellery can also be used.

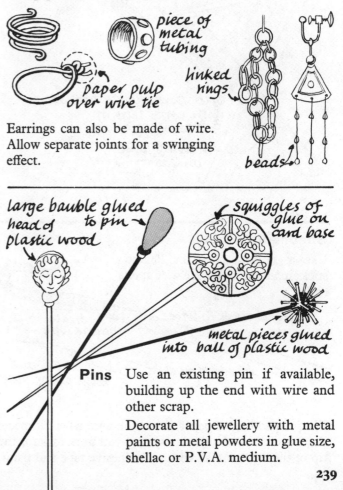

piece of metal tubing

paper pulp over wire tie

linked rings

Earrings can also be made of wire. Allow separate joints for a swinging effect.

beads

large bauble glued to pin

head of plastic wood

squiggles of glue on card base

metal pieces glued into ball of plastic wood

Pins Use an existing pin if available, building up the end with wire and other scrap.

Decorate all jewellery with metal paints or metal powders in glue size, shellac or P.V.A. medium.

ITEMS FOR A SCHOOL NATIVITY PLAY

Nativity plays require little or no scenery – perhaps a hint at a stable or, preferably, a cave-like dwelling. The properties required are described below.

A simple crib

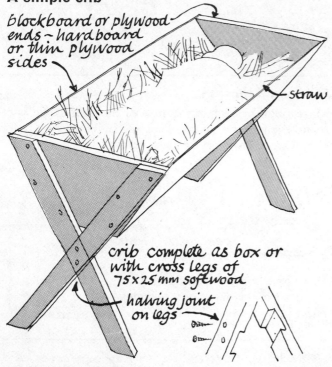

blockboard or plywood ends – hardboard or thin plywood sides

straw

crib complete as box or with cross legs of 75 x 25 mm softwood

halving joint on legs

Shepherds' crooks

Use a 25 mm dowel or bamboo stick; insert heavy-gauge wire at one end.

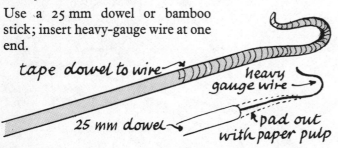

tape dowel to wire

heavy gauge wire

25 mm dowel

pad out with paper pulp

Wrap a padding of paper round the wire where it meets the dowel or bamboo, narrowing as you work towards the tip of the wire. Finish with self-adhesive tape and paint.

Angels' wings

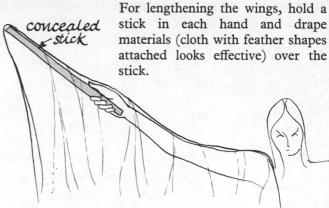

concealed stick

For lengthening the wings, hold a stick in each hand and drape materials (cloth with feather shapes attached looks effective) over the stick.

More traditional wings: use a wire frame attached to straps to tie across the chest.

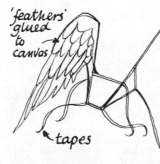

'feathers' glued to canvas

wire frame – cover with light canvas, etc.

tapes

Build up wire frames for the wings themselves and cover with fabric stretched tightly. Attach 'feathers' if desired.

Primary school Nativity Play: note the use of simple sheeting for angels at the sides.

The gifts

Look at pages 160–163 for examples of various pots and page 168 for boxes. The important thing is to aim at variety of shape, the decoration can be quite simple.

Here are shown a sphere, an oblong box and a chalice-like shape. Many other possibilities can be tried – but differences in shape should be obvious from a distance.

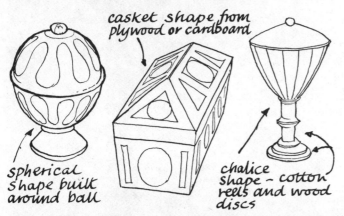

casket shape from plywood or cardboard

spherical shape built around ball

chalice shape – cotton reels and wood discs

Crowns

See pages 226–229 for method of construction.

Crowns càn be elaborate or very simple but variety of shape is important as it is for the gifts. Here are three basic shapes:

cone and ring of stiff card

velvet inside

decorative cake band on card

A star

Make a wire frame, stretch tissue paper over it and place a lamp behind; alternatively, cover wire or card with silver foil.

paper star - score and fold

wire frame - tissue covered lamp and battery behind

ITEMS FOR A SCHOOL PASSION PLAY

Passion plays can be most effective if performed in the open, weather permitting. It is rewarding to work with large crowd movements in a natural environment.

The essential items for a Passion play are: Three crosses; Pilate's throne; Roman arms and armour; and small props – a crown of thorns, a bowl for washing and some stage blood. A stretcher will be useful if Christ is to be carried away.

A simple form of Roman armour is shown below:

1 Cut four lengths of card 5 cm wide, long enough to encircle the waist.

2 Cut eight lengths of card 40 cm long for each soldier's shoulder armour.

pierce holes for joining bands

3 Cover each card strip with thin foil, glueing it on with P.V.A. medium and folding the surplus foil to the back of each strip – one side only need be smooth.

fold over and glue metal foil

4 Each set of shoulder strips can be curved together and stapled, then sewn to the garment.

The waistband is secured at the front by lacing or press studs.

any convenient fasteners, press studs, etc...

secure with paper fasteners or tapes

Helmets and body armour are shown on pages 202–203, arms on page 213. (continued on next page)

Items for a passion play (continued)

The crosses

Ensure that they are strong in structure to carry the weight of actors. Cut lengths of timber and assemble as shown. Allow extra length for the depth of the hole. The Christus figure should be raised into position from the ground so it is important to place the cross base conveniently close to the hole. Ropes can effectively be used to pull the cross into a vertical positon. A wedge can be inserted at the rear of the cross to prevent movement.

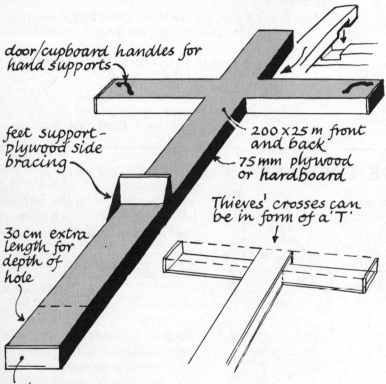

door/cupboard handles for hand supports

feet support – plywood side bracing

200 × 25 m front and back

75 mm plywood or hardboard

Thieves' crosses can be in form of a 'T'

30 cm extra length for depth of hole

ends – 200 × 75 mm softwood or thick plywood

Throne

A throne suitable for a Passion play is shown on page 150.

A crown of thorns

Use either medium gauge wire or light ash twigs as a base – intertwine suitable twigs with this base.

Christus figure on Cross – rehearsal for an outdoor Passion play.

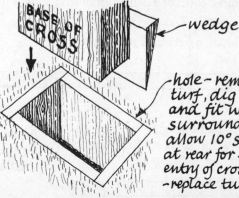

BASE OF CROSS

wedge

hole – remove turf, dig hole and fit wood surround – allow 10° slope at rear for easy entry of cross – replace turf.

242

Make-up and masks 10

MATERIALS · CHARACTER CREATION · AGEING
· RACIAL TYPES · MASKS

Basic requirements 244
Straight make-up for male and female . . . 246
The eyes and eyebrows 248
The mouth 249
The nose 250
The hand 250
The body 251
Lengthening and broadening the face . . . 251
Creating character 252
Ageing 253
Racial types 255
Hair 258
Other beings (fairies, etc.) 260
Artificial features (scars, etc.) 263
Masks 264

BASIC REQUIREMENTS

Lighting in the dressing room

A large mirror set on a wide bench or table is ideal for making-up. Try to avoid any direct glare from naked lamps. Position them so that they reflect light from the mirror. Neon strip lighting is very effective, or adjustable desk lamps, as shown in the illustration.

Make-up materials

The basis for a simple make-up kit is as follows:

1 A strong box of wood or metal (enamelled metal boxes are obtainable from suppliers) with several compartments and a lift-out tray.

2 Greasepaint: available in stick and tube form, with liners for detail work (the colour range is shown on the opposite page).

3 Liquid make-up for limbs and body. The colours are numbered to match the greasepaint colours.

4 Blending powders, used for completing facial make-up and for blending in hair for ageing. They are available in five shades.

5 Crepe hair and false eyelashes, eyebrow pencil and sable brush. Always use best-quality brushes.

6 Spirit gum for fixing crepe hair for moustaches and beards, and for fixing gauze when padding out the face.

7 Tooth enamel for blocking out teeth.

8 Putty for altering the shape of the nose or for deforming the face.

9 Stage blood, available in liquid or cake form.

10 Creams for foundation and for removal of make-up.

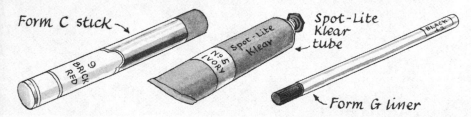

Basic greasepaint forms: stick, tube and liner

Basic list of greasepaint colours:

Colour	Form C Stick	Spot-Lite Klear Tube	Form G Liner
Light Tan	$3\frac{1}{2}$	$3\frac{1}{2}$	—
Brownish Tan	$4\frac{1}{2}$	$4\frac{1}{2}$	—
Ivory	5	5	—
Sallow Pink	6	—	—
Light Olive	$6\frac{1}{2}$	$6\frac{1}{2}$	—
Coffee Brown	7	7	—
Golden Tan	8	8	—
Brick Red	9	9	—
Black	12	12	42
Deep Brown	16	—	—
White	20	20	20
Lit K (5 and 9)	50	50	—
Chrome Yellow	59	—	—
Gold	—	57	—
Silver	—	58	—
Crimson Lake	—	—	25
Dark Brown	—	—	28
Light Grey	—	—	31
Dark Grey	—	—	32
Carmine 1	—	—	320
Carmine 2	—	—	321
Carmine 3	—	—	322
Light Blue	—	—	326L
Dark Blue	—	—	326D
Green 3	—	—	336
Dark Mauve	—	—	337D

Beginners' kit is listed in heavy type. The make-up described here is from Leichner of London. For equivalent shades in other brands of make-up, refer to chart on pages 281–82.

Some modifications to skin tone are necessary on the stage because of the effect of stage lighting. The intensity of the lights tends to bleach out the natural colouring of the face, making the flesh look very pale. This bleaching effect is rectified by selecting a foundation that restores the colour.

As the arrangement of lights about the stage tends to neutralise natural shadow under brow, chin and cheek, these features need strengthening with appropriate shadow areas and highlighting. The basic make-up will restore the natural structure of the face which would otherwise look flat and two-dimensional under the lights.

Spread greasepaint Nos. 5 and 9 in stripes as shown, blending the colours with finger-tips

Applying the basic foundation

Make-up is an art. Practise and experiment on yourself or others to achieve the effects you desire. You do not want a mask but a make-up that reflects and searches out the character being played.

Think first of the character and then look at the face, considering the structure, cheekbones, shape of nose, brow, jawline – then decide how to use the features to create visually the part to be acted.

STRAIGHT MAKE-UP FOR MALE AND FEMALE

Straight make-up is the term used to describe the simple, basic make-up for male and female. Before applying any make-up see that the skin is free from greasiness.

1 Using the finger-tips, rub in a little of the foundation cream well into the face until the whole surface has a smooth even look. Wipe off any surplus with a sponge or facial tissues.

2 Apply foundation colour (numbers given in separate illustrations for male and female). Blend carefully together until the required shade is obtained. Cover the whole face – the forehead up to the hairline, under the nose and under the chin are areas often neglected.

3 Apply colour to the cheeks as shown in both illustrations – avoid leaving a hard edge to the colour.

4 Next concentrate on the eyelids. Blue, green or brown, or any combination, should be used to match the eye colouring. Fade the lid colours at the sides and do not take up to the eyebrow. The space between eyebrow and top of lid should be of the same colour as the foundation, with a slight shading of No. 9 at the centre.

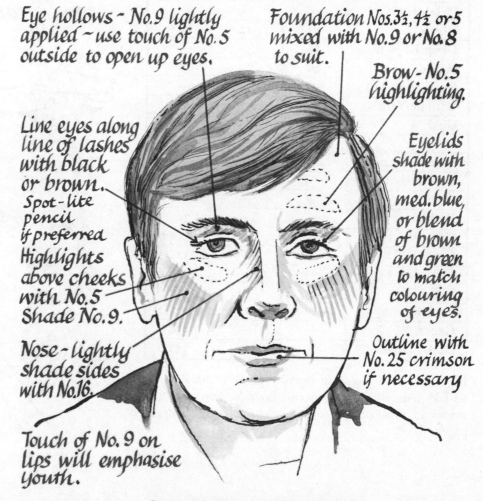

Eye hollows - No.9 lightly applied - use touch of No.5 outside to open up eyes.

Foundation Nos. 3½, 4½ or 5 mixed with No.9 or No.8 to suit.

Brow - No.5 highlighting.

Line eyes along line of lashes with black or brown. Spot-lite pencil if preferred Highlights above cheeks with No.5 Shade No.9.

Eyelids shade with brown, med. blue, or blend of brown and green to match colouring of eyes.

Nose - lightly shade sides with No.16.

Outline with No.25 crimson if necessary

Touch of No.9 on lips will emphasise youth.

Straight make-up: young man

246

5 Shade both sides of the nose lightly with No. 16, blending gently into foundation colour towards the cheeks. Also shade below cheekbone, blending, downwards. Women should lightly colour cheeks with Carmine or rouge before shading.

6 Apply appropriate lip colour with Carmine 1, 2 or 3.

7 Use blending powder lightly over the whole face, selecting a shade to match the foundation colour. This powdering will stabilise the greasepaint before adding lines and highlights. Steady, well-defined lines will always be preferable to casual smears and will produce a clear-looking make-up.

8 Thin lines are now applied with a brush along the line of the lashes. These can be black or brown and can be extended slightly at the outer end to enlarge the eye.

9 Strengthen the eyebrows with a black or brown liner.

10 Highlight gently above the cheekbone, brow and bridge of nose – the highlighting is more important to male make-up.

11 Add a small red spot in the corner of the eye by the tearduct – also behind each nostril in female make-up.

12 In female make-up apply mascara carefully to the upper lashes.

13 Complete the make-up by a good powdering to fix all colours.

Eyebrows—strengthen with No. 16 under, and line with black or brown

Foundation—Nos. 5 and 9 or 2 and 2½ for pale tints

Lower lash line with No. 16 or Spot-lite pencil

Eyehollow—light touch of No. 9

Eyeshadow—to match eye—dark blue, black or brown along lashes

Nose—shade sides with No. 16

Lips—Carmine 1, 2 or 3, to suit colouring

No. 9 on cheekbones fading to Carmine 1

Foundation colours must be selected to suit type of character and one's own skin colouring

Straight make-up: young woman

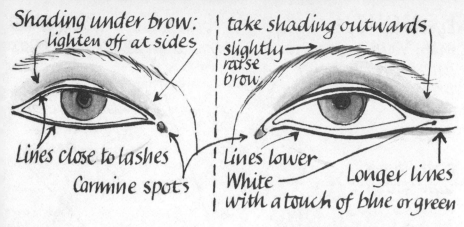

Shading under brow: lighten off at sides

take shading outwards | slightly raise brow

Lines close to lashes

Carmine spots

Lines lower

White with a touch of blue or green

Longer lines

Normal eye make-up

'Enlarged eye' make-up

THE EYES AND EYEBROWS

As the eyes reflect the thoughts of a character, it is most important that they should be clearly seen at a distance.

1 Enhance and strengthen the eyes by a careful selection of colour for the eyelid – use a colour, or combination of colours, that will match or bring out the colour of the eye. Use liquid mascara on the top lashes.

2 To enlarge the eyes, the colour must be spread further out over the lids. Extend the lines along the lashes outward and slightly upward, placing the line beneath the lower lashes rather lower than in straight make-up. A touch of White No. 20 mixed with a minute spot of Green I or Light Blue and placed between the lines at the outer end will help to highlight and enlarge the eye. Arch the eyebrow a little if desired. Apply mascara, allow to dry and apply a second coat.

3 The eyebrows can considerably change the shape of the face and therefore the character.

If a major alteration is considered, it is possible to blank out the existing brows and to make new ones. Dip a piece of hard soap in water and rub across the brows, starting from the nose. This fixes the hair firmly to the skin and foundation colours can be applied over the brows.

The new eyebrow lines are then painted in with a brush or liner.

Above: illustration shows the effect of eye make-up for a young girl – beauty spots of No. 16.

For a thick, bushy effect crepe hair can be fixed with spirit gum. A change can also be achieved by brushing the natural eyebrow from the outer end inwards to give a bushier look – then apply black or brown colour for younger faces or a light grey for a more aged look.

4 To sink the eye into its socket, use Lake No. 25 and/or No. 16 above the eyelid colour, blending upward and outward to the eyebrow.

If the reverse effect is required, a deepset eye can be 'brought forward' by using No. 5 above the eyelid colour.

5 To age the eyes, use more subdued colours on the lid. Grey the eyebrows with talcum powder or by applying No. 5 and/or No. 20 lightly. Drop the line under the lower lid and shadow above the line with No. 16, lightly applied. Take care over the placing of wrinkles, hollows and 'crowsfeet' in the eye area – screwing up the face in a grimace will often reveal such lines. Use thin lines at the edges of the eyes.

THE MOUTH

The most mobile part of the face is the mouth area stretching from the nose to the chin, involving the lips and surrounding muscle area.

The colour, shape and set of the mouth suggest the temperament and mood of a character. It is very important that the make-up of the mouth does not detract from the eyes – this often happens because the lips are made too red, so that they stand out obtrusively.

Before applying any colour, rub the lips with tissues to remove any grease. Then apply the colour with a liner, brush or finger-tip. Bite on a tissue to remove surplus colour and then powder to set and to remove the shine. Women should use Carmine 1, 2 or 3, men No. 9 lightly applied, possibly with a little Carmine 3 mixed in. Never use the brighter reds for men. Lake No. 25 can be lightly applied to give an effect of age.

Changing the shape

1 To make the lips fuller, over-paint the shape with the appropriate Carmine and then highlight with a very thin line of white No. 20 or No. 5 to strengthen the new shape. (See illustration below.)

2 To make the mouth appear thin and drawn, blot out the natural shape of the lips with foundation colour. Paint the new outline inside the lips with No. 16. Fill in new shape with appropriate lip colour for the character.

3 To widen the mouth, carry the lip colour to the outer corners and then extend the outline from the corners of the mouth outwards.

4 A twisted mouth can be achieved by redrawing the shape, lowering slightly on one side and raising on the other. A slight variation in colour from side to side will help to distort the shape further.

5 To age the mouth, the lips should become thinner and lose much of their colour – use a mixture of Lake No. 25 and Carmine 3. Draw fine vertical lines in Lake just below the line of the lips to give the puckered effect. Extend the corner lines further down and mark in lines from nose to mouth. Shade and highlight all lines.

6 Teeth can be made to look brighter by use of tooth enamel or dulled by rubbing No. 16 over dry teeth. Black tooth enamel can be used for blotting out teeth or for giving them a chipped look (see illustration on page 262).

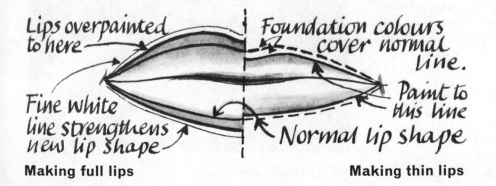

Lips overpainted to here

Fine white line strengthens new lip shape

Making full lips

Foundation colours cover normal line.

Paint to this line

Normal lip shape

Making thin lips

249

THE NOSE

1 Narrow the nose by shading with No. 16 on the sides, bringing the shadows closer together near the ridge.

2 Widen the nose by shading with No. 7, taking the shadows away from each side of the ridge. Slightly raise the tip of the nose with a shadow under and lighten nostrils with a touch of No. 5.

3 Lengthen the nose by painting the tip with No. 5, taking the shadow further under the tip. Highlight the bridge of the nose with a thin line of No. 5.

4 Shorten the nose by painting the tip wider with No. 16.

5 A snub nose needs a lighter tip area.

6 To make more aquiline, the highlight on the ridge must be widened at the centre and faded off gradually towards the tip.

7 To change the profile outline, the only method is to use nose putty. It is obtained in stick form and is softened by working between damp fingers to prevent sticking. Only a small amount is needed to make a drastic change to the nose shape, so use it sparingly. A touch of spirit gum will help the putty to adhere.

When applied, model to the required shape and view from all angles. Allow to set firm and apply foundation over it to blend with the face colour.

Nose paste is also useful for warts and other deformities (see page 260). It can be used again if carefully removed and stored.

8 A twisted nose can be effected in a similar way to the twisted mouth – when shading, take the lines down the ridge slightly askew and move the shadow under the tip to one side.

Remember always to paint the lines between nostrils and cheeks to define the shape of the nose. These lines can vary their position and change the appearance of the character as desired.

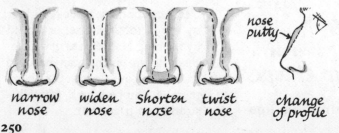

narrow nose | widen nose | shorten nose | twist nose | change of profile

THE HAND

The hand of a player should always reflect the age of the character he is playing. Be sure that the make-up of the face, if aged, is truly echoed in the lines and colour of the hands. Follow the drawing and the photograph below:

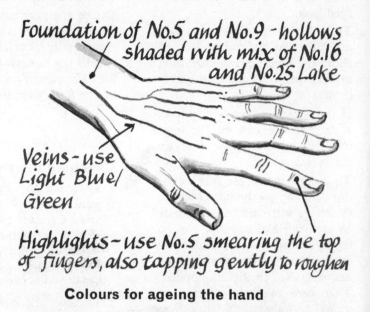

Foundation of No.5 and No.9 – hollows shaded with mix of No.16 and No.25 Lake

Veins – use Light Blue/Green

Highlights – use No.5 smearing the top of fingers, also tapping gently to roughen

Colours for ageing the hand

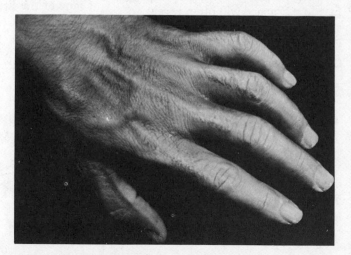

The hand under stage lighting.

250

THE BODY

The body must always fit in with the character being played. Body make-up, in the form of a liquid in varying shades, is used to change the colour of any exposed skin. It is unnecessary to powder after application and it can be easily washed off with soap and water. Detailed make-up is rarely required. An emaciated look can be given by a light colour followed by a darker shading along muscle and bone structures. Ribs need clear definition. The neck needs more care: the greasepaint should be applied to match the face.

THE FACE: Lengthening and broadening

It is important to experiment with shadow and highlight so that the contours of the face can be brought out and the basic shape appear to alter.

Below are two illustrations showing the main points for lengthening or broadening the face in order to express more fully the character to be portrayed by the actor.

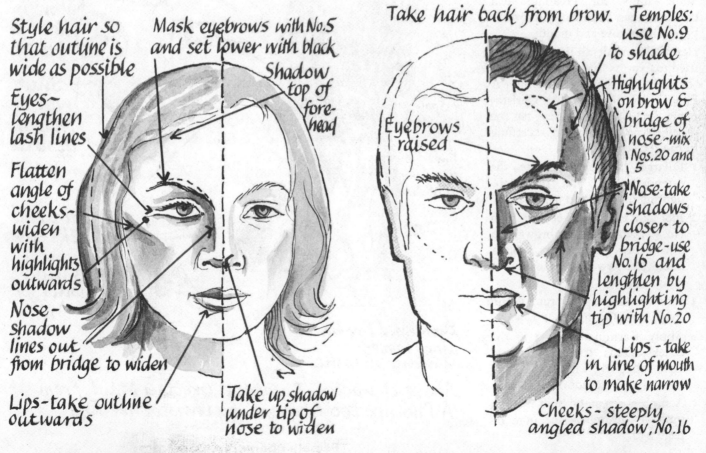

Style hair so that outline is wide as possible

Eyes—lengthen lash lines

Flatten angle of cheeks—widen with highlights outwards

Nose—shadow lines out from bridge to widen

Lips—take outline outwards

Mask eyebrows with No.5 and set lower with black

Shadow top of forehead

Take up shadow under tip of nose to widen

Method of broadening the face

Take hair back from brow.

Temples: use No.9 to shade

Highlights on brow & bridge of nose—mix Nos.20 and 5

Eyebrows raised

Nose—take shadows closer to bridge—use No.16 and lengthen by highlighting tip with No.20

Lips—take in line of mouth to make narrow

Cheeks—steeply angled shadow, No.16

Method of lengthening the face

251

CREATING CHARACTER

In creating a character with make-up, we attempt to reflect the basic nature and peculiarity of an individual through the facial and bodily structure.

Sir Andrew Aguecheek ('Twelfth Night') is obviously a lanky fellow with thin features and a long nose. Falstaff, by contrast, is obese, ruddy of complexion and very well padded. Some hints for creating such characters can be found on previous pages about nose and mouth.

Here follow in detail the techniques used to express the spirit of comedy shown in the character of Doto ('A Phoenix too Frequent' by Christopher Fry). The features can be modified or exaggerated according to the type of comedy.

1 Enlarge the eyes – note the extended lines and the highlighting (see note on page 248).

2 Blot out existing eyebrows with No. 5, then paint new brows with a brown or, occasionally, a black liner. The new shape should give a higher arch.

3 Lips should be fully rounded in shape – use Carmine 2 or 3.

4 Apply Carmine 2 or 3 to the cheeks. This colouring should look obvious without looking 'clownish' – do not overdo.

5 A snub nose can be built up with putty if desired – see note on page 250.

Foundation - blend Nos. 3½ or 5 with 9

Hair - for this character styled to suit a Grecian Maid

Highlighting with No. 5

Eyebrow covered over with No. 5 ~ new brow above is lined in brown.

Snub nose of putty if desired

Eyes – blue eye shadow or Spot-lite pencil

Highlight use touch of No. 20

Mouth and cheeks - use Carmine 2 or 3 with touch of No 9

Eyes lined brown along lashes - mascara on lashes

Above character 'Doto', the Grecian Maid, from 'A Phoenix too Frequent' by Christopher Fry.

Female character—comedy

AGEING A YOUNG PERSON

It is difficult to age effectively. Inexperienced players often overpaint the wrinkle lines and greying effects. Always err on the side of understatement.

The illustration on this page shows how to make up a young person to look old.

All the lining must be done slowly and carefully, and with a steady hand. Lines should be drawn as thinly as possible. Fade off at the ends of lines, blending into the basic make-up – hard edges spoil the appearance.

Start by asking the player to wrinkle his face. This will reveal some of the natural creases. Apply the make-up within the natural lines.

Each individual produces different lines as he frowns, so search out those that suggest age lines for that particular person – especially around the eyes and mouth.

A sequence for creating age:

1 Apply the foundation colours No. 4½ (or 6) with No. 9 to suit.

2 Apply the shadow areas under brows, under eyes between lash line and lower lid, on the cheeks, along the sides of the nose and finally under the chin. Use Brown No. 16.

3 Brush eyebrows backwards with No. 5.

4 If you stipple very lightly on cheeks and just below the eyes with Lake No. 25, it gives the impression of broken veins. This can be a very effective addition to the make-up of an old character.

5 Powder lightly – see note 7 on page 247 concerning the application at this stage.

6 Draw lines of No. 16 on the forehead, close to eyelashes, under the eyes and at the outer corners. Also draw short vertical lines between the eyebrows, following natural frown lines.

7 Draw lines with No. 16 from above lobes of nose to corners of mouth, fading slightly towards the mouth. Then draw again from corners of mouth downwards, fading out towards the chin. Draw another line in the groove formed by the top of the chin meeting the underside of the mouth.

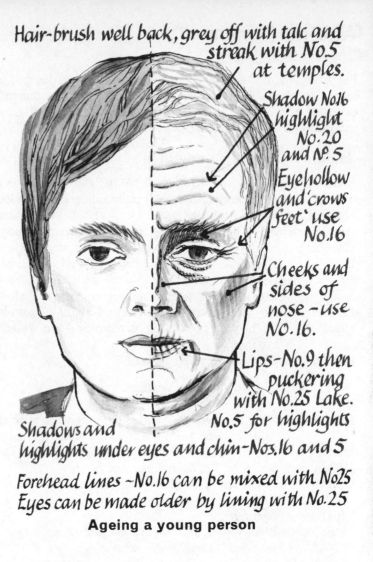

Hair-brush well back, grey off with talc and streak with No.5 at temples.

Shadow No.16 highlight No.20 and No.5

Eyehollow and 'crows feet' use No.16

Cheeks and sides of nose – use No.16.

Lips-No.9 then puckering with No.25 Lake. No.5 for highlights

Shadows and highlights under eyes and chin-Nos.16 and 5

Forehead lines ~No.16 can be mixed with No.25
Eyes can be made older by lining with No.25

Ageing a young person

8 Apply No. 9 to the lips, then draw fine vertical lines with Lake No. 25 to give the effect of puckering. Highlight between these lines with No. 5.

9 Powder the hair with talcum powder or a dry shampoo. Alternatively, streak the hair with No. 5 and No. 20 greasepaint.

10 Powder the whole face with facial powder.

(continued on next page)

Ageing (continued)

For adults the make-up problems of ageing are less demanding, but the same care should be taken in the application. Always remember not to overstate the lines of age. Use the same technique of frowning and grimacing to discover all the potential ageing lines.

Middle-aged and elderly man

Foundation: No. 3½ and a touch of No. 9; No. 4½ for a more rugged appearance. No. 6 for a more sallow elderly colouring.
Shading: No. 16 with No. 25. A touch of No. 32 for elderly look.
Highlights: No. 5 – add a touch of No. 20 for strong lighting.
Cheeks: No. 25 with No. 9. No. 25 only for an older man.
Eyes: No. 16 with No. 25 or No. 32 on eyelids. Brown Spot-lite pencil on lashes. Use No. 20 on eyebrows of older man and add more shadow on inner corners of eyehollow.
Lips: No. 9 for middle age. More of No. 25 for an older man.
Hair: Slight grey powdering at temples – add white powder as age increases.
Powder with Neutral Blending Powder.

Middle-aged and elderly woman

Foundation: No. 52 or No. 53 – some No. 2½ gives a pink appearance. Add No. 6 or No. 5 with No. 59 as age increases.
Shading: No. 16 mixed with No. 25. Touch of No. 31 for ageing.
Highlights: No. 5, or No. 2, and No. 20.
Cheeks: No. 9 and a touch of Carmine 1. Apply a light touch of Carmine 2 for an older woman.
Lips: Carmine 2 or 3.
Eyes: Blue, Green and Mauve eyeshadow or Brown and Grey required. More Mauve with No. 16 for an older woman. Colour lashes with Brown Spot-lite pencil. No. 32 for an an older woman, without mascara.
Hair: Light grey or white powder.
Powder with Rose or Neutral Blending Powder.

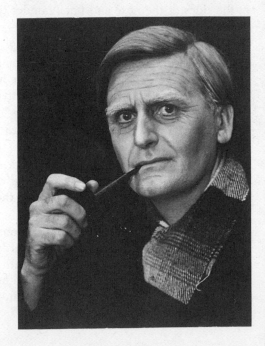

The two illustrations on the right show a man made up to look approximately 55 years old. One can only aim at a general age group – this make-up, with very small variations, could cover an age range of 45–60 years.

Top right: the make-up under the artificial light of a dressing room.
Bottom right: the same make-up under stage lighting.

RACIAL TYPE

To make up to look a member of another race, look for the accepted racial characteristics. Colour is the most important quality – followed by shape of feature, hair style and colour of hair.

Study carefully racial types as depicted in photographs and paintings. Ideally, meet and talk with someone of the race you wish to portray.

On this and the next two pages are some suggestions for creating a number of racial types not infrequently required in theatrical make-up.

Latin Basically the same as straight (European) make-up (pages 246–247) but with more olive complexion.
Foundation colour: No. 6½ with No. 8

Indian

The Northern Indian has fine clear-cut features with a fairly narrow nose. Southern Indian features are generally rounder and broader.

1 Use No. 8 foundation: mix with Nos. 7 or 16 for Southern type; with No. 5 for the paler Northern type.

2 Cheeks and lips: use Carmine 3 or No. 16 mixed with Lake No. 25. Men should use the combined colour.

3 Eyelids: use Dark Brown No. 28 for men, Green 3 or mauve for women. Paint eyebrows in Dark Brown or Black – they need a fairly straight appearance.

4 Line round the eyes with Black. Mascara the lashes.

5 Shade the sides of the nose in order to narrow its appearance. Use No. 16 mixed with Lake No. 25. Place a spot of Carmine at the side of each nostril.

6 Place caste mark at the centre of the forehead (Carmine 3).

7 Add highlights of No. 5 where necessary – but apply lightly.

8 Hair should be black and straight, tight against the skull.

9 Body: use liquid make-up on the body where required – Dark Brown for the Southern Indian and Island Tan for the Northern.

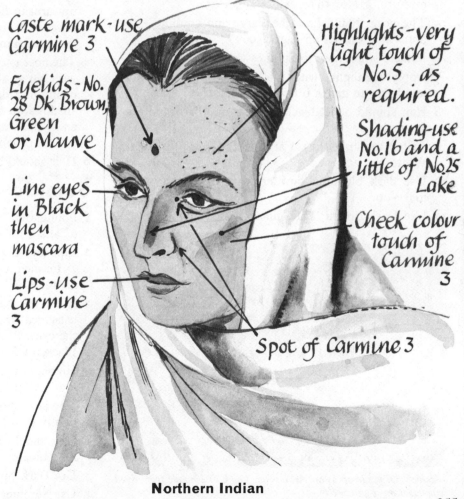

Foundation – use No. 8 mixed with 7 or 16 for darker Southern Indian skins. Add touch of No. 5 for paler skins

Caste mark – use Carmine 3

Eyelids – No. 28 Dk. Brown, Green or Mauve

Line eyes in Black then mascara

Lips – use Carmine 3

Highlights – very light touch of No. 5 as required.

Shading – use No. 16 and a little of No. 25 Lake

Cheek colour touch of Carmine 3

Spot of Carmine 3

Northern Indian

255

Racial type (continued)

Red Indian

1 Foundation either No. 8, No. 6½ mixed with No. 8 – or No. 4½ mixed with No. 8 or No. 9.

2 Cheeks and lips: use Lake No. 25. Mouth should be firm and broad.

3 Eyes: use No. 28 on the lids. Eyes are deepset, so shadow well. Paint eyebrows lightly with Dark Brown No. 28 and Black. Line around the eyes with Black. Blacken women's lashes with mascara.

4 Sharply cut features need angular shadows – use a mixture of No. 16 with Lake No. 25.

5 The nose should be rather large and aquiline – see notes about noses on page 250.

6 Make distinct nose to lip lines with No. 28.

7 Apply highlights with No. 5 – put in cheekbone highlights to give a broadening effect.

8 Hair should be jet black, straight and flat. Men may wear plaits.

9 Tribal markings: use Carmine 2, Green, Black and White No. 20.

10 Use dark blending powder to complete the facial make-up.

11 Use Dark Brown liquid make-up for the body.

Above: girl made up as an Arab type. The hair is made from dyed rug-wool on a gauze cap.

Semitic: Jew

1 Foundation No. 6, mixed with No. 5 for a paler appearance or with No. 8 for a darker. For women use No. 5 with 4½.

2 Cheeks: use Lake No. 25 and Light Grey. For an older man, use Grey No. 31 which helps to give the effect of a beard – add crepe hair if required.

3 Full lips: paint with Lake No. 25 and No. 9. For women, use Carmine 3.

4 Shade eyelids with Lake No. 25 and Grey No. 31 or Dark Brown No. 28. For women, use Green. Eyebrows should be black and arched. Lines round the eyes should be black, and taken slightly outwards and upwards to elongate the eye. Put Carmine dots slightly lower at the corners to aid the effect. Blacken women's lashes with mascara.

5 The nose is commonly arched. Highlight on the ridge with No. 5, starting from the summit of the ridge and continuing down to the underside of the tip. Place shadows on the sides and under the tip with No. 16 and No. 25 mixed. Nose putty can be used to produce a more pronounced arch.

6 Hair should be Dark Brown or Black.

Semitic: Arab

1 Foundation Nos. 4½ and 8, or No. 6½ for men; Nos. 6½ and 8 for women.

2 Lips and cheeks: Carmine 3 for women; Nos. 9 and 25 for men. Use Lake No. 25 to create high cheekbones for men.

3 Eyes: use No. 16 for men's lids, with black brows; use green on women's lids and black for the lines round the eyes. Brows should be black and slightly arched. Blacken women's lashes with mascara.

4 Highlight eyelids and cheeks lightly with a mixture of No. 5 with No. 20.

5 The nose should be long and narrow. Shade the sides lightly with No. 16 (mixed with No. 25 for men).

6 Hair should be black. Wigs can be made – or hired for women.

7 Use Dark Brown blending powder.

8 Use Summer Tan body liquid as required.

256

Negro

1 Foundation No. 8 with No. 16 or No. 12 added to make the degree of darkness required.

2 Cheekbones should be rather high – use Lake No. 25 for shadows and No. 5 for highlights.

3 The mouth should be large with thick lips overpainted as described on page 249. Outline lips with No. 5 as a highlight, filling in with No. 25 for men, Carmine 3 for women.

4 Eyes: use Dark Brown No. 28 or Black No. 12 (or Spot-lite pencil) on the eyelids. Shorten outer ends of brows and lightly join them in the middle with the 'same colours. Paint black lines around the eyelashes. Blacken women's lashes with mascara.

5 Nose: flatten by shading the ridge with No. 12 and No. 7 (according to the colour for the foundation). Broaden the nose by highlighting with No. 5 on each side, well away from the ridge, and on upper lip and nostrils. Use nose putty on each side of nostrils to enlarge them.

6 Hair: short, black, curly wig is essential for authentic shape and colour.

7 Use dark blending powder and body liquid.

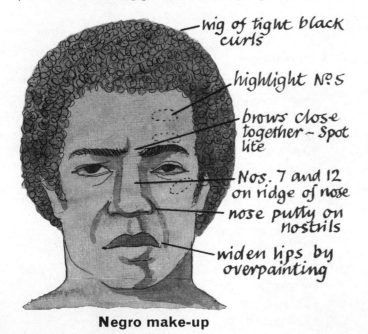

- wig of tight black curls
- highlight No 5
- brows close together ~ Spot lite
- Nos. 7 and 12 on ridge of nose
- nose putty on nostrils
- widen lips by overpainting

Negro make-up

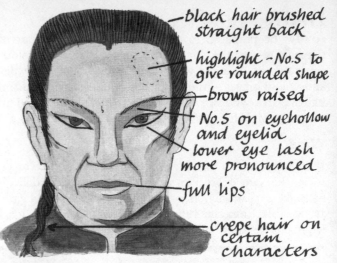

- black hair brushed straight back
- highlight ~ No.5 to give rounded shape
- brows raised
- No.5 on eyehollow and eyelid
- lower eye lash more pronounced
- full lips
- crepe hair on certain characters

Oriental
Oriental make-up

1 Foundation:
  Japanese – No. $6\frac{1}{2}$ and No. 8 with cheeks painted with No. 8 for men, Carmine 2 for women.
  Use foundation Nos. 20 with $3\frac{1}{2}$ for Geisha Girls.

  Chinese – No. $6\frac{1}{2}$ and No. 8 with a little No. 59 (Chrome Yellow).

2 Lips: use No. 9 with No. 25 for men, Carmine 2 or 3 for women (Cupid-bow shape for Geisha Girls).

3 Soap out eyebrows and cover with the foundation colour. Then paint in slanting eyebrows with black (Japanese brows bushier and not so upward-slanting). Draw black lines round the eyes, sloping downwards at inner corners and upwards at outer corners. Blacken women's eyelashes with mascara.

4 The nose should be fairly flat, particularly for the Japanese. Shade with No. 16 mixed with No. 25 on the lower sides of the nose in order to increase the width of the lower part.

5 Enlarge the cheekbones, shading underneath with Nos. 16 and 25. Highlight above with No. 5.

6 Hair:
  Chinese – black, oily and straight.
  Japanese – black, and flatter than the Chinese.

7 Use a pale blending powder.

8 Use liquid make-up on neck, limbs and body.

257

HAIR

Always be prepared to change the style and colour of the hair to suit the character being played. The colour can easily be changed with hair powder, talcum powder and colour rinses – the latter are readily available from hairdressers who are also likely to be very helpful in creating a style for a particular character.

Wigs

If it is possible to avoid wearing wigs, it is better to do so as they are expensive to rent and extremely difficult to make realistically. If one is necessary, order as early as possible from the supplier (see page 276) or a local wigmaker to allow plenty of time for preparation. (The wigmaker will provide a measurement form on which to note details of correct measurements, character, period and style). Take great care of any properly made wig, storing carefully after each performance stuffed with tissue paper.

Wigs are made of natural hair or synthetic fibres fixed to a lace scalp shape. When fitting a wig to the head, hide the edges by covering with No. 6 greasepaint and then blend in with a light powdering. *Then* apply foundation make-up in the usual way.

Cheap modern wigs are very suitable for converting boys into girls. Made of synthetic fibres mounted on nets, they slip comfortably over the head – with elastic tapes to grip snugly at the sides.

Moustaches and Beards

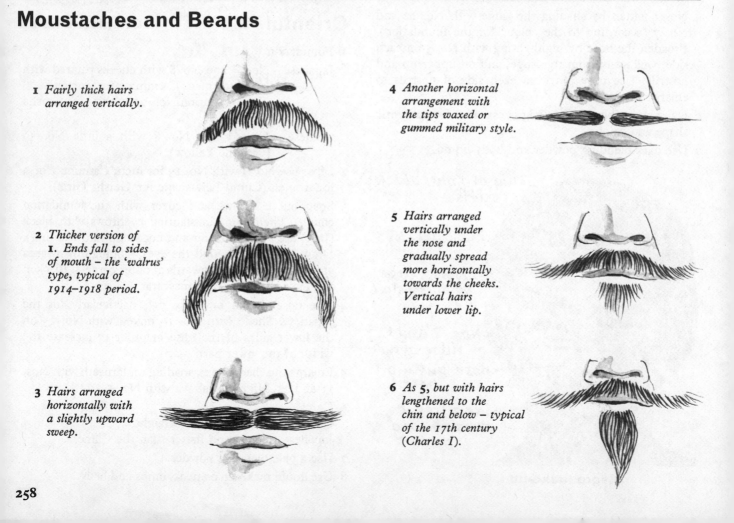

1 *Fairly thick hairs arranged vertically.*

2 *Thicker version of 1. Ends fall to sides of mouth – the 'walrus' type, typical of 1914–1918 period.*

3 *Hairs arranged horizontally with a slightly upward sweep.*

4 *Another horizontal arrangement with the tips waxed or gummed military style.*

5 *Hairs arranged vertically under the nose and gradually spread more horizontally towards the cheeks. Vertical hairs under lower lip.*

6 *As 5, but with hairs lengthened to the chin and below – typical of the 17th century (Charles I).*

Stage 1 - fix hair under the chin.

Stage 2 - add to front of chin and jaw line

Stage 3 - jaw, to lower lip and moustache if required

Method of making a beard

Beards and other surface hair can be mounted on lace in the same way as wigs. For most purposes, however, crepe hair is used and is secured to the face with spirit gum. Crepe hair is available in a wide variety of shades and is supplied in plaited form:

← skein   steam

Pull a length from the skein and stretch tightly over the steam from a kettle. Gently open out crepe by rolling between fingers. Press beneath a weighted book or iron out.

The crepe is fixed to the gummed area of the face in the direction required – see the various illustrations.

Crepe hair can be removed from the face with alcohol, spirit gum remover, or acetone.

Moustaches are comparatively simple to apply – the hair is held against the gummed area until secure and pressed firmly on with a damp cloth. Trim with scissors if necessary.

Beards are more difficult and have to be built up carefully. Study the illustrations above:

1 Start under the chin and work outwards along the jawline.

2 Place a second piece on the front of the chin under the lower lip and take to the sides above the previous application. (It would be necessary to trim both stages 1 and 2 if the beard were required for the chin only.)

3 For a full beard, continue from 2, applying more hair under the lower lip and thickening the 'sideboards' running up the sides of the face.

4 If a moustache is required in addition, follow suggestions on the opposite page and blend in with the beard.

5 Blend into face make-up with a few brown or black pinhead dots or a grey liner – in order to graduate the hair tones into the skin.

259

OTHER BEINGS

Creating a style of make-up for a sub- or non-human character depends very much on the imagination of the actor, director and make-up artist. There is no standard make-up. Remember to experiment as much as possible.

Fairies and sprites

In general terms, fairies need a paler foundation than that normally used for human beings.

Lines should be drawn on the face from the centres of expression: mouth, eyes and nostril area of the nose. Use greens, blues, blacks and metallic colours. Metallic sprays and powders can be used over a well-greased face or body. Remember to keep the eyes shut and the hair protected. Gold No. 57 and Silver No. 58 Spot-lite tubes are useful.

Glitter can be very effective, especially in combination with the metallic colours.

The illustration below gives one example of 'fairy' make-up.

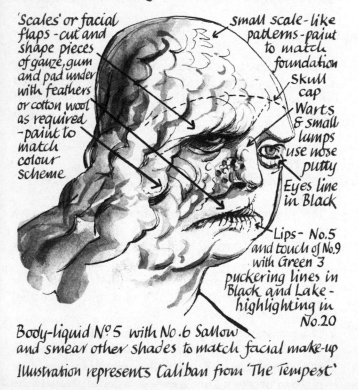

Foundation~ use No.5 with touch of No.9 then either Green 3, No.31 Lt. Grey or Chrome Yellow to suit character

'Scales' or facial flaps - cut and shape pieces of gauze, gum and pad under with feathers or cotton wool as required - paint to match colour scheme

small scale-like patterns - paint to match foundation

Skull cap

Warts & small lumps use nose putty

Eyes line in Black

Lips - No.5 and touch of No.9 with Green 3 puckering lines in Black and Lake - highlighting in No.20

Body - liquid Nº 5 with No.6 Sallow and smear other shades to match facial make-up

Illustration represents Caliban from 'The Tempest'

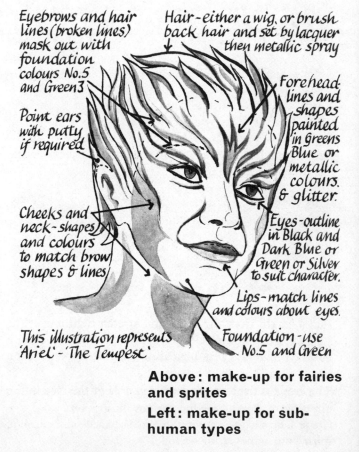

Eyebrows and hair lines (broken lines) mask out with foundation colours No.5 and Green 3

Hair - either a wig, or brush back hair and set by lacquer then metallic spray

Forehead lines and shapes painted in Greens Blue or metallic colours. & glitter.

Point ears with putty if required

Cheeks and neck - shapes and colours to match brow shapes & lines

Eyes - outline in Black and Dark Blue or Green or Silver to suit character.

Lips - match lines and colours about eyes

This illustration represents 'Ariel' - 'The Tempest'

Foundation - use No.5 and Green

Above: make-up for fairies and sprites

Left: make-up for sub-human types

Sub-humans

The lower illustration on the opposite page shows a possible make-up for Caliban, in 'The Tempest' by Shakespeare. Note the use of nose putty and gauze to build up grotesque effects. Wigs can also be made of unusual materials.

Ghosts

Ghosts need an ethereal and transparent look. No. 5 makes a useful foundation, mixed with a little green. No lip make-up is required. It is important to have cold lighting for ghosts: if behind a transparent gauze the ethereal quality will be strengthened.

Creatures from outer space

The increasing interest in science fiction and drama (notably on television – 'Dr. Who' and such odysseys) demands further experimenting in this field.
The use of metallic colours can be explored, using combinations of facial hair, half masks, nose putty, etc. with metallic sprays.

Witches and ancients

The illustration shows a possible make-up for the Conjur Woman from 'The Dark of the Moon' by Howard Richardson and William Berney. Again note the use of nose putty, this time in combination with crepe hair.

Foundation - Use No. 5 with small amount of No. 9

Wrinkles, 'crow's feet' – shadows heavy use of No. 16 with No. 25 Lake highlights in No. 20 with touch of Blue or Green

Eyebrows - hair brushed down - lighten with talc and No. 20

Nose and warts - putty and crepe hair down one side of face to meet jawline

Lips - No. 9 with No. 25 Lake for puckering, highlights in No. 20

Hair - wig of string or cord.

'Conjur Woman' from 'Dark of the Moon'

Make-up for witches and ancients

Witches and ancients (continued)

The witch make-up below is basically No. 5 mixed with green.

Eyes: green with or without blue for the shadows below the brows. Brush eyebrows the wrong way to raise the hair and darken with black if necessary.

Shadow areas: use No. 16 on the sides of the nose, round the eyes and under the cheeks.

Lips are blotted out with foundation colour and redrawn with a No. 16 outline. Fill in the lips with Lake No. 25. Teeth can be blacked either with tooth enamel or No. 16.

Below: young girl before make-up.

Right: young girl made up as witch, using the greasepaint suggested in the notes above.

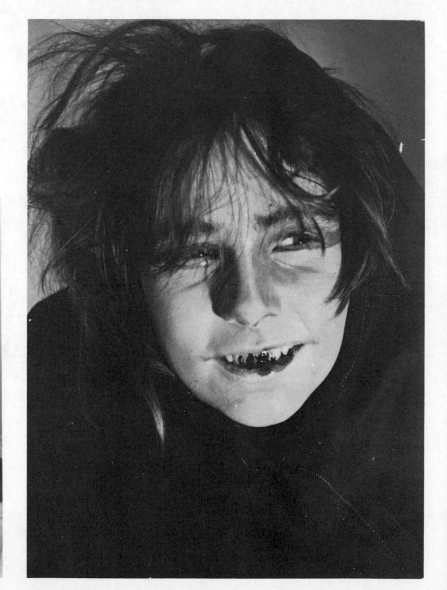

262

ARTIFICIAL FEATURES: Scars

Scars are marked over the foundation colour with greasepaint liners. The illustration below shows a scar made with Lake No. 25 mixed with a blue liner. The main line is drawn down the cheek first. Cross lines are then added – to be highlighted with White No. 20.

A liquid called Collodion which contracts on drying is also useful for scar effects.

Facial padding

Characters such as Falstaff or Henry VIII need padding. This can be produced with gauze cut to shape and gummed to the face at the edges.

Padding is then inserted under the gauze before it is finally secured – use feathers or cotton wool. Edges can then be buried in natural or artificial hair. Experimenting is essential if a realistic effect is to be achieved.

Paint to match foundation colour.

For very large noses it may be necessary to gum on a false nose of rubber, which should be painted to match the foundation colour.

Blood

Stage blood is sold in liquid form available in small bottles.

Seal up the required quantity in a small rubber or cellophane bag and attach to the skin with sticky (fabric-surfaced) plaster. Cover with grease-paint to match the surrounding area.

For use, prick with a sharp point – see page 218 for an alternative method, attaching 'blood' to dagger.

Blood from the mouth is simulated by using gelatine capsules. Small blood patches can be made by rubbing Carmine 3 in removing cream. For weals and lash marks, use No. 9 on the tips of the fingers and pull across the skin.

Perspiration

Perspiration can be simulated by spraying liquid paraffin or glycerine on the skin with a fine spray.

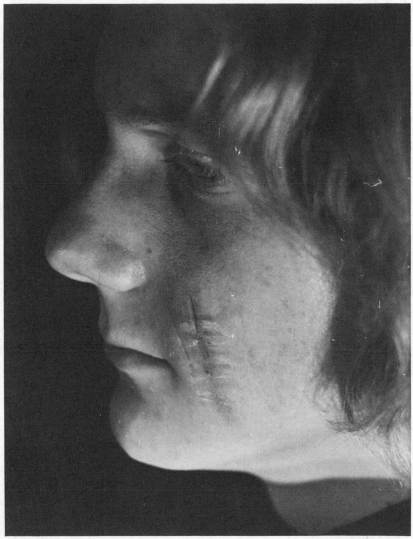

Scar tissue on cheek.

MASKS – 1:
Papier mâché method

Masks have always played an important part in the theatre. Primitive man used to wear a mask for hunting, disguising himself as the animal he was stalking.

Egyptian priests used animal head masks to represent gods. Roman tragic actors wore large head masks – some of terrifying aspect according to contemporary reports.

The medieval mystery plays also made use of masks to portray devils; actors portraying buffoons also wore masks.

Masks of various shapes and kinds were frequently worn for masked balls (as in 'Romeo and Juliet') and are today enjoying a revival in the form of the carnival heads used by travelling players in America (Bread and Puppet Theatre and other groups).

Clay model method of construction

One of the most practical methods of making masks is on a clay model mould. The illustrations here show the materials and process of making a full-face mask:

1 You will need a smooth, flat board, sufficient clay for the size of head (Plasticine can be used if available), Vaseline or any thick oil, newspaper and tissue paper, cold-water paste and brush, string and elastic for tying, and paint.

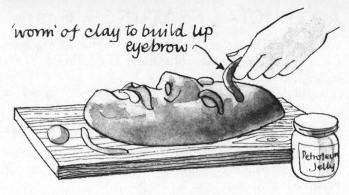

'worm' of clay to build up eyebrow

2 Using the board as a base, model the shape you require. Work coils and lumps of clay to make bold vigorous shapes – avoid undercutting which would allow the mask to stick to the clay.

When modelling is complete, allow the clay to dry then grease the surface thoroughly. Alternatively, if time is short, build up tissue on the moist clay immediately.

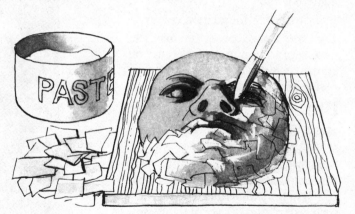

3 Cover the greased surface with a single layer of torn, unpasted tissue paper. A damped brush is ideal for picking up the small pieces of tissue. When the clay has been covered, paste the whole surface. This first layer acts as a smooth barrier between the clay model and newspaper.

Start building up the paper layers – six are sufficient – with torn squares of newspaper (about 25 mm square).

To ensure even distribution, alternate layers of white and coloured newspaper (colour with dye or ink by soaking pieces in a bowl). A layer of butter muslin on the fifth layer will help to strengthen the mask.

gently
lift mask
from mould

mould

4 Prise the mask from the clay model when the paper is quite dry. Take care not to damage the clay if a repeat is required.

turning edges over and
pasting down

PASTE

5 Mould papier-mâché round all the edges, pasting down loose bits of paper inside. Cut out eye-holes and paste the edges smooth. Leave the mask to dry thoroughly.

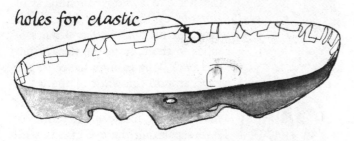

holes for elastic

6 Smooth the mask with fine sandpaper and apply shellac all over. The shellac will bind together any loose pieces and prepare the surface for painting.
Pierce holes at temple position to carry elastic.

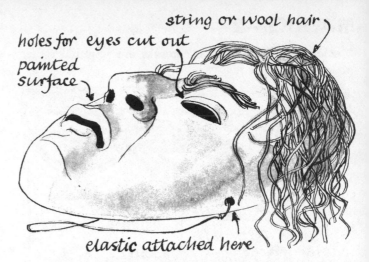

string or wool hair

holes for eyes cut out
painted
surface

elastic attached here

7 Paint mask to suit the character desired. Add hair with string, coarse wool or other materials – colour the hair to match the face before glueing. Attach elastic.

Wire mask

A stronger mask can be built on a wire frame as illustrated below:

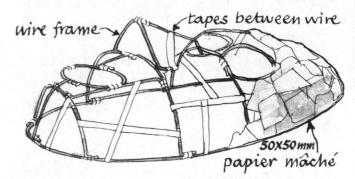

wire frame

tapes between wire

50x50mm
papier mâché

Build a wire contour to the shape required. Strengthen between the wires with self-adhesive masking tape.

Apply five or six layers of newspaper pieces (as described on the opposite page) and complete as before.

Add hair and other features with string, felt or other materials.

MASKS – 2

Sometimes half-face or eye masks are required rather than the full-face masks.

Eye masks

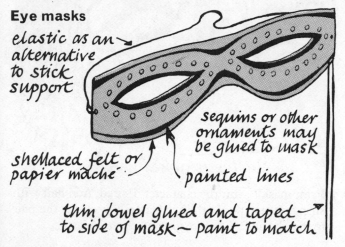

elastic as an alternative to stick support

sequins or other ornaments may be glued to mask

painted lines

shellaced felt or papier mâché

thin dowel glued and taped to side of mask – paint to match

Small eye masks do not require a model or mould, but felt can be shaped to the face by stiffening with shellac for self-supporting types (see illustration) or can be fitted with elastic and not stiffened for wearing on the head.

Half-face masks

These masks allow freedom to speak. Make-up must be adjusted to suit the colouring of the mask.

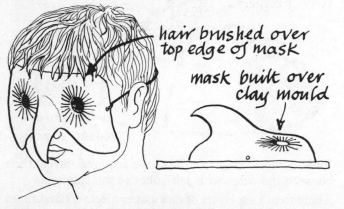

hair brushed over top edge of mask

mask built over clay mould

Half-face masks need more modelling. Make a clay or Plasticine model on a board and build up in papier-mâché as described on the previous two pages.

266

Carnival masks

Very large heads, used mainly for carnivals but occasionally in the theatre (see page 268) can be built over a wire-mesh framework.

Cut a piece of wire-mesh approximately 1 m × 1.30 m and shape into a cylinder; overlap and bend over the edges and thread through with string or wire to fasten. Make up individual features with added pieces of wire-mesh, joining and fastening with additional wire.

flap down

Cut slits in the cylinder from the top and bottom edges and shape with mesh over the top of the head, overlapping as necessary – also draw in the mesh round the neck area over an upturned bucket. Tie together all overlapping areas and flatten out all points.

separate mesh pieces for each feature

bucket for stability whilst constructing

Cover the whole head with 5 or 6 layers of newspaper in 20 cm squares, using cold-water paste. Allow to dry thoroughly.

Secure foam rubber or plastic inside the neck to avoid scratching. Cut suitable eye-holes and cover with gauze or muslin. Add two pairs of tapes to the base of the neck, front and back, long enough to secure the head around the waist of the actor.

Paint to suit the character, adding materials for hair, etc. if required. Avoid painting the eye gauzes with thick colour.

gauze eye-holes
foam rubber protection
tapes for securing to armpits or waist

Animal masks

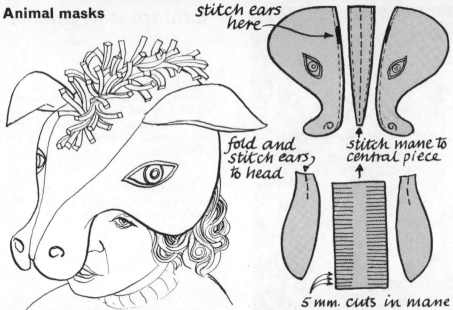

stitch ears here

fold and stitch ears to head

stitch mane to central piece

5 mm. cuts in mane

make up face to match mask

These masks can be made by the methods already described, or with foam rubber.

The donkey mask above shows a method that can be used and adapted to suit most animals. The advantage of foam rubber is the ease with which masks can be made and decorated. Foam rubber takes colour extremely well – all features can be added with fibre and felt-tip pens.

The cutting pattern given above is intended only as a guide to structure. Design and make shapes by experimenting.

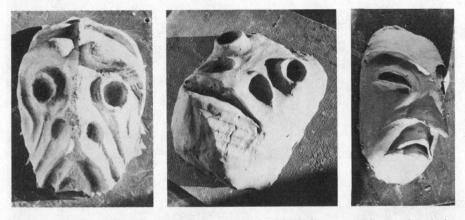

Above: papier mâché masks taken from clay models before smoothing and painting (see also 264).

Decorative masks

Should a purely decorative mask be required for fixing on a wall or large flat area, use expanded polystyrene. It is easy to cut this material with hot wires (page 147) and build it up in light relief. It can then be painted – see example below. A useful thickness to work with is 25 mm. Pieces can be glued on with P.V.A. medium or polystyrene adhesive.

See overleaf for more examples of masks

Examples of masks

Left: carnival masks.
A group of young children in masks made by 12 year old boys. In rehearsal for a carnival procession which opened a school production of 'Twelfth Night' (see page 266).

Below: animal masks. A scene from 'Noah' by André Obey. Masks are of canvas but similar ones could be built up from foam plastic.

Glossary **11**

STAGE TERMS · LISTS OF MATERIALS AND SUPPLIERS · BOOK LIST · INDEX

Glossary 270
Complete list of materials, tools and sundries . . 273
Suppliers 276
Book list 277
Index 278
General Information 281

GLOSSARY

Technical terms related to the stage

Apron The forestage extending into the auditorium beyond the proscenium arch. Usually at stage level but sometimes built lower. (see page 5)

Arena An acting area surrounded by the audience, either totally or on three (sometimes two) sides. (see pages 5 and 6)

Backcloth Sometimes called a backdrop. A scene canvas across the width of the upstage, fixed at the top and bottom. (see page 23)

Backing Any flat or cloth behind doors or windows to mask parts of the stage that should not be seen. (see model stage on page 77)

Bar or **Barrel** An iron pipe above the stage for carrying lighting equipment and scenery. Fastened in a vertical position, it is called a boom. (see page 180)

Batten 1 Electrical: the compartment trough carrying a set of lamps divided into 3 or 4 circuits. (see page 176); commonly known as a borderlight.
2 Scenic: lengths of timber for tautening backcloths at top and bottom. The top edge of a cloth is gripped between two battens, termed sandwich battens. A batten is often slotted through a canvas hem.

Book flats Two flats hinged together to fold to any angle. (see page 51)

Boom See **Bar**.

Border Horizontal flat or curtain, hanging from bar or grid to mask lights and/or ceiling from the audience. (see diagram and page 18)

Box set An enclosed setting that has three walls and usually a ceiling. (see page 88)

Brace An extending rod with attachments to support flats (see page 55). A **French Brace** is hinged. (see page 55)

Brail The rope and adjusting part of hanging scenery. (see diagram)

Centre line A line from front to back of stage on the ground plan drawing – chalked on the stage itself for correct placing of settings and props. (see page 79)

Cleat Metal fitting on the back of flats to which a throw-line is attached. (see page 54)

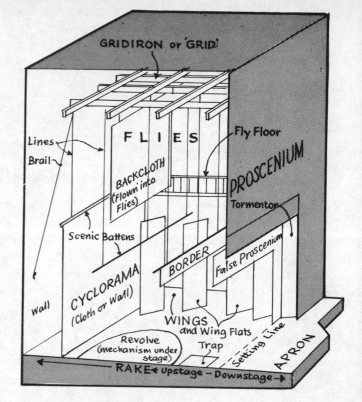

Section cut through centre line showing parts of traditional theatre stage. All terms included on the drawing are explained in the glossary.

Cloth see **Backcloth**.

Cut-out A cloth with parts cut away to suggest foliage etc. (see pages 24 and 58)

Cut-out flat A flat with a plywood or hardboard edge cut away to suggest foliage, etc. (see page 51)

Cyclorama Either a permanent plaster wall or, more frequently, a curved or straight backcloth hung at the rear of the stage. Used as sky or background, usually painted white and lit as required. (see pp. 26 and 92)

Dimmer (correct electrical term: a **rheostat**) An electrical appliance which varies intensity of light. (see page 179)

Dip Metal trap in the stage floor for electrical sockets – used for plugging in stage floor lights. (see page 181)

Dock Backstage storage area for scenery.

Downstage Towards the audience.

Elevation Side view drawings of units or parts shown on the ground plan. (see page 80)

False proscenium A smaller temporary 'proscenium' of flats or cloths behind the main proscenium arch to make the stage area smaller:

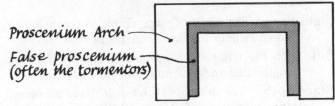

Proscenium Arch

False proscenium (often the tormentors)

Flat A rectangular wooden frame covered with canvas, hardboard or other material. The unit of which most scenery is composed. (see pages 47–70)

Flies The space above the stage where sets can be 'flown' or taken up (not usually provided in school theatres).

Floats see **Footlights**.

Flood Lamp giving a wide spread of light. (see page 175)

Fly floor Galleries above stage on side walls used for securing, raising and lowering lights and scenery – only found over large, traditional stages. (see illustration on this page)

F.O.H. see **Front of House**

Footlights An electrical batten at the front of the stage at floor level. (see page 180)

Fresnel A spotlight with a soft-edge lens. (see page 177)

Front cloth A movable cloth immediately behind the proscenium arch (see page 18)

Front of House Term sometimes applied to the auditorium area, usually abbreviated to F.O.H.

Front of House lighting Spotlights positioned in or above the auditorium area to illumine the forestage. (see pages 181 and 182)

Frost A gelatine ('gel') lighting filter that resembles frosted glass – for diffusing light. (see page 186)

Gauze A transparent cloth for scenic effects – called also a transparency. (see pages 24–25)

Gelatine ('gel') A colour filter for lighting. (see page 186)

Grid Wooden or steel framework above large stages for suspending all equipment, scenery and lighting; used for storage between scenes. (see illustration on this page)

Ground plan A scaled drawing of a setting seen from above. (see page 79)

Ground row 1 Electrical: batten lighting for a cyclorama at stage floor level. (see page 181)
2 Scenic: a flat lying on its side across the stage concealing lighting, and giving impression of ramparts, undulating ground, etc. according to the shape of its cut-out top edge. (see page 58)

Hang iron Ring on iron plate secured to the back of flats – used on stages where scenery can be flown. (see **Flies**) (see page 56)

House curtain The proscenium curtains, also called 'front tabs' or 'house tabs'. (see page 18)

House lights Lights in the auditorium: the normal hall lights, not to be confused with lights placed F.O.H. for stage lighting purposes.

Inset A small scene within a larger setting. (see page 106)

Legs Canvas wings, hanging vertically as side maskings. (see page 116)

Lines Hemp ropes used for raising and lowering scenery and lights. They are fastened to cleats on the sides of the stage, on the fly galleries – or to a grid when scenery and battens are held in permanent place. The lines run through a series of pulleys:

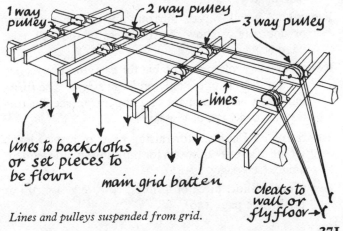

1 way pulley

2 way pulley

3 way pulley

lines

lines to backcloths or set pieces to be flown

main grid batten

cleats to wall or fly floor

Lines and pulleys suspended from grid.

271

Glossary (continued)

Mask   To hide parts of the stage from the audience.

Opposite prompt (Stage Right)   The right-hand side of the stage when facing the audience.

Plate   A reinforcing corner, usually of plywood, for strengthening the frames of flats at butt corners. (see page 49)

Pre-set (pre-setting)   **1** In large lighting control systems, the capacity to set up in advance any lighting arrangement. By pressing different master switches one scenic effect will be cross-faded for another.

2 The lighting seen on stage before the play begins.

Priming   Coat of thin size and paint as a preparation for painting. (see page 113)

Prompt side (Stage Left)   The left-hand side of the stage when facing the audience

Properties ('**props**')   All objects on stage too small to be classified as scenery – they include all furniture. (see pages 133–172)

Proscenium   The stage opening that separates the audience from the actors on the traditional type of stage.

Rail   Horizontal part of the framework of a flat. (see page 48)

Rake   The slope of the stage floor from the back down to the front on some larger stages. (see illustration on previous page of glossary)

Return   A flat leading off at right angles to another. (see page 57)

Reveal   A small 'return' surrounding an arch, window or doorway to show the thickness of the wall. (see page 60)

Revolve   A revolving turntable for carrying two scenes for a quick change – only on large stages. The turntable can be permanent or temporary. (see illustration on page 270 of glossary)

Rostrum   **1** Platform for raising parts of a stage level. **2** One of a series of rostra for building an independent stage. (see pages 27–46)

Set piece   Short piece of 'ground row,' e.g. a shrub or bush. (see page 156)

Setting line   A line set back from the front edge of the stage, slightly behind the proscenium (except on an apron stage) drawn on the ground plan and chalked on the stage floor in order to position scenery and props. (see page 79)

Sight lines   The limits of stage visible to the audience – shown as lines on plans. (see pages 16–17)

Sill   Iron bar screwed to the bottom of door flats for strengthening and securing. (see page 62)

Stage cloth   A cloth laid over the stage to reduce noise, seldom used on small stages. Where used it is often painted to match the setting.

Stage left   Right of stage, looking from auditorium.

Stage right   Left of stage, looking from auditorium. (see plan)

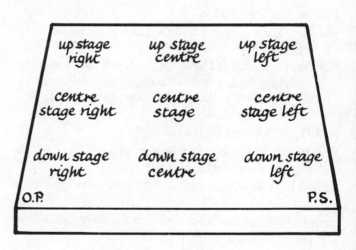

Stage screw   Screw for fixing braces to the stage floor – not recommended except for strong permanent stage floors. Alternative is a **stage weight** for holding brace in position. (see page 55)

Stile   Vertical part of the framework of a flat. (page 48)

Tabs   Curtains.

Throw-line   Line for lashing two flats together. (see page 54)

Toggle On large flats, the supports to the centre rail. (see page 48)

Tormentor A black masking flat behind the proscenium at right angles – or angled upstage. Sometimes used as a false proscenium. (see glossary illustration on page 270)
The setting line is usually drawn from the upstage edge of the tormentors.

Trap A door in the stage floor for special effects and entrances – usually in large theatres. (see glossary illustration on page 270)

Traverse tabs Tabs on a track across the stage, on a line with a set of wings and borders. (see page 18)

Truck A mobile rostrum carrying a section of the setting – resting on wheels or ball-castors. (see page 42)

Upstage Towards the back of the stage.

Wings 1 The flats masking the sides of the stage. (see glossary illustration on page 270)
2 The sides of the stage masked from view by the wings or wing flats.
3 Legs – hanging canvas wings.

COMPLETE LIST OF MATERIALS, TOOLS AND SUNDRIES
Basic materials

Wood

Softwood (pine, etc.) – see chart on page 69 for metric sizes

Plywood – assorted thicknesses and sizes

Hardboard – assorted thicknesses and sizes

Composition boards

Balsa wood for modelling

Bamboo and *cane* for properties

Metals

Thin sheet aluminium and alloys for properties, arms and armour.

Wire – thin gauge 1 mm
medium gauge 1.6 mm
thick gauge 2.5 mm

Wire mesh – for use in constructing set pieces of shrubs, sculpture, etc.

Foils – all colours for scenic effects, properties, etc.

Metal scrap – small pieces of chain, bottle caps, coins, sequins, glitter, fine binding wire: all ideal for decorating properties, etc.

Paper and card

Newspaper for general purposes

Grey sugar paper for papier mâché (stronger than newspaper)

Brown parcel paper – for properties

Tissue for papier mâché and details such as imitation glass

Cartridge paper for sketches and plans

Corrugated cardboard – general purpose material for scale models and properties

Cardboard – useful for leg armour and large properties

Strawboard – useful for the stiff parts of properties

Cloth

Flax canvas – for flats and backcloths

Scenery hessian – cheap form of covering for flats; also useful for properties

Bolton twill – used for curtain settings

Scenery gauze for transformation

Felt and underfelt – available in various qualities; used for properties and armour

Old blankets – armour-making

Sheeting – generally useful for properties and armour

Buckram – useful for making helmets and other headgear

Gauze bandages for small properties

Butter muslin – ideal for strengthening and supporting irregular properties: sculptures, masks, etc.

Hessian scrim – about 75 mm wide; open mesh scrim useful in combination with plaster for sculptural properties

Muslin scrim – about 50 mm wide; fine mesh scrim for sculptural details and as a reinforcement for plaster moulds

Continued overleaf

Modelling materials

Plasticine – useful general-purpose material for smaller items

Clay – ideal for mask models

Papier mâché

Fine paper pulp

Plaster – used with scrim, ideal for large properties

Expanded polystyrene – versatile plastic material for properties, textured surfaces and printing blocks

Making and shaping
Essential tools

Hand saw

Coping saw

Fretsaw

Hacksaws, large and small

Plane

Chisels – assorted sizes

Mallet

Shaping files and planes

Claw and tack hammers

Hand stapler

Screwdrivers – assorted

'G' clamps and cramps

Brace and bits

Hand-drill and set of twist drills

Pliers and pincers

Tin snips and wire cutters

Adjustable wrench

Files and rasps

'Stanley' trimming knife

T-square

Mortice gauge

Dividers and a pair of large compasses

Nail punch

Bucket – assorted sizes, some at least of galvanised metal

Useful tools

An electric drill and attachments

Jig-saw

Rip-saw for large pieces of wood

Grinding wheel

Fillers

Materials for use in filling holes, shaping awkward areas, curves, etc. in small items of scenery and in properties

Alabastine, plaster of Paris – very fine, tough, white plasters

Fibre-glass – specialist material suitable for those with knowledge of its uses in boat-building, etc. Can be used as a basic structure for helmets, armour and properties

Papier mâché – can be home-made or can be bought from certain craft or toy shops (expensive)

Wood filler – plastic wood. Can be useful in detailed model-making

Sawdust and glue – home-made mixture for large gaps and cracks in rough work.

Smoothing materials

Garnet paper – long-lasting and tough abrasive

Sandpaper (*or glasspaper*) – graded from very fine to coarse, abrasive for general purposes

Files (see *Tools*) – various

Fixing and fastening
Adhesives

Animal glues – traditional glues ideal for wood joints but not waterproof. Sold by weight as 'pearl' crystals, sheet or solid bars and in branded containers such as Lepage's Liquid Glue.

Size powder – for scenic painting

Casein glue – stronger wood glue than animal glue where very strong joints required – sold in powder form.

Contact cements – the two surfaces are glued and, when brought together, 'impact' and are difficult to move.

Epoxies – compound adhesive for very strong fixing; ideal for repairs to glass, china, etc. (slow drying).

Latex – excellent for fabrics, paper and card; very quick drying.

SYNTHETIC RESINS: PLASTIC RESINS

Under this general heading are some of the most versatile of adhesives: P.V.A., P.V.C. and Acrylic.

P.V.A. (*Polyvinyl acetate*)

The most versatile for general theatre work, ideal for strong adhesion of wood, fabric and plastic.

Thinned slightly with water, it also a useful painting medium for mixing powder colours.

P.V.C. (Polyvinyl chloride)
Useful for flexible plastics – curtains, etc.

Acrylic (Polymethyl acrylate)
A painting medium and an adhesive for fabrics, card and paper.

All synthetic resins can be thinned in water but are waterproof when dry. The solvent to use for hardened brushes is methylated spirit.

Tapes and string

Cellophane tape – plastic tape (clear or coloured) sticky on one side

Masking tape – similar to cellophane but less strongly adhesive. Useful for masking areas not to be painted, etc. and removable.

Gummed paper tape – for paper and card.

Insulating tape – similar to cellophane but more pliable. Used for covering wire – electrical or otherwise.

String and cord – picture cord, nylon, hemp, etc. all useful for binding and holding.

Rope – hemp or nylon for scenic purposes

Elastic bands – to hold materials while modelling

Cotton and synthetic thread – for sewing and fastening costumes and props

General ironmongery

Screws Countersunk steel: $1''$, $1\frac{1}{4}''$, $1\frac{1}{2}''$, $1\frac{3}{4}''$, $2''$, $2\frac{1}{2}''$ and $3''$
Round head: $\frac{1}{2}''$ and $1''$

Nails Oval: $1''$, $1\frac{1}{2}''$, $2''$ and $2\frac{1}{2}''$
Round: $1''$, $1\frac{1}{2}''$, $2''$ and $2\frac{1}{2}''$

Assorted nuts and bolts

Pins – veneer and panel (or gimp), all useful for small, detailed work

Tacks – for fastening canvas

Corrugated fasteners – useful for simple butt joints

Ball catches – quick and efficient for door fixing

Hasp and staple (gate hook and eye) – for large boxes, trunks or doors

Hinges – assorted collection

Brackets – assortment for supporting shelves, joining pieces of wood at a right angle, etc.

Angle (mild steel) – useful for supports, reveals, etc. Less strong than brackets.

Stapler and staples of various sizes

Decorating

Paint

Decorator's powder (scenic) – colour for scene-painting

Powder colour (tempera) – general-purpose colour for props

Enamel and Lacquer – for detailed props requiring high gloss

Metallic powders – powders in gold, silver, green, blue and mauve shades

Dyes – aniline dyes for fabrics.

Medium, thinner and solvent

P.V.A. medium – versatile liquid base for mixing colour or metallic powders – and for glueing fabrics and papers (see *Adhesives*).

Gold Size – for mixing metallic powders

Varnish – use clear varnish for a high gloss finish on some props, jewellery, etc.

Shellac (available flake or liquid) – a varnish for stiffening felt and for waterproofing and hardening props and armour (clear type for props)

Turpentine (turps), white spirit, methylated spirit – all essential solvents for paints, cleaning brushes and thinning – there may be special thinners to accompany some new products

Wax: beeswax, polish – if required, use instead of varnish on props to reduce reflection of light

Vaseline (or motor oil) – useful when making moulds and taking plaster casts

Brushes and rollers

Use sable brushes for painting scale models, hog's hair for general painting of props and larger bristle brushes for scenery. Wool or foam plastic rollers can also be used for scenery though brushes will still be required for detail.

For glue, use 18 mm or 25 mm round pure bristle brushes.

Electric or gas stove

A heat source is required for the heating of water, some kinds of glue, etc.

SUPPLIERS

Simon's Directory (New York: Package Publicity Service) provides an extensive listing of theatrical suppliers in the United States and Canada.

Art materials
paints, sable brushes, sprayers, adhesives

M. Epstein's Son, Inc.
809 Ninth Ave.
New York, N.Y. 10019

Rosco
11420 Ventura Blvd.
Studio City, Cal. 91604

Cardboard and polystyrene
Try appliance dealers and furniture stores for discarded cartons and packing.

Costumes
Eaves Costume Co.
423 W. 55th St.
New York, N.Y. 10019

Krause Costume Co.
2445 Superior Ave.
Cleveland, Ohio 44114

Broadway Costume House
15 W. Hubbard St.
Chicago, Ill. 60610

Make-up
The Make-up Center
80 Boylston St.
Boston, Mass. 02116

Bob Kelly
151 W. 46th St.
New York, N.Y. 10036

M. Stein Cosmetic Co.
430 Broome St.
New York, N.Y. 10013

Scenic Colors and Dyes
Playhouse Colors
771 Ninth Ave.
New York, N.Y. 10019

Gothic Color Co.
727 Washington St.
New York, N.Y. 10014

Sound effects
Carroll Sound, Inc.
351 W. 41st St.
New York, N.Y. 10036

Special effects
Special Effects Unlimited
18 Euclid Ave.
Yonkers, N.Y. 10705

Stage draperies, flame-proof textiles
Novelty Scenic Studios
40 Sea Cliff Ave.
Glen Cove, N.Y. 11542

A. F. Runnel Studios
4767 14th St.
Detroit, Mich. 48208

Stage Hardware
J. R. Clancy, Inc.
1010 W. Belden Ave.
Syracuse, N.Y. 13204

Paramount Supplies
32A W. 20th St.
New York, N.Y. 10011

L&M Stagecraft, Inc.
2110 Superior Ave.
Cleveland, Ohio, 44114

Stage Jewelry
All Woolworth stores

Invincible Sales
2303 W. Ninth St.
Los Angeles, Cal. 90006

Stage lighting
American Scenic
11 Andrews St., Box 283
Greenville, S.C. 29602

Capitol Stage Lighting
509 W. 56th St.
New York, N.Y. 10019

Grand Stage Lighting
630 W. Lake St.
Chicago, Ill. 60606

ATC
307 W. 80th St.
Kansas City, Mo. 64114

Stage props and armour
Kenmore Furniture Co.
152 E. 33rd St.
New York, N.Y. 10016

Costume Armour
Stewart Airport
Newburgh, N.Y. 12550

Bob's Military Antiques
208 Santa Monica Blvd.
Santa Monica, Cal. 90401

Lumber
All lumberyards and hardware stores. Also try demolition contractors, junkyards, second-hand furniture stores, etc.

BOOK LIST

PROPERTIES	Stage Properties and How to Make Them, by Warren Kenton	Drama Books	Practical illustrated handbook on useful, and unusual props
	Handbook of Ornament, by Franz Sales Meyer	Dover Publications	A grammar of ornament, especially the 'antique' – lavishly illustrated
COSTUME	Making Costumes for School Plays, by Joan Peters and Anna Sutcliffe	Plays, Inc.	Excellent book on basic design and improvisation. Use of new and scrap materials
	Designing and Making Stage Costumes, by Motley	Watson-Guptill	Practical advice on all aspects of costume-making
	Western European Costume, by Iris Brooke	Theatre Arts Books	For those interested in the trends in costuming from the 13th Century to the present; 2 volumes
	Historic Costume for the Stage, by Lucy Barton	Baker's Plays	Traces development of dress of all peoples and periods in history with practical application to the stage. Useful information on properties for earlier periods
	Five Centuries of American Costume, by R. Turner Wilcox	Scribner's	Useful to all those seeking information about the origins of American dress; over 460 illustrations
MAKE-UP	Stage Make-up, by Herman Buchman	Watson-Guptill	A complete manual, with many step-by-step demonstrations
	Stage Make-up, by Richard Corson	Prentice-Hall	A classic in the field, with excellent illustrations covering every aspect of make-up application
PRINTING TECHNIQUES	Ideas for Fabric Printing, by Peter Gooch	Scribner's	Step-by-step advice on a wide variety of printing methods. A useful introduction to such techniques
LIGHTING	The Art of Stage Lighting, by F. Bentham	Taplinger	Informative book on all practical aspects of stage lighting
ARMS AND ARMOUR	Arms and Armour, by Frederick Wilkinson	Hamlyn	Excellent small handbook, informative and profusely illustrated

INDEX

acting area 3–26
adhesives 274
ageing (make-up) 253–4
angels 240
angle (metal) 4, 11–13
animal masks 267–8
apron stage 5, 15, 270
architectural details 144
architectural friezes 147
arena setting 4, 6–7, 82
arms and armour 193–224
  archer 204
  armature 194, 196
  armplate 207, 209
  arquebusier 210
  arrows 198, 215
  axes 198–9, 205, 215, 217
  bows 198, 215
  breastplate 201–3, 208–11
  cannon (hand) 222
  cavalier 211
  chainmail 204–6
  crossbow 206, 215, 217
  dagger 218
  dagger with bloody device 218
  device for sticking spear into body 212
  dummies 194–7
  gauntlets 206, 209
  gorget 211
  greaves 201, 203
  guns 222–4
  halberd 219
  helmet 196–200, 202–6, 208, 210–11
  leather jerkin 199, 207
  mace 217, 219
  musket 224
  Passion Play 241
  pike 219, 221
  pikeman 210
  plate armour 202–3, 206–11
  pole-arms 221
  quiver 198, 215
  rapier 220
  scabbard: sword 216
        dagger 213
  scale armour 198, 200–2, 205
  shield 212–14, 217
  spear 213, 219
  standard 213
  standard bearer 202
  swords and swordbelts 198, 212, 214, 216, 218, 220–1

war hammer 219
auditorium 4–7, 9, 17, 82–3, 180

backcloth 18
  rolling up 23
  flying 270
  quick assembly 22, 26
  painting 116
backing 77
balustrade 149
barrels (bars) 180
battens
  lighting 176
  scenic 23
beards and moustaches 258–9
belt (sword) 213–14, 216
benches 152
bishop's mitre 229
bollards 154
book flats 51
boom 180
boots 229
borders 16–19, 23, 59
boxes and chests 168–9
box sets 88–91
braces 54–8
  making of weights for 55
  extending 54
  French 56
brail 270
brazier 137
brooches 239
brushes, for painting 109
buttons 239

candelabrum 138
candlesticks 139
canvas 52–3, 276
  pliers 52
  stretching 53
capstan 155
castors 43
cave 148
ceilings (box set) 88–9
centre line 79
chalice 162
chandelier 139
chests 168–9
clasps 239
cleats 21, 54
clocks 159
cloths 18
coffin 169
columns and pillars 102, 145
compartment batten 175

composite setting 94–5
concertina screen 66
coronet 229
costume accessories 225–42
crook 240
crowns 226–9
  basic construction 226–8
  Nativity Play 241
  oriental 228
  Passion Play 242
  tiered 229
  traditional 228
crucifix 144, 242
curtains and cloths 18–23, 86
  set 86–7
  supports 19, 22
  tracks 13, 19, 21
  traverse 18–20
cut-outs
  border 59
  flats 59
  ground-rows 58
cyclorama 270
  fixing temporarily 26
  sets 92–3

design 71–106
  model theatre 78
  rough model 76–7
  rough sketches 75
  design terms 73
dimmer (rheostat) 178
doors 60–3
downstage 270
drums 167
dummies (armour) 194–7
dyes 111

elevation (drawing) 80
eyes and eyebrows (make-up) 248

fans (hand) 232
fences 149
fire
  fireplace 50, 137
  fire hydrant 154
  precautions 173, 281
  log fire 137
flats 47–70
  backing 77, 79–80, 88, 90, 96
  book 51
  braces and weights 54–5
  canvas stretching 52–3
  construction 48–53
  doors 60–3

fireplaces 50
  French 56
  joints 49
  profile 51
  return 57
  reveal 60–1
  supports 54–7
  tormentor 270, 273
  types of flat 50–1
  windows 62–5
floodlight 175
flowers and leaves 156–7
fly floor and flying 270–1
foliage 156
food 172
footwear 229
  (see also **armour** section)
fountains 142–3
Fresnel lanterns 177
FOH (front of house) lights 180

gauntlets (see **armour**)
gauze (make-up) 263
gauzes and cut-cloths 24–5
  transformation scenes 25
gelatine filters ('gels') 186
girdle 239
glossary 270–3
glues (see adhesives)
goblets 160–2
greasepaint 244–5
grids
  scaling up drawings 114–15
  suspension 270–1
ground plans 79, 81, 83, 88, 90, 92, 94,
  96, 101, 103
ground rows
  lighting 181
  scenery 58, 181
guns (see **arms**)

hair (make-up) 258–9
handbags and purses 233
hang-iron 56
helmets (see also **armour** section)
  fireman's 231
  policeman's 231
house lights 192
house (mobile) 44
hydrant 154
inkwells 171
inset 85, 106

jewel boxes 168
jewellery 234–9

joints
  flats 49
  rostra 29
jugs and pitchers 164–5

lamps 135–6
lanterns 135–6
legs 116
letters and documents 171
lighting 173–192
  arena stage 183
  back 188
  battens 175–6
  colour mixing 184–5
  colour selection 186
  colour theory 184
  control systems 178–9
  cyclorama 187–9
  dimmers (rheostats) 178–9, 192
  dip 181
  ellipsoidal spots 177
  filters ('gels') 184–6
  floods 175
  FOH (front of house) 180–2
  footlights 176, 180
  Fresnel spots 176–7
  lamps 174
  layouts 187
  plots 192
  positioning 180–3, 189–91
  rehearsals 191–2
  switchboards 178
lines 271
lining (painting) 132
lute 166
lyre 166

mace 217
make-up and masks 243–68
make-up 244–63
  ageing 253–4
  basic requirements 244–5
  blood 263
  body 251
  character 252
  crepe hair 259
  eyes and eyebrows 248
  face: broadening 251
        lengthening 251
  fairies and sprites 260
  foundation 245
  ghosts 261
  greasepaint 244–5
  hair, beards, etc. 258–9
  mouth 249

nose 250
  perspiration 263
  racial types 255–7
  scars 263
  straight 246–7
  sub-human 261
  witches and ancients 261
masks 264–8
  animal 267–8
  basic construction 264–6
  carnival 266, 268
  clay models 264
  decorative for wall 267
  eye 266
  half-face 266
metal frame
  staging 10–11
  setting 104–6
milestone 155
mirror 158
mirror frames 158
mobile scenery 42–6, 103
model settings 76–8
model theatre 78
modelling materials 274
money (stage) 170
monumental sculpture 140–5
moulds
  stage weights 55
  jewellery 234–6
musical instruments 166–7

Nativity Play 240–1
naturalistic setting 116–17
necklaces 238

occupational costume accessories 230–1
opposite prompt (O.P.) 272

pail 230
painting and printing 107–32
painting
  backcloths 116
  blending in edges 132
  chalking lines for 114
  cloths 116
  colour matching 113
  colour mixing 112–13
  cut-outs 117
  gauze 127
  lining 132
  materials 108–11
  metallic colour 111
  pigments 110–13, 184
  priming 113

ragroll 120
roller 121
scenic colour (see pigments)
scumbling and drybrush 119
spatter and splash 119
spraying (aerosol) 111
paper pulp 234
papier mâché 264–5
Passion Play 241–2
permanent sets 96–106
pendants 237
perch (see boom)
perspective drawing 80
pillar box 154
pillar (column) 33, 102, 145
pince-nez 233
pitchers 164–5
plan (drawing) 79–81
plan (stage) 272
plan symbols 81
polystyrene (expanded)
    block 123, 172
    print 123
    sheet 123, 146–7, 158
    wall 129
pomander 233
pots 160–3
pre-setting (lighting) 272
printing
    batik 124–5
    block 123
    paper money 170
    patterned surfaces 122
    polystyrene 123
    screen 126
    stencil 122
properties 133–72
proscenium 5, 14–15, 59, 85–99
pump, village 155
purses 233
putty, nose (make-up) 250

quills 171

rail 48
railings 149
rake (of stage) 270, 272
ramps 32
rehearsal (lighting) 191–2
relief (sculptural) 146
return 57
reveal 60
revolve 270, 272
ring (jewellery) 239

rocks 148
rostra 27–46
    basic system 40–1
    collapsible 29–31
    construction 28–46
    curved 38–9
    fascia boards 9
    pillar 33
    semi-circular 33, 39
    steps and staircases 36–9
    triangular 33
    trucks 42–6

sandwich batten 23
scale models 76–8
scaling-up 114–15
screens
    arched 67
    concertina 66
    printing 126
    setting 85
    sliding 68
scrolls 170
sculpture 140–7
    heads 140–1
    fountain 142–3
    relief 146–8
    trophies 147
set-piece 58, 156
sets
    box 88–91
    composite 94–5
    curtain 86
    cyclorama 92–3
    permanent 96–106
    wing and cloth 87
setting line 77, 79
shoes 229
shrub 156
sight lines 16–17
signpost 155
sill 62
sketches, rough 74–5
sketch methods 75
softwood sections 68–9
spectacles 233
stage
    (ground) cloths 10–11
    design 82
    'stage left' 272
    'stage right' 272
    screw 55
    superstructure 4, 12–13
    weights 54–5

staircases 36–8
steps 34–9
    spiral 38
stiles 48
street furniture 154–5

tabs (see curtains)
tankards 163
theatre-in-the-round 4, 6–7, 82–4
    lighting 183
    seating 7
thrones 150–3
    canopied 153
    Gothic 152
    oriental 151
    Pilate's 150
    simple 150
    Snow Queen's 150
throwline 48, 54
thrust stage 83
toggle rail 48
tools, complete list of 273–5
torches 137
tormentor 273
transformation effects – see gauzes
trap 270, 273
trees 156–7
tree stumps 157
trucks (see rostra) 42–6
    revolving 44–6
trumpet 167
trunks 169
tubular steel 10–13

undercoating 118
upstage 273
urns 142

weights (for braces) 55
whiting 110, 112–13
wigs 258
winch/windlass 20–1
windows 63–5
    French 63
    frame for 62–4
    sash 63
    stained glass 65
wings – see angels
wings 270, 273
wing and cloth set 59, 87
wire and wire mesh 134
working area for the construction of
        properties 134
working drawings 79–80
working space for scene-painting 108

EQUIVALENCY CHART FOR LEICHNER OF LONDON GREASEPAINTS

I. Foundations

LEICHNER GREASEPAINT: FORM C STICK OR SPOT-LITE KLEAR TUBE	BOB KELLY STAGE COLORS	MAX FACTOR SUPREME GREASE PAINT MAKE-UP FOUNDATION	MEHRON FOUNDATION COLORS	STEIN SOFT GREASEPAINT	BEN NYE CREME FOUNDATIONS
2 Pale Pink	S–2	4–A	2	X	X
2½ Light Rose	SR–1 or 2	X	X	X	X
3½ Light Tan	S–6	7–A	6	7F	M–1
4½ Brownish Tan	S–14	UC 8–A	6½	10	L–5
5 Ivory	S–21	X	C	22	Ultra-Fair
6 Sallow Pink (Stick only)	X	X	16	Greasepaint Stick #23	23
6½ Light Olive	SL–15	X	M	X	X
7 Coffee Brown	S–19	16	14	16	30
8 Golden Tan	S–16	8–A	X	9	29
9 Brick Red	S–15	10	12	14	27
12 Black		ORDER BLACK			
16 Deep Brown (Stick only)	S–18	11	14	19	30
20 White		ORDER WHITE			
50 Lit K (5 and 9) Yellowish Brown	S–9	12	F	5½	X
52 Peach I	S–4	X	3	2½	L–2
53 Peach II	S–4	X	3	7F	L–3
59 Chrome Yellow	Yellow (a bit dark)	X	4½	12 (a bit dark)	X
57 Gold (Tube Only)	Gold	X	X	Liquid Make-Up 25 Gold	X
58 Silver (Tube Only)	Silver	X	X	Liquid Make-Up 26 Silver	X

X=Brand has no acceptable color equivalent in greasepaint make-up.

EQUIVALENCY CHART FOR LEICHNER OF LONDON GREASEPAINTS

II. Liners and Shading Colors

LEICHNER LINERS FORM G	BOB KELLY CREME SHADING COLORS (LINER, EYESHADOW, ROUGE)	MAX FACTOR	MEHRON SHADO-LINERS AND LIP ROUGE	STEIN SOFT SHADING COLORS	BEN NYE CREME SHADING COLORS (LINERS AND CREME ROUGE)
42 Black	SL–9		X	17	X
20 White	SL–12		X	15	X
25 Crimson Lake	SL–17		Lip Rouge Crimson	13	Dark Maroon
28 Dark Brown	SL–7	Not Available	8	2	Beard Stipple
31 Light Grey	SL–10		X	3	X
32 Dark Grey	SL–11		7	4	Grey
320 Carmine 1	SR–5		Lip Rouge Light	14	Creme Rouge Red
321 Carmine 2	SR–5		Lip Rouge Medium	14	Maroon
322 Carmine 3	X		Lip Rouge Cherry	Moist Rouge 4	Dark Maroon
326D Dark Blue	SL–3		X	10	Blue
326L Light Blue	X	Not Available	X	11	X
334 Green I	SES–6		X	Moist Eye-Shadow 6	X
336 Green III	SL–6		4	Moist-Eye-Shadow 3	Green
337D Dark Mauve	SL–4		X	23	X

X=Brand has no acceptable color equivalent in greasepaint make-up.